The cast brass numberplate of *Channel Packet*, at the naming ceremony, 10 March 1941. The designer, O. V. S. Bulleid is pictured in the background – at the cab window is Lt.-Col. J. T. C. Moore-Brabazon, M.P., Minister of Transport

LOCOMOTIVES

OF THE

SOUTHERN RAILWAY

PART 2

D. L. BRADLEY

ISBN 0 901115 31 2

CONTENTS

INTRODUCTION

For a number of reasons the railways of this country were slow to adopt the 4-6-2 wheel formation for locomotives. Indeed, from 1908 to 1922, the Great Western was the only British company to possess a locomotive of this type, the ill-fated No. 111 *The Great Bear*. When this locomotive was built, pacifics were well established in North America and Europe, while representatives could be found in most other parts of the world, including South Africa and Australasia. Having gained admission to the club, the Great Western might with reason have been expected to have built more of the type, but this failed to occur and after a period of experimentation *The Great Bear* was relegated to comparatively mundane duties until rebuilt as a Castle class 4-6-0.

In 1922, however, this apparent reluctance on the part of British locomotive engineers was finally overcome with the appearance on the Great Northern Railway of the first Gresley pacifics, to be followed at the end of the year by two locomotives of similar type from Darlington Works of the North Eastern Railway. After Grouping both classes were augmented but, whereas the Gresley design was adopted as the standard LNER express class, and was multiplied and developed until Nationalisation, the North Eastern class was restricted to five and quickly withdrawn.

In the years following the Grouping of railways in 1923 the Great Western, after its early digression, remained totally committed to 4-6-0's for express work while the strife-torn LMS was able to make few progressive measures before the appointment of William Stanier as Chief Mechanical Engineer in January 1932. He at once appreciated the need of large and powerful locomotives for the Anglo-Scottish expresses and being master of his domain had No. 6200 *The Princess Royal* in service within seventeen months. Other pacifics followed from Crewe, each series incorporating progressive improvements, until the LMS possessed express power comparable to that of the LNER.

At this period the Southern Railway was wholly committed to main-line electrification and had little interest in steam power until war clouds gathered over Europe and the dynamic O. V. S. Bulleid arrived as Chief Mechanical Engineer. Various schemes were prepared for new express power and as quickly discarded until the Merchant Navy pacifics gained favour, with the first entering traffic from Eastleigh Works in 1941. Later the class was increased to thirty while in 1945 came the generally similar but smaller West Country class which eventually totalled no less than 110. Therefore, the Southern Railway, despite its belated start, in course of time possessed more pacific locomotives than the LMS and almost as many as the LNER.

From the outset the two Bulleid classes received more comment, eulogy and vituperation than any express locomotives since the Webb compounds at the turn of the century. They embodied many features new to British practice, including welded steel fireboxes, power-operated firedoors, 280 lb./sq. in. working pressure and box-section wheels, while details new to any country were the encased radial valve-gear with chain operation and pump lubrication, the outside admission piston valves with between-head drive and the oil-bath enclosure of the inside big-end, main rod and crosshead. There was also little enchantment for the air-smoothed casing which embraced the smokebox, boiler and cab with such a devastating effect on appearance and accessibility.

Unfortunately, experience proved many of the misgivings valid, and much expenditure of resources and time was necessary before the Running Department found either class fully acceptable. Much of this occurred in the early years when both commodities were at a premium and the overriding demand was for reliability and simplicity. However, once the worst idiosyncrasies had been mastered, the Merchant Navies and West Countries gave such an excellent account of themselves that they completely revolutionised the Southern Railway express services.

In this book the complete history of the 30 Merchant Navies and 110 West Countries/ Battle of Britains is given. Dimensions are quoted together with full lists of detail alterations, dates of building, renaming, renumbering, rebuilding and withdrawal. Full coverage is also given to the early difficulties and the remedial measures introduced before and after Nationalisation, while accounts are offered of the rebuilding programme instigated by British Railways in 1951-6 when 90 of the 140 Bulleid pacifics were equipped at great expense with Walschaerts valve-gear and other conventional features. Detailed accounts are similarly presented of the 1948 locomotive exchanges and other trials involving these classes, including material hitherto not readily available to the non-railway fraternity.

A large proportion of the information has been obtained from official sources and in a number of instances disagrees with previously published accounts. In such cases the greatest care has been taken to have the details verified and the author believes that the version now presented is authentic. The records kept at Ashford, Eastleigh and Brighton Works were not on a uniform basis, particularly in the period before Nationalisation, and on several occasions this has prevented full documentation of some minor modifications.

Over the last seven years many friends have contributed to the preparation and illustrating of this book. First and foremost, I am indebted to Mr. Robert Cogger, late of the Transport Museum, Clapham, for making available the general arrangement and detailed drawings of the Bulleid pacifics as well as the engine, boiler, frame, cylinder, axle and tender record cards. Much moral and factual assistance also came from Messrs. Barry Fletcher, Sid Nash, George Woodward and Eric Youldon, while yet again Ted Fry has supplied many of the illustrations. To them all I am most grateful.

The line drawing of No. 21C101 *Exeter* was produced by Mr. D. Rodgers, to whom the Society is indebted.

The MERCHANT NAVY Class

There is little doubt that Oliver Vaughan Snell Bulleid on appointment as Chief Mechanical Engineer found the Southern Railway's steam power at a particularly low ebb and that critical remarks made by him at the time were fully justified. The cause of this unfortunate state of affairs was the benevolent, if bureaucratic, rule of Sir Herbert Walker, who as General Manager had led the Company from an undistinguished pre-grouping record to become the most successful British railway and one capable of paying regularly a dividend of 5 per cent. With the private motorist not yet a serious menace, he had proved that a railway could be made to pay and at the same time remain positively attractive to its customers.

This success was founded on suburban and main-line electrification at a period when office workers in London were being edged away from the centre by congestion and a rise of property values in many middle-class districts. Status could only be maintained by migration to the home counties. Under Sir Herbert's guidance and zeal, the Southern led the resulting assault on the Kent, Surrey, Sussex and Hampshire countryside by creating a network of electrified commuter services. Once these became operational, thousands of new houses were constructed and sold, connecting farms, villages and market towns into the vast subtopian sprawls of today.

The trade depression of the early 1930's left southern England less affected than the remainder of the country and, although money was lost by the steam services, the receipts from the electrified lines increased steadily, for the City workers much appreciated their cleanliness, punctuality, frequency, comfort and speed.

Not satisfied with modernising the inner suburban services, Sir Herbert cast the Southern Railway's net further afield and electrified to Brighton and Worthing in 1933, Sevenoaks, Eastbourne and Hastings in 1935, Portsmouth in 1937 and Bognor Regis in 1938. At once these lines, too, recorded sizeable receipt increases and gave rise to visions of complete electrification, with the steam locomotive becoming a necessary evil until it could be eradicated. Funds, therefore, were only sparingly allotted for maintenance, re-boilering, modernising and new construction; thus, by 1937, much of the steam stock was elderly and underpowered, and unless conversion to electricity could be significantly hastened there was the distinct possibility of a breakdown in steam services.

Therefore, even with allowance for the differing customs and backgrounds of the London & North Eastern and Southern Railways, there existed a vast contrast in direction of thought. Above all, it existed in the respective approaches to the steam locomotive which, at King's Cross, had developed in stature until it had become the most important factor of the Company's image. This, Bulleid fully appreciated and understood; the attitude adopted at Waterloo to all things steam, he certainly did not.

A change of official attitude was essential if steam was to survive efficiently, although just how this was to be achieved must have caused Bulleid much deliberation. Fortunately, two factors offered material assistance, his own tact and impeccable manners, and the retirement of Sir Herbert Walker in favour of Gilbert Szlumper. The latter shared the enthusiasm for all things electric, but he appreciated that as an intermediate measure some improvement in steam stock was necessary. Behind the scenes, Bulleid astutely encouraged this appreciation, as well as suggesting that a handful of swallows did not make a summer and likewise that a few modern steam locomotives did not rejuvenate those already growing grey in service. Nevertheless, he was only partly successful, for at the Rolling Stock Committee meeting of 22 March 1938, the thirty express locomotives requested were reduced to twenty of an unspecified design. This decision was formally approved by the Locomotive & Electrical Committee on 30 March 1938, the cost being estimated as £110,000.

The way was now open for Bulleid to commence his steam modernisation scheme, admittedly on a very moderate scale, but at least the need of such action had been officially accepted and with perseverance there was no reason why further steam orders could not be gained. By this date, outside influences were also working for Bulleid, first Munich, and then the knowledge that war with Hitler's Germany was inevitable. Coal and steam power rapidly regained respectability, and a further meeting of the Locomotive & Electrical Committee agreed, without comment, to extend the number of locomotives on order to thirty.

All now required was a decision on the basic details of the new locomotives, but, unfortunately, these were not immediately forthcoming, for Bulleid had been outpaced by events and had not determined the precise form that construction should follow. In part this was the result of attempting to reconcile the diverse motive power requirements of the

Eastern and Western Sections, for although the latter could be worked reasonably satisfactorily by the modified Lord Nelson's, the former could not. Bulleid envisaged working the Eastern Section with its sharp gradients and heavily-loaded "Night Ferry" and "Golden Arrow" expresses by eight-coupled locomotives, and the Western Section by pacifics and Lord Nelsons.

Further investigation and thought hardened these feelings and since the Eastern Section's need for new locomotives was more urgent, Bulleid had drawings prepared for a three-cylinder 2-8-2, with 6ft. 0in. coupled wheels and a weight of 112 tons in working order. In December 1938 details were passed to the Civil Engineer for comment and, after modification to 4-8-2, in order to remove the objection to the leading truck, the design was rejected in March 1939. The long rigid wheelbase and the weight received adverse comment, while the size of the coupled wheels was also questioned. In view of later developments, it is interesting to note that both designs included a number of Doncaster features, although the BFB wheels, steel fireboxes and three sets of Walschaerts valve-gear were not standard Doncaster fittings.

As long as the chance remained of placing a number of new express locomotives in service on the Eastern Section at an early date, Bulleid was prepared to accept conventional features, in particular, those of Gresley's that he had found acceptable on the LNER, the derived motion not unexpectedly being tactfully forgotten. However, once delays occurred, he decided not only to place his faith on a pacific suitable for service on both Eastern and Western Sections, but also to incorporate a number of revolutionary ideas of his own. This in turn made further delays unavoidable, especially when the 4-8-2 boiler required major modification to suit the new design and the incorporation of a steel firebox. It appears that at this period the Rolling Stock and Locomotive & Electrical Committees had little idea of what was afoot, while the Civil Engineer was vainly requesting detailed drawings of the new locomotives as late as October 1939, two months after the first boilers had been ordered from the North British Locomotive Company.

Much of the design was undertaken by Brighton, but Eastleigh and Ashford Works also played an important role. From the various reference numbers of the drawings and their distribution, it is difficult not to conclude that Bulleid deliberately intended to restrict full knowledge of the new class to a limited selection of personnel. Indeed, the secret was so well maintained that the ability of Eastleigh to contruct the proposed locomotives was not fully examined, and when this finally occurred, the equipment and techniques available there proved unequal to the boiler size and the all-welded inner steel firebox. These had to be ordered at a cost of £2,850 each from the North British Locomotive Company with the thermic syphons being sub-contracted to Beyer Peacock & Co.

Before the locomotive and tender design had been finalised and the boilers ordered, the European nations were on the brink of hostilities and, with War Department commitments, construction could not be hastened. Similarly, Eastleigh Works became inundated and was forced to pass construction of the tenders and the preparation of the main framing to Ashford Works. Trouble was also met obtaining delivery of the cylinder castings and, when these did arrive, most had to be rejected as below standard.

Under these circumstances, when lesser mortals would have quietly accepted defeat and cancelled assembly until more propitious times, Bulleid merely postponed part of the order and continued with the remainder as labour and materials became available. Little serious work, however, was possible before the first of the North British boilers reached Eastleigh in November 1940, but thereafter steady progress was made until 17 February 1941, when the first Bulleid pacific left the Erecting Shop for steaming in the yards. On the following day two return journeys were made to Winchester, while on 22 February a trial train of ten coaches was worked to and from Bournemouth West. Various minor adjustments were then made before other test runs were made to Brockenhurst, Basingstoke and Salisbury, the last of these with a sixty-three wagon goods and two brake vans.

For some years the notation employed by European railways to describe the wheel arrangement of steam locomotives had been based on a logical and easily-manipulated system of letters denoting the number of coupled wheels and figures describing the location and number of carrying axles. A pacific, for instance, was recorded as 2C1 and an atlantic as 2B1. Bulleid evidently was impressed by the system and decided to adopt it for his new express class, although for reasons best known to himself he introduced at the same time a number of modifications which made the end product bizarre and of limited value. So it came about that the Southern Railway's first pacific entered traffic as 21C1, the final figure denoting the running number.

The original intention had been to name the class after British land, sea and air victories of the Second World War. Since these, by 1941, had been few and of doubtful authenticity, the idea had to be abandoned, but not before a trial rectangular nameplate had been prepared in wood. This was entitled *The Plate* and commemorated the destruction of the German pocket battleship *Graf Spee* by H.M. cruisers *Exeter*, *Ajax* and *Achilles*. Capital cities of the United Kingdom and Commonwealth were then given consideration, but failed to satisfy the critics, and resort was finally made on the suggestion of the Chairman of the Union Castle Line, to the names of shipping companies which regularly called in peacetime at Southampton. Both left- and right-handed circular centre plates were provided to ensure that the companies' house flags flew correctly while the locomotives were running forwards. Despite the nameplates being lettered "Merchant Navy Class", Bulleid preferred the classification 21C1 and, on his insistence, this was entered on the record cards and other official documents, this applying also to the second series of 1944-5. No. 21C1 was named *Channel Packet* after the Southern Railway's own cross-Channel fleet, the ceremony being performed by the Minister of Transport, Lt.-Col. J. T. C. Moore-Brabazon, at Eastleigh Works on 10 March 1941.

During April and May 1941, No. 21C1 *Channel Packet* was employed on a wide range of Western Section goods and semi-fast passenger duties, interspersed by several visits to Eastleigh Works for adjustments, minor modifications, and the fitting of larger sand containers and a new regulator of improved design. The tender also gave considerable trouble, the leading axle boxes regularly running hot and the tank welding proving inadequate to withstand the surge of water when partly filled. Modifications were also necessary to the drawgear and handbrake mechanism. As a temporary measure in May 1941, it was exchanged for T3112, which was awaiting the second locomotive of the series. Regular revenue-earning service was entered from Salisbury on 4 June 1941, where it was joined by No. 21C2, *Union Castle*, twelve days later. On 4 July 1941, No. 21C2 *Union Castle* was officially named at Victoria and later hauled a four-coach special conveying guests via the Quarry Line to Earlswood. From there it retired to Redhill for turning and servicing before working the train back to Charing Cross in the early evening.

The budgeted cost of the class underwent several revisions, but even the final £16,000 each was handsomely exceeded by No. 21C1 *Channel Packet*. On the date that it entered revenue-earning service it had cost no less than £23,840, while an additional £11,368 was debited to design and allied expenses. No. 21C2 *Union Castle* cost £20,146, and the remaining eight members of the original series between £18,470 and £19,144 each.

The dimensions were as follows:

Cylinders (3) ..	18″×24″
Piston valves ..	11″
Bogie wheels ..	3′ 1″
Coupled wheels ..	6′ 2″
Trailing wheels ..	3′ 7″
Wheelbase ..	6′ 3″+5′ 6″+7′ 6″+7′ 6″+10′ 0″=36′ 9″
Boiler diameter ..	5′ 9¾″ to 6′ 3½″
Boiler length ..	16′ 9½″ (tube length 17′ 0″)
Firebox length ..	7′ 10½″
Heating surfaces:	
Tubes (124×2¼″)	1,241.6 sq. ft.
Flues (40×5¼″)	934.3 sq. ft.
Firebox and thermic syphons..	275.0 sq. ft.
Total evaporative	2,450.9 sq. ft.
Superheater ..	665.0 sq. ft.
Combined total	3,115.9 sq. ft.
Grate area ..	48.5 sq. ft.
Working pressure	280 lb./sq. in.

The estimated working order weight was 92½ tons of which 63 tons were carried by the coupled wheels. This the Civil Engineer found acceptable, although he intimated that 3 tons less adhesion would be preferable, if it was intended to employ the class regularly on the Eastern Section. Most prototypes weigh more than the totals written into their specification, although it is doubtful whether many suffered to the degree Bulleid achieved with Nos. 21C1 *Channel Packet* and 21C2 *Union Castle*, for both turned the scales at over 99½ tons. On being appraised of this, the Civil Engineer insisted that immediate measures were taken to reduce the weight of the next eight locomotives. As a result, their assembly was halted and not recommenced until the practical degree of reduction was apparent and had received approval.

Much of the excess weight was found in the massive cast-steel frame stretchers, where a reduction of three-sixteenths of an inch in thickness offered a worthwhile saving of 23½ cwt. The lightening holes in the main framing were also found capable of enlargement, while others could be cut with little loss of strength. With the same aim, thinner plating was worked into the casing top, cab sides and smokebox, "limpet" board used for the casing sides, and the king-size numberplates discarded in favour of transfer numerals. By such means a saving of 4 tons was anticipated, although when weighed in working order No. 21C3 *Royal Mail* scaled 96 tons 8 cwt., an actual reduction of 3 tons 4 cwt. Detailed working order weights of Nos. 21C1/2/9 were as follows:

Locomotive	*21C1*	*21C2*	*21C9*
Date	4.6.1941	3.6.1944	25.6.1942
Bogie	16 tons 10 cwt.	16 tons 12 cwt.	16 tons 18 cwt.
Leading coupled wheels ..	22 tons 12 cwt.	21 tons 10 cwt.	21 tons 5 cwt.
Centre coupled wheels	22 tons 12 cwt.	21 tons 14 cwt.	21 tons 8 cwt.
Trailing coupled wheels ..	22 tons 12 cwt.	21 tons 10 cwt.	21 tons 5 cwt.
Trailing wheels	15 tons 6 cwt.	15 tons 12 cwt.	15 tons 12 cwt.
Locomotive total	99 tons 12 cwt.	96 tons 18 cwt.	96 tons 8 cwt.
Tender	47 tons 19 cwt.	47 tons 19 cwt.	47 tons 16 cwt.
Locomotive and tender.. ..	147 tons 11 cwt.	144 tons 17 cwt.	144 tons 4 cwt.

In all cases the weighing cards showed three inches of water in the glass, a light fire burning, about 100 lb./sq. in. boiler pressure and the tender fully laden. No. 21C1 *Channel Packet* in December 1943 and No. 21C2 *Union Castle* in June 1944 were similarly modified, although it was not until October 1949 and January 1950 respectively that their number and Southern plates were finally discarded.

The dates that the remaining locomotives entered traffic were: 1941 Nos. 21C3 *Royal Mail* (September), 21C4 *Cunard White Star* (October), 21C5 *Canadian Pacific*, 21C6 *Peninsular & Oriental S.N.Co.* (December); 1942 Nos. 21C7 *Aberdeen Commonwealth*, 21C8 *Orient Line*, 21C9 *Shaw Savill* (June), 21C10 *Blue Star* (July).

Nos. 21C1 to 21C5 were painted malachite green with a matt surface in an attempt to conceal the small irregularities inherent in large areas of thin metal plating. Three horizontal yellow bands ran the length of the air-smoothed casing and were continued along the tender. The matt paintwork quickly became grimy and unattractive, and was not repeated. Nos. 21C6 to 21C10 entered traffic painted plain black. Nos. 21C5 *Canadian Pacific* quickly lost its malachite livery, for black was applied prior to the official naming ceremony in March 1942. The others lost their malachite livery as follows: 21C1 *Channel Packet*—December 1943, 21C2 *Union Castle*—June 1944, 21C3 *Royal Mail*—June 1942, and 21C4 *Cunard White Star*—July 1943. By 1943 those retaining the green had assumed a streaky khaki hue with much of the yellow bands obscured by grime or erased by the elements.

Bulleid's original instructions for painting the class involved the top horizontal yellow band passing along the casing just below the bottom washout plug and thence across the cab side sheets, level with the top framing of the side windows. No. 21C1 *Channel Packet* is known to have been painted in this manner while being completed in the Erecting Shop, but before being removed to the yards for steaming and the taking of official photographs, this band had been raised above the washout plug and over the cab windows. It was then level with the top of the tender and was extended along the sides of the coal space. It also appears likely that, had the country not been at war, Bulleid would have used chromium-plated numberplates, tender plates, external piping and handrailing. One drawing shows a rectangular nameplate bolted A4 fashion to the casing above the cylinders, and another above the centre coupled wheels where they were eventually placed.

Most of the design work was undertaken at Brighton, although that of the boiler and firebox was shared with Ashford, while Eastleigh dealt with the tender. The three cylinders were prepared separately to simplify the casting and machining. All drove the centre coupled axle, the outside pair being inclined at 1 in 40 with centres ahead and lower than the inside cylinder which was inclined at 1 in 7¾ to provide clearance for the inside connecting rod above the leading coupled axle. This gave main rod lengths of 8ft. inside and 11ft. outside. Incoming steam entered the casting at the top flange which led to the cored feedpipe, giving passage through to either end of the steam chests. The volume of this pipe and the two end steam-chests was 2.6 cu. ft. or 5 per cent greater than the cylinder volume with full cut-off. The port area through the valve liners was 40.7 sq. in., and this opened to an area of 254.5 sq. in. through the cylinder barrel, the clearance volume being 9.8 per cent. The exhaust of the inside cylinder was directed into the cavity below the blastpipe, while that of the outside cylinders passed through the exhaust pipe flange and thence via a fabricated external pipe to the centre cylinder casting, where the three exhausts joined under the blastpipe.

Unusually for the period, the piston valves had outside admission, while even more unexpectedly they did not have circular-section spindles connecting the two heads, nor were they spindle-driven at the rear end from the valve motion. Instead the valve heads were connected by means of a double girder welded to the end plates, while a cross-pin in this girder took the drive from a rocker shaft and arms, which in turn were driven by a 50in. rod from a guided plunger off the combination lever of the valve motion. This eliminated the normal valve-spindle stuffing box, but, unfortunately, did not prove entirely successful in regular traffic, as the arm of the rocking spindle was prone to failure. The arrangement of the cylinders and valve chest was neatly symmetrical, with valve heads of 11in. diameter or 61 per cent of the cylinder diameter, which was probably the highest ratio employed in the country. At 18in. by 24in., the three cylinders were equal in piston-swept volume to two of 21½in. by 26in. Their small diameter was made possible by the high steam pressure which in turn reduced the reciprocating weight and kept the outside cylinder well within the loading gauge. To gain the best from small diameter high-pressure cylinders, steampipes and passages must, of necessity, be ample and direct, with the valve events arranged to offer a high expansion ratio, yet avoiding over-compression and heating of the big-end brasses. All was provided, at least on paper and when locomotives were in good mechanical order. Because of this, the class was exceptionally free-running, with speeds of 90-95 m.p.h. easily obtainable without any particular effort or preparation by the crew.

Bulleid, like Gresley, did not favour divided drive, and the increased frame length and short connecting rods unavoidable with inside cylinders driving on the leading coupled axle. Equally, Bulleid disliked the use of derived motion for inside cylinders, he had seen this at first-hand on the LNER. Standard Walschaerts motion could not be accommodated between the frames if the middle cylinder drove the second coupled axle on account of the leading axle's intervention. Maunsell overcame this difficulty in his three-cylinder 2-6-0's by the introduction of twin eccentrics and a very short combination lever, but in traffic, maintenance of this was heavy and the failure rate higher than normal. This left Bulleid with little choice but to evolve an entirely new type of valve motion. Various layouts were investigated at Brighton, including one which employed derived motion direct from the driving axle, but when all proved impracticable Bulleid turned to a separate three-throw crankshaft. This had the advantage of permitting the total enclosure of all three sets of valve motion within an oil-bath and offered economies in maintenance and preparation. The intention was to drive the crankshaft by means of gears and a propeller shaft, as with the rotary-cam poppet valve motion, but the necessary gears could not be obtained in wartime. A chain drive was substituted in which the crankshaft working the expansion links was driven by two chains, one horizontally from the crank axle to an intermediate sprocket wheel, and the other vertically down to the crankshaft at the bottom of the oil-bath sump, an arrangement which allowed for the up-and-down movement of the crank axle on its springs and did not disturb the working of the valve motions. The crankshaft, revolving at the same speed as the crank axle and having each crank phased with its own big-end, imparted the motion to the three piston valves. On account of the confined space into which the three sets of valve motion had to be fitted, the maximum throw of the expansion links was restricted to 37½ per cent of the maximum valve travel, the difference being made good by a proportionately unequal length of the rocker arms.

The inside crosshead and slide bars, the inside connecting rod with its big-ends, the crank axle and all three sets of valve motion were contained within the oil-bath with a sump holding 40 gallons of lubricating oil. From the sump, two gear pumps driven off the three-throw crankshaft passed oil continuously at 18 lb./sq. in. through perforated pipes over the moving parts not actually immersed in the lubricant. The sprocket on which the pair of chains operated was designed for adjusting in position to take up the stretching likely to occur in regular service.

The weight of one set of standard Walschaerts gear of suitable dimensions for the Merchant Navy was estimated as 1,150 lb., whereas a single set of Bulleid's gear was only 945 lb. But to three sets of the latter had to be added 330 lb. for the oil contained in the bath and the bath itself. Therefore, although the unsprung weight of the Bulleid gear was less, the total weight was much the same as that of conventional Walschaerts gear. Another unusual feature was the absence of any reciprocating balance. On all locomotives it is necessary to fully balance the rotating parts, but opinion differed as to the proportion of reciprocating parts which should be balanced. Too great reciprocating balance increased the hammer-blow on the track, while too little led to severe lateral oscillation. Bulleid dispensed entirely with reciprocating balance and, with the assistance of the three-cylinder propulsion, successfully counteracted any tendency for rough riding at speed. There was no normal hammer-blow in the wheels caused by excess mass of revolving weight, but there was "true" hammer-blow from the vertical thrust of the inside cylinder. This, however, would decrease rapidly as the speed increased and above 50 m.p.h. would have little noticeable effect.

Reversing was by steam, not because Bulleid particularly favoured the method, but on account of the wide firebox and triple ashpans not permitting a reasonable arrangement of screw reversing gear. Fine adjustment, unfortunately, was not provided.

The boiler also contained unconventional features, for the front ring tapered on the underside while the rear ring was parallel, and the inner firebox was of steel instead of copper. Welding was not used for the boiler barrel, but the outer firebox shell, the inner firebox and combustion chamber, and the two thermic syphons were welded throughout, the inner and outer fireboxes being welded together at the firehole. The use of a steel inner firebox came about for a number of reasons, among which the saving of copper was not included, for the decision had been made before the war. The saving of weight was obviously important with such a large boiler, and the steel welded firebox saved some 1½ tons over a riveted copper box. At temperatures in excess of 440° F. loss of strength and elasticity would occur on the water side of the copper side plates, but not with steel. This presented another reason, as did the desirability of avoiding the use of steel tubes and copper tube plates. Syphons may have improved circulation, but Bulleid was more concerned with promoting greater safety with low water in view of the exceptionally high pressure. The latter was deemed necessary to limit cylinder size and reciprocating weight and yet retain a high tractive effort.

The smokebox was fabricated instead of being circular and supported by a saddle. Because the inside valve chamber projected well into the base and the top front was cut away for smoke lifting, the final shape was irregular and led, incidentally, to the unusual shaped door. Although over 8ft. long, the interior was well encumbered by the extra piping required by the outside admission piston valves, as well as large-diameter steampipes, the blower pipe and the exhaust pipe coming out of the tube plate.

One of Bulleid's earliest innovations on the Southern was the use of Lemaître multi-jet blastpipes on the Lord Nelsons. The same principles were adopted on the pacifics, with five 2⅝in. diameter nozzles discharging upward through a 25in. choke. The nozzles were 15⅝in. below the boiler centre line and exhausted through a large-diameter prefabricated chimney.

The main frames with welded hornblocks were centred above the axleboxes, thereby giving one centre line for the frames, boxes, guides and springs, and cut-out offset thrust. Hitherto, this had been one of the main advantages of bar framing, and was a feature perpetuated by the BR standard classes. Exceptionally good horizontal cast-steel racking stays were provided, although the bracing was weakened when holes had to be enlarged, and others cut, and lighter fabricated stays and plates substituted in order to reduce weight.

A further break with tradition occurred in the design of the wheels. In North America much use was being made of cast steel wheel centres of the Boxpok type, instead of the spoked wheels preferred in the United Kingdom. Their employment avoided the necessity of providing retaining rings, set bolts and the like, as well as offering greater and more continuous support to the tyre. The fastening depended entirely on shrinkage, with but a single turned lip on the outside and a small lip on the inside cold-rolled over the centre with the tyre positioned. Rather than adopt a proprietary wheel, of which several were on the market, Bulleid, in alliance with Thos. Firth & John Brown, steelmakers of Sheffield, made a number of variations and evolved the BFB pattern (Bulleid-Firth-Brown). The centres were lightened by a series of cavities and holes, the former having the resemblance of eight large-size half spokes. By these means the weight was 12 per cent less than similarly-sized spoked wheels.

Although the 6ft. 2in. coupled wheels were of smaller diameter than those of the LNER pacifics, among which much of Bulleid's professional life had been spent, the coupled wheelbase and engine wheelbase were actually longer. This was necessary to keep the locomotives within the lower lineal loading necessitated by the Southern Railway bridges, in particular those of the Eastern Section. As a result, ample space was available between the coupled wheels and this was used to advantage by fitting clasp braking with each intermediate hanger carrying two blocks, one for the wheel ahead and the other for the wheel behind. Only the coupled wheels were braked, this by means of a pair of 8in. steam cylinders, which gave a maximum pull on the blocks of about 57 tons, equal to 97 per cent of the adhesive weight and 60 per cent of the working order weight. Some saving of weight was achieved by the use of steam instead of vacuum braking, and probably accounted for the preference. No such limitations applied to the tenders and these were vacuum fitted. The sanding arrangements for such large and powerful locomotives was particularly meagre, it being applied only to the centre coupled wheels and with no provision whatsoever for tender-first working. A sand container was inconveniently sited on either side within the air-smoothed casing, where replenishment was only possible by means of a ladder or staging, as each filler hole was level with the nameplate top. Access was by means of sliding covers, but these, too, proved an embarrassment by either jamming at one or other extremity, or working so slack that they opened and closed with movement on the road.

The leading bogie was similar to that of the Lord Nelsons, though the 7ft. 6in. wheelbase was shortened to the LNER standard of 6ft. 3in. The pivot had a side play of 3¼in. controlled by spiral springs having an initial compression of 3 tons, rising to 5¾ tons at maximum throw-over. The trailing truck structure was of one-piece cast steel and contributed greatly to the steady running of the rear end. It was of delta pattern with three-point suspension, spring side control and the weight transmitted through sliding pads.

Externally there was no superstructure of the kind normally found in locomotive practice, although hidden from sight were splashers and a running-plate. The boiler was concealed under a steel casing which at the rear conformed to the profile of the Belpaire firebox and at the leading end extended ahead of the smokebox in two wings intended to function as smoke deflectors. This casing was supported by bearers of channel section, attached to the main frames. The smokebox was of the same shape as the casing and was fabricated from thin steel plate with its top supporting an equally lightly-constructed chimney.

For British locomotives the crews were offered an unusual measure of comfort, for in addition to the large roomy cab with two sliding side windows, the front of the tender was raised to the height of the cab roof and connected by flexible sheeting to make the footplate most habitable. So comfortable, in fact, that in warm weather, firemen found the almost total enclosure somewhat overpowering when travelling slowly and firing heavily. A small steam-driven generator provided power for the electric lighting which illuminated the steam reverser, cut-off indicator, water gauges and injectors. To avoid interference with night vision, ultra-violet bulbs were used so that the figures, pointers, etc., glowed faintly and left the remainder of the cab interior dark. Lamps were also available as route indicators after dark on both the engine front and the rear of the tender, and inside the boiler casing to facilitate oiling and inspection. For day use brackets were provided for the standard Southern white route boards and shed duty numbers.

The fireman's task was eased by the fitting of a power-operated firedoor. By means of a small steam cylinder, operated by a pedal on the cab floor, the fireman, by pivoting on the foot depressing the pedal, could swing round with his shovel of coal from the tender and feed the fire without having first to open the firebox door. This also avoided the necessity of leaving the door open during lengthy spells of firing, air being emitted via a series of small holes. Both injectors were sited on the fireman's side of the cab so they could be attended without his having to cross the footplate or disturb the driver.

The tender profile conformed with that of the latest coaching stock and was fabricated from steel plating $\frac{3}{16}$in. thick. Construction was undertaken in the Paint Shop at Ashford Works, where modern welding equipment was available and the latest techniques employed. The estimated cost was £770 each, but by the time service was entered this had risen to £945. They ran on six wheels, had an equally-divided 13ft. 0in. wheelbase, and a capacity of 5,000 gallons of water and 5 tons of coal. The tare weight was 20 tons 10 cwt. (Nos. 21C1/2 20 tons 13 cwt.), and that fully laden 47 tons 16 cwt. (Nos. 21C1/2 47 tons 19 cwt.). The 3ft. 7in. diameter wheels, like those of the engine, were of BFB pattern and were clasp-braked by means of two 21in. vacuum cylinders to a force equivalent to 115 per cent of the tare weight.

As on the later Maunsell tenders, the vacuum cylinders were grouped on the tank top to the rear of the coal space and in front of the filler opening. Two further filler holes were provided at the front end to relieve the fireman of the chore of climbing on top of the tender when replenishing and to enable the water level to be checked in safety on the road, without the provision of gauges.

The intention of the air-smoothed casing enclosing the smokebox, boiler, firebox and cab was to lift the exhaust gases, in particular steam, away from the lookout windows. In No. 21C1 *Channel Packet* the side casings were swept round higher than the chimney and had the front plate of the smokebox rising vertically to meet them. In this front plate a large horizontal slit was cut over the smokebox door so that air forced through by the passage of the locomotive along the track was released violently upwards via a smaller slit in the casing top just forward of the chimney and lifted the exhaust. Unfortunately, in practice no such effect occurred, for the air overflowing from a shallow recess behind the smokebox front plate created areas of low pressure along the casing sides and these drew the exhaust gases downwards to drift rearwards and loiter around the cab windows. As soon as this became apparent, the incomplete No. 21C2 *Union Castle* had its smokebox front cut away above the door to expose the top plate which sloped back to the chimney centre line. On the casing top the rectangular slot and the chimney opening were combined to give a single square aperture with rounded corners. On trial, reasonable clearance was obtained and the modifications were applied to Nos. 21C3 to 21C10 during construction.

When new, No. 21C1 *Channel Packet* was equipped with a circular plate pivoted at the circumference, which could be rotated to cover the chimney when standing out of steam in the shed. No. 21C2 *Union Castle* was to be similarly fitted, but this proved impracticable after the smokebox modifications. The provision of such fittings in wartime yet again illustrates the vast gulf that existed between Bulleid and the men who had to operate his locomotives, for no practising railwayman could imagine a stabling crew with an out-of-steam locomotive bothering to find a ladder to cover the chimney. Even if they should, then the chance of the lighting-up gang recalling the chimney encumbrance appears even more remote until the freshly-lit fire went out.

Other detail changes were also made to the front end. No. 21C1 *Channel Packet* had a lightly constructed bar-iron footstep on the left-hand side only with a foot block above it on the buffer casing to give access to the running plate below the smokebox door. Almost at once these fittings were duplicated on the right-hand side, and they appeared on Nos. 21C2 to 21C10 when new. There were also minor differences between the first two locomotives, inasmuch that No. 21C1 *Channel Packet* had the hinged flat running plate below the smokebox door secured by front hasps.

Large cast brass plates inscribed "Southern" were attached to the smokebox doors of Nos. 21C1 and 21C2; these were of circular form with a gap at the base, having the appearance of horseshoes hung the wrong way up. Some crews objected to this traditionally unlucky symbol, and, when this was brought to Bulleid's notice, he had the emblem changed to fully circular—No. 21C1 in February 1942 and No. 21C2 in December 1941—while Nos. 21C3 to 21C10 were so equipped when new. The additional space was gainfully employed to record the date and place of construction.

Differences also occurred in the positioning of the front numberplates. On No. 21C1 *Channel Packet* it was attached to the sloping section of sheeting where deciphering could prove difficult; therefore on the second locomotive it was re-sited lower down on the vertical sheeting and the lights-cum-disc brackets moved above to the sloping section. No. 21C1 *Channel Packet* was modified to conform in August 1941. This followed a minor mishap at Templecombe during the blackout, when timber on a passing goods train struck the casing a glancing blow.

The electric lamps could be switched on or off individually to present at night the route codes employed by the Southern Railway. Each light incorporated a vertical bracket to support the white discs carried for the same purpose by day, one of which displayed the locomotive duty in black figures. Similar lights and brackets were positioned on the rear of the tender, these being mostly required when working light engine to and from running sheds at the beginning or end of journeys. By mischance the second tier of locomotive front lamps and brackets were so sited that, when carrying discs, there was a projection outside the air-smoothed casing which proved dangerous for passing trains, or high winds tore them adrift. As high-speed missiles, these discs could cause a surprisingly large degree of damage. There was also some obscuring of the lookout ahead, especially as regards low-positioned signals. Nevertheless, all the first twenty of the class were similarly fitted, and it was April 1946 before the first, No. 21C4 *Cunard White Star*, had the offending brackets transferred to the smokebox door.

In revenue-earning service at Salisbury No. 21C1 *Channel Packet* quickly developed a host of minor troubles which kept it on shed for days, or even weeks, on end. As a result, only 11,069 miles were run between 4 June 1941 and 6 January 1942, when it entered Eastleigh Works for the fitting of new valve-gear chains and a modified oil-bath. Further trouble in September 1942 led to a second visit to works for the fitting of a new right-hand cylinder. No. 21C2 *Union Castle* did marginally better and, when sent to Eastleigh for attention to the main steampipes on 27 January 1942, had run 15,411 miles. Few express duties had been worked, most of the mileage having been accrued on the Salisbury-Exeter or Salisbury-Southampton goods services. No. 21C2 *Union Castle* on main freight duty was reported as burning 80 to 85 lb. of coal per mile.

During the delayed construction of Nos. 21C3 to 21C10 great efforts were made to reduce the many troublesome features, and their entry into traffic between September 1941 and July 1942 was not fraught with quite so many difficulties. Nevertheless, extra fitters had to be allotted to Salisbury to maintain Nos. 21C6 to 21C10 and to Exmouth Junction for Nos. 21C1 to 21C5, those for the latter mainly coming from Kentish sheds where their presence was no longer essential. Salisbury estimated that for every hour spent working on a King Arthur no less than 4½ were necessary for a pacific.

On account of the unusually high working pressure, it was considered necessary to supply steam to the class while standing on shed and when lit up from cold after washout. To provide this, withdrawn Adams 4-4-0 No. 657 was converted to a stationary boiler in February 1941 and despatched to Salisbury. Later, Adams 0-4-2 No. 646 took over this task and No. 657 was transferred to Exmouth Junction. Both locomotives had their pistons and valve rods removed, modified brick arches fitted, and steam hose connections on the dome. No. 657 was in use at Exmouth Junction on 11 October 1942, raising steam on No. 21C9 *Shaw Savill* following a boiler washout, but when Salisbury was visited on 2 July 1943, No. 646 was lying derelict and appeared not to have been steamed for many months. Experience had shown that their use was quite unnecessary.

Once all ten locomotives were in general service and being handled by a cross-section of crews, the strengths and weaknesses of the class became readily apparent. The steaming capacity and output appeared almost unlimited despite the moderate quality wartime coal; there was more power available than ever before on the Southern, while the riding at all speeds was impeccably smooth. Against this was the difficulty in starting even with moderate loads, slipping at speed, restricted lookout, high fuel consumption, time-consuming maintenance, oil bath leaks and numerous niggling minor faults which kept engines on shed. Much was done to reduce these failings to acceptable levels, but to some extent all remained until re-building in 1956-59.

During 1941-42 various test trains were worked to supply Bulleid with data regarding haulage capacity and fuel consumption. One on 9 November 1941 had No. 21C3 *Royal Mail* heading a sixteen-coach special from Waterloo to Salisbury, while later in the month 800-ton goods trains were worked between Salisbury and Exeter. Similarly Nos. 21C2 *Union Castle* and 21C4 *Cunard White Star* on various occasions had charge of 18-coach and 20-coach specials between Waterloo and Exeter, while No. 21C3 *Royal Mail* worked to and from Bournemouth West with a 17-coach train. Coal consumption, mileages and availability details dated 31 December 1942 are as follows:

Locomotive No.	*Mileage Run*	*Coal Burnt per mile (lb.)*	*Months in Traffic*	*Days in Works*	*Days Stopped on Shed*
21C1	35,082	56.2	18	96	213
21C2	39,892	57.8	18	102	197
21C3	38,548	56.7	15	106	168
21C4	25,911	59.1	13	108	172
21C5	29,688	60.3	12	81	103
21C6	35,992	61.5	12	36	88
21C7	23,892	58.6	6	33	47
21C8	24,625	57.4	6	27	46
21C9	26,802	58.7	5	5	34
21C10	24,224	56.3	4	6	29

On 18 November 1942, No. 21C4 *Cunard White Star* very nearly ended its career on the Southern, for while heading a goods it was shot up by a low-flying German fighter-bomber near Whimple. Most of the cannon shells missed the locomotive and hit two covered vans loaded with bacon and hams next to the tender. Both immediately burst into

flames, giving off a mouth-watering aroma of frying bacon, a wartime rarity, but not one fully appreciated by the locomotive crew and guard, who had to part the train and tackle the blaze as best they could with water from the tender, until assistance eventually reached them.

In the following month, on 17 December 1942, it was the turn of No. 21C6 *Peninsular & Oriental* to come to grief when working the evening Exeter-Salisbury goods. About half-a-mile east of Honiton a chain parted and, thrashing around in the oil-bath, caused absolute havoc until the engine came to rest. The scattered oil quickly ignited, setting the boiler cladding, sleepers and lineside bushes ablaze, and leaving the crew helpless until the local fire brigade reached the scene. A similar but less damaging mishap occurred to No. 21C1 *Channel Packet* on 7 October 1943, when backing-down from the running shed to the station at Salisbury. The resulting fire was quickly brought under control, but lengthy delays affected other traffic until fitters arrived and made it possible for the culprit to be removed to the shed.

Trouble was also met from the oil-baths. These held forty gallons of lubricating oil and extended between frames to enclose not only the chain drive and oscillating levers, but also the connecting rod big-end and crank webs, the slide bars, crossheads and piston rods. At speed these thrashed around creating immense pressure if the vents were not clear, which led to distortion and fracturing of the casing. Much oil also escaped from these vents, as well as via the axle seals and plungers, while fractures along the casing top gave entry to water and grime. Much of this leakage reached the wheel treads, causing slipping, and the boiler lagging where it provided a ready source of ignition. Various modifications were made to the oil-baths in 1942-43, but apparently without great success until a new pattern was fitted to No. 21C6 *Peninsular & Oriental* in April 1944. Some oil loss still occurred, although the loss via the seals and vents was greatly reduced, while an attempt was made to channel any water dripping off the boiler fittings away from the top of the bath. This, however, proved only partially successful and varying quantities of water which still got in had to be drained off daily by means of a cock at the base of the sump. Nevertheless, some remained, which led to corrosion of the motion pins, big-ends, etc., until a higher grade non-emulsifying oil was substituted for the standard grade. Even so, if locomotives were stored for any length of time it was necessary to drain the bath and refill with fresh oil, the expense being considerable.

The chains themselves proved expensive items, costing £128 each (in 1944) and having to be scrapped when they showed considerable wear at the 30-36,000 miles valve and piston examination. The longer chains comprised 118 links, and wear on the pins and holes, added to wear on the sprocket teeth, amounted to almost six inches of elongation in many instances. Thoughts of this sag in the chain as engines set back, and the horrible snatch at it when from the slack condition it was suddenly jerked taut by a violent slip on starting, are really startling. By 1956 these chains cost £200 each, a price which had risen to £280 when the last were purchased in 1965.

Failure of the rocker shaft keyways of the middle piston valves also caused concern in 1943. No. 21C1 *Channel Packet* failed twice from this cause in the early months of the year, while No. 21C3 *Royal Mail* was incapacitated on one of the demonstration runs. When the locomotives were new, damage was generally restricted to sheared keyways, but later, fracturing of the rocker arms also occurred. At the time, Eastleigh had little knowledge of stresses and strains set up in locomotive piston valves, so Bulleid instigated a thorough investigation of the failures. By January 1944 the cause had been traced to momentary inequalities of steam pressure on the piston valve heads which placed excessive strain on the valve-operating mechanism. A cure was achieved by adding balancing pipes to equalise pressure between the ends of the steam chests. No. 21C4 *Cunard White Star* in January 1944 was the first modified, with the others being dealt with as routine repairs became necessary. At the same time additional bearings were provided to support the rocker shaft, while changes to the piston-valve liners were intended to stop valve-head breakages. When new cylinders became necessary the equalising pipes were incorporated within the castings, dates being as follows:

Locomotive No.	*Date*	*Mileage*
21C1	12/1945	143,639
21C2	7/1945	139,675
21C3	2/1944	91,235
21C4	7/1945	124,306
21C5	1/1946	158,606
21C6	2/1946	173,100
21C7	8/1945	138,575
21C8	11/1944	113,569
21C9	9/1945	153,174
21C10	3/1947	205,633

Around the same period, consideration had again to be given to exhaust clearance, for time had proved the earlier modifications less successful than anticipated in all weather conditions. After further thought on the subject and lineside observation at localities where crews found the problem worst, it was concluded that the phenomenon was the result of the soft blast and low-pressure pockets along the firebox top and sides. On other Southern Railway locomotives large smoke-deflector plates fitted alongside the smokebox had proved beneficial in lifting exhaust gases, but it was not thought practical to apply the same remedy to the larger-boilered pacifics, until other solutions had been tested and found wanting.

In December 1942 No. 21C10 *Blue Star* was transferred to Eastleigh for employment as a mobile testbed, given a more sharply-angled gap for air flow above the smokebox door, and a chimney lowered by 2$\frac{13}{16}$in. This proved disastrous, especially in cuttings and when leaving tunnels, as the exhaust failed to rise clear of the casing top and gathered like smog around the cab. Changes were then made to the chimney lip and, when these offered no improvement, resort was made to the wind tunnel at Southampton University where tests were carried out with a scale model, using vaporised paraffin to simulate steam and smoke. Various modifications and additions were made to the model until a workable solution was found. Drawings were then prepared and in April 1943 No. 21C10 *Blue Star* was taken into works and equipped with a separate top cowl extending ahead and across the smokebox front plate and short individual smoke-deflector plates standing clear of the side casing and like the latter, curved noticeably inwards. This curving was added by Eastleigh Drawing Office without reference to the wind tunnel in an attempt to make the front end of the locomotives less severe, but it was a serious error and was not perpetuated on Nos. 21C1 to 21C9, their dates of modification being as follows: 1943 Nos. 21C1 (December), 21C8/9 (June); 1944 Nos. 21C2 (June), 21C3 (September), 21C4 (January), 21C5 (March), 21C6 (April), 21C7 (August).

Prior to the wind tunnel experiments, Bulleid had considered various alternative front-end layouts and drawings of three of these were found at Eastleigh Works in August 1964. The most interesting was the provision of small steam jets along the casing top at the rear of the chimney to break up any low-pressure pockets and instil lift to the exhaust. Control of the jets was left to the crew who, presumably, were to have activated them when the lookout became obscured. The other drawings showed the class with front ends approximating in profile to the LNER A4's and *Cock o' the North* as originally built. The last-mentioned transformation was not only highly impressive, but harmonised remarkably well with the remaining Bulleid features. Other drawings not directly concerned with exhaust clearance illustrated cab exteriors, including one having a V-front and three side windows, thereby suggesting that these alterations were in mind long before implementation.

The standard Maunsell-Urie double-bogie 5,000-gallon tenders constructed successfully by Eastleigh since 1918 were built like Dreadnoughts and seldom gave cause for concern in service. Indeed, they withstood the ravages of time and rough usage remarkably well and took occasional minor accidents as part of the day's work. Such, unfortunately, was not the case with the Bulleid tenders, for the slightest knock invariably had dire consequences and led to withdrawal from traffic until repairs could be executed. Trouble was also experienced with the thin and inadequately-braced tank plating, which bulged and split along the welds when heavy braking caused surging of the contents. On occasions, the leakage was so widespread that tenders had the appearance of water carts once employed by local authorities to lay dust in the streets. In an attempt to counteract surging the tender from No. 21C4 *Cunard White Star* (T3114) was fitted in January 1944 with additional wash-plates and in April 1944 returned to traffic attached to No. 21C7 *Aberdeen Commonwealth*. No noticeable improvement occurred, so further thought was given to the problem; when No. 21C2 *Union Castle* was in works for its first general repair between 27 March and 3 June 1944, its tender (T3112) had the wash-plates re-sited, the side bracing strengthened, and much of the welding relieved of excessive stress. This proved more successful and by December 1945 all ten tenders had been similarly modified.

As built, Nos. 21C1 to 21C10 had no rearward sanding, but as much slipping took place when stock was being backed out of stations or into carriage sidings, some provision was essential. This was undertaken as simply and economically as possible by the addition of manually-operated and gravity-fed sand containers on the tenders which deposited their contents on the rails between the locomotive trailing wheels and the tender leading wheels. In service these boxes frequently clogged, while much of the sand in windy weather was swept clear before reaching the coupled wheels. Sanding on the locomotives in view of the low adhesion factor and oil-throwing propensity was also far from satisfactory, for it was only available to the front of the centre coupled wheels. Operation was by steam from containers placed part way up the casing with sliding covers to the filler holes. To augment supply, sanding was applied at first to the leading coupled wheels and, when this still proved inadequate, later to the rear coupled wheels also. The containers, in particular those supplying the front of the leading coupled wheels, were again sited inconveniently high in the casing.

The partial transfer of weight from the coupled wheels when starting away with a heavy train was a failing of all pacifics, but on the Merchant Navies this was accentuated by the low adhesion factor, the insensitive regulator, and oil seepage. As a result, inspectors were instructed to impress on drivers the absolute necessity of closing the regulator almost as soon as it was opened and then pumping it gently until a train was well on the move. In course of time this led to some improvement, although bouts of violent slipping on starting and at speed remained a characteristic until re-building. Buckled or broken coupling-rods were common, and by 1953-54 had reached such a pitch that a new and more robust pattern was prepared. However, in view of the pending re-building, little positive action was taken and only a few unrebuilt locomotives ran with plain rectangular-section coupling-rods.

Once the slipping propensities became known to signalmen, they tried to avoid stopping the class where restarting was likely to be a problem. Of course, this was not always possible and then onlookers often had an amusing few minutes watching the crew frantically trying to get on the move. One such place was on the sharp curve over the Bourne Valley viaduct leading to Bournemouth West station. Here, the check rails, camber and proximity of the rival Somerset & Dorset Section motive power depot made the task of restarting particularly taxing of nerve and skill. The class frequently came to grief here, yet an LMS Class 5 or GWR Hall similarly loaded pulled away without any fuss, slipping, or apparent effort.

Less worrying, though an ever-present irritant, was the tendency of the steam reversing gear to creep. This would not have been unduly troublesome to drivers using fully-open regulators and making cut-off changes to adjust their power output, but unfortunately this method of driving was seldom practised with the class until after re-building because of severe vibration when cut-offs were appreciably shortened. Equally wasteful of fuel was the lack of fine adjustment which frequently saw a locomotive working less efficiently than the circumstances necessitated. In an attempt to stop the creep, No. 21C6 *Peninsular & Oriental* was experimentally fitted, in August 1944, with a modified hydraulic locking-cylinder and given several test runs between Woking and Exeter to evaluate its effectiveness. Much better control was possible, though creep still existed, but to a degree unlikely to seriously inconvenience drivers on normal express duties. Good maintenance of the reverser was essential and this tended to be wasteful use of fitters' time, while steam leakages were present even on locomotives freshly despatched from the Works. Later members of the class were equipped with the modified locking-cylinder when new, but it appears from the records kept at Eastleigh that in addition to No. 21C6 *Peninsular & Oriental*, only Nos. 21C5 *Canadian Pacific* (June 1950) and 21C10 *Blue Star* (February 1945) were similarly modified before re-building.

The reversing gear creep was not alone in affecting the valve openings, for the final drive rocking levers which multiplied the intended movement by 2⅝ to 1 magnified any inaccuracy or wear up to plus or minus the same ratio. Therefore, if the valve-gear was not maintained in top condition, the valve openings would vary while the locomotive was running, without the driver altering the cut-off, so that one valve could be barely opening and another offering twice the aperture intended.

Despite the many troubles that beset these ten locomotives when new, there is no doubt whatsoever that by 1944 they were giving some astonishingly fine performances, both as regards speed and haulage power. Many crews were willing to forget their heavy fuel consumption, oil spillage and other foibles in view of the free-steaming boiler and power reserve. No other British express locomotives rode so well and, as one Nine Elms driver exclaimed on leaving his first Britannia, the comparison was akin to a Mini hopping from bump to bump and a Rolls Royce gliding over the top. Considering that the design was new and included many unconventional features, the mileages run to the first general repair were reasonably good and compared favourably with other Southern express classes, details being as follows:

Locomotive No.	Intermediate Repair Miles	Months	General Repair Miles	Months
Merchant Navy Class				
21C1	65,074	28	89,995	37
21C2	41,691	12	97,212	33
21C3	91,235	27	162,307	47
21C4	73,236	22	124,306	41
21C5	85,357	24	158,606	47
21C6	64,009	17	100,140	25
21C7	59,311	12	100,647	24
21C8	58,698	10	113,569	27
21C9	53,603	12	103,501	22
21C10	74,891	15	120,033	28
Lord Nelson Class (1943-44)				
851	51,263	13	125,655	34
856	85,610	16	102,683	22
857	66,807	21	121,807	37
862	96,411	24	148,476	38
863	66,065	14	118,508	24
Schools Class (1943-44)				
901	55,219	21	102,140	36
906	58,952	16	141,782	46
911	75,857	26	139,558	44
926	85,651	21	111,545	27
939	81,446	22	126,004	31
King Arthur Class (1943-44)				
770	77,022	18	107,086	28
777	79,003	19	112,613	25
780	69,996	20	123,444	26
792	84,624	17	133,250	29
800	61,469	16	130,614	32

Average mileages and time between repairs:

Type of Repair	*Merchant Navy*	*Lord Nelson*	*Schools*	*King Arthur*
Mileage to intermediate repair	66,711	73,231	71,425	74,423
Time to intermediate repair (months)	17.9	17.6	21.2	18.0
Mileage to general repair	117,031	123,426	124,206	121,399
Time to general repair (months) ..	33.1	31.0	36.8	26.8

Since the availability of the Merchant Navies in 1942-3 was poor, these figures suggest that when serviceable the class more than held its own with the other Southern express classes. The actual mileage run in 1941 to 1944 shows a progressive improvement, details of which are as follows:

Locomotive No.	*1941*	*1942*	*1943*	*1944*	*1945*	*Total 31/12/1945*
21C1	11,069	24,013	29,992	38,921	39,644	143,639
21C2	13,223	26,669	36,443	50,877	31,469	158,681
21C3	3,888	34,660	40,787	43,047	40,525	162,907
21C4	1,415	24,496	48,740	39,664	32,035	146,350

Locomotive No.	1941	1942	1943	1944	1945	Total 31/12/1945
21C5	—	26,688	38,664	49,640	43,614	158,606
21C6	—	35,992	49,248	48,127	39,733	173,100
21C7	—	23,892	45,838	39,402	39,867	148,999
21C8	—	24,625	47,179	41,765	37,847	151,416
21C9	—	26,802	44,658	54,131	30,303	155,894
21C10	—	24,224	50,667	45,142	34,948	154,981
Yearly totals	29,595	272,061	432,216	450,716	369,985	1,554,573

No general repairs were necessary in 1942-3, but thereafter the yearly mileages were affected as the locomotives passed through works, Nos. 21C1/2/6/7/8/9/10 receiving their first overhauls in 1944 and Nos. 21C3/4/5 in the following year. Because of hostilities and the need to apply various modifications, the time spent in shops tended to be lengthy, the period varying from 51 to 120 days, with an average of 79. This radically reduced mileages, which otherwise would have shown progressive increases from 1942 to 1945. Actual dates, mileages and time under repair for these general repairs are as follows:

Dates and mileages at first General Repair:

Year	*Loco-motive No.*	*Period in Works*	*Mileage*	*Days in Works*
1944	21C1	13/7 to 9/9	89,995	58
1944	21C2	18/3 to 3/6	97,212	77
1945	21C3	11/8 to 3/11	162,307	84
1945	21C4	30/3 to 28/7	124,306	120
1945	21C5	1/11 to 26/1/46	158,606	86
1944	21C6	15/2 to 27/4	100,140	74
1944	21C7	29/5 to 17/8	100,647	80
1944	21C8	14/9 to 4/11	113,569	51
1944	21C9	18/4 to 17/6	103,501	60
1944	21C10	18/11 to 24/2/45	120,033	97

By good fortune, the Salisbury duty register for the six months November 1943 to April 1944 has survived the ravages of time and is available for research. At the time Nos. 21C6 to 21C10 were stationed there and were employed on both passenger and goods duties with Nos. 21C9/10 being the most consistent performers. Seldom were there more than two in traffic at the same time, although when serviceable it was not uncommon to find them working twice the mileage of the same shed's King Arthurs, for after completing their passenger duties, they were commandeered for main-line goods services, in particular the Nine Elms-Exeter partly-fitted freight which left London nightly at 10 minutes to midnight.

From mid-October 1943 there were four regular Merchant Navy express workings out of Waterloo at 10.50 a.m., 12.50 p.m., 2.50 p.m. and 5.00 p.m. On Tuesdays, Wednesdays and Thursdays, the 10.50 a.m., the wartime equivalent of the "Atlantic Coast Express", was made up to sixteen or seventeen coaches with the locomotive working right through to Exeter. The corresponding up train similarly loaded to eighteen coaches, and in order to handle conveniently such a lengthy rake of coaches at Waterloo a stop was made at Clapham Junction to detach the six coaches forming the Plymouth portion, which was then worked separately up to the terminus by any convenient M7. On Mondays, Fridays and Saturdays, reliefs followed the main trains in both directions and the loads were correspondingly less. A relief was also provided for the 5.00 p.m. Waterloo-Exeter, the main train consisting of ten coaches with limited stops being Merchant Navy hauled, and the extra of fourteen coaches with additional stops being entrusted to a King Arthur, usually of the 448 to 457 series. By the New Year, however, the roles had been reversed and the pacific was taking the heavier train. Should a Merchant Navy be unavailable, then Nine Elms invariably provided No. 755 *The Red Knight* as a substitute, with its large cylinders and Lemaître blastpipe it was a firm favourite. On the Bournemouth line it had the reputation of being the only express locomotive capable of completing the journey without having to take water en route.

Boilers for Nos. 21C11 to 21C20, the ten postponed members of the class, had been ordered from the North British Locomotive Company in November 1940 at £2,855 each, a mere £5 more than the original series despite the increased costs brought about by the War. When construction of these locomotives was considered in February 1943, the North British made it known that no work had been possible on the boilers because of War Department commitments, so their construction was transferred to Eastleigh Works, where suitable equipment had been installed. On receiving the order, Eastleigh estimated the cost as £3,700 each, which proved reasonably accurate, for the actual costs ranged from £3,745 to £3,900. The use of thermic syphons had regained favour, but the ten cancelled North British boilers were without them, and these again were supplied by Beyer Peacock & Co. Work on these boilers commenced at Eastleigh in February 1944, but lack of manpower and the complicated techniques delayed completion of the first one until the autumn. To ensure all the steel firebox welding was faultless, each inch was scrutinised radiographically, although experience showed that a 25 per cent inspection offered sufficient safeguard.

The first boiler was tested successfully on 10 October 1944, and assembly of No. 21C11 commenced towards the end of the month, with completion taking place on 31 December 1944. The other nine followed at regular intervals, with the last entering traffic on 30 June 1945. Taking inflation into account, the average cost of £23,740 was an improvement on the first series. Construction details were as follows: 1944 No. 21C11 *General Steam Navigation* (December); 1945 Nos. 21C12 *United States Lines* (January), 21C13 *Blue Funnel*, 21C14 *Nederland Line* (February), 21C15 *Rotterdam Lloyd*, 21C16 *Elders Fyffes* (March), 21C17 *Belgian Marine* (April), 21C18 *British India Line* (May), 21C19 *French Line CGT*, 21C20 *Bibby Line* (June). All entered traffic painted black, but No. 21C12 *United States Lines* broke a chain in its oil-bath on 29 January 1945, and was returned to works where, in addition to repairs, it was re-painted grey with three parallel white lines running along both engine and tender.

Generally they followed the 21C1 to 21C10 series, although advantage was taken to reduce the weight by using $\frac{1}{32}$in. thinner frame plates, reducing the casing sheeting to 22 s.w.g. thickness, carefully controlled steel casting sizing, and a major constructional difference to the boiler. The front ring was parallel and the rear one tapered along the bottom, whereas on the earlier series the front ring was the one with the tapering. This change had no beneficial significance, it being introduced solely to save weight in the barrel shell and to lower the water capacity of the boiler without altering the heading surface or steam-generating capacity. By these means the empty weight of Nos. 21C11 to 21C20 was lowered to 86 tons 11 cwt. and that in working order to 95 tons 5 cwt. Some of the weight savings were lost by the addition of the top cowling, extra sandboxes and piping, and the fitting of smoke-deflector plates and cab alcoves, but, nevertheless, the final figures were a credit to the design staff.

All wheels were again of BFB pattern, but the coupled wheels of No. 21C18 *British India Line* differed by being fabricated from separate pieces welded together, and not cast whole like those fitted to the remainder of the class. Presumably they did not prove successful, because in April 1947 they were removed and replaced by the standard variety.

More obvious to the casual observer were the straight smoke-deflector plates which commenced a little higher than the slightly convex pattern fitted after the wind tunnel experiments to Nos. 21C1 to 21C10. They remained short, but later, like the earlier series, had them lengthened to conform with Nos. 35021 to 35030. This not only made them more effective, but also gave the front end a more balanced look, something which hitherto had been lacking.

No changes were made to the lamp and disc bracket layout, this despite the known danger of the discs being swept away by passing trains or high winds. The lower tier of three lights with brackets above remained spaced across the sloping section of the plating, the second tier of two attached to the casing where the discs partly protruded outside the smoke deflectors, and the single top lamp on the cowling with the bracket below on the smokebox door. Like Nos. 21C1 to 21C10, the disc brackets of the second tier were later removed to the smokebox door where they no longer impaired the driver's lookout or were lost en route. If the smokebox door disc brackets had been fitted when the locomotives were new, then no doubt the right-hand one would have been employed as an aid to opening and closing the door during ash-clearing operations. However, their non-availability led to grab handles being welded on to the doors of Nos. 21C16 to 21C20 before entry to traffic and to Nos. 21C11 to 21C15 when returned to works for attention. No catches were provided on the right-hand side of the smokebox doors as they were on Nos. 21C3 to 21C10 when new and Nos. 21C1/2 after commencing work. Of the first series only No. 21C7 received a smokebox door grab handle.

In Nos. 21C1 to 21C10 much trouble had been met with the 7in. smokebox steampipes which had proved much too rigid and frequently fractured at the flanges. No. 21C6 *Peninsular & Oriental* was by far the worst affected, and in April 1944 was fitted experimentally at Eastleigh Works with corrugated steel piping. This proved effective and became a common feature of the class, Nos. 21C11 to 21C20 having it when built.

The sanding layout followed that provided finally for Nos. 21C1 to 21C10, that is forward steam sanding to all three pairs of coupled wheels and gravity feed on the tender for running backwards. The sand containers on the engines remained enclosed and inaccessible within the casing.

The enclosed footplate of Nos. 21C1 to 21C10 was generally well received except in respect of draughts on exposed sections of line, with the result that commencing with No. 21C11 *General Steam Navigation* the cab side sheets at the rear were turned inwards for about 16in. to give the seats of the driver and fireman shielded recesses. Glazed lights were inserted in the upper portion to avoid loss of light and visibility. Another necessary improvement concerned the narrowing of the tender coal box at the top to form a tunnel with the high-curved topped tank side plates, along which a backward view was possible for tender-first running. Use of these tunnels was made to stow the fire-irons, although their removal or return while locomotives were in motion tended to be fraught with difficulties and some risk to life and limb.

Once again, three tank-filler openings were provided, one conventionally sited at the rear and the other two either side at the forward end of the rear-viewing tunnels mentioned above. Access to them and the fire-irons was by means of hinged lights, although the latter's presence was no real preventative to water flooding the footplate during replenishing operations or when braking with full tanks. To avoid this undesirable intrusion Nos. 21C18/19/20 had their forward filler holes plated over before entry to traffic, while those on Nos. 21C1 to 21C17 were similarly dealt with in 1946, many by the running sheds before authorisation was granted. The capacity was officially given as 5 tons of coal and 5,100 gallons of water, although under test at Eastleigh Works on 14 March 1945, tender T3125 (locomotive No. 21C16) was found to hold 6 tons and 5,194 gallons respectively. The long unadjustable spring hangers of the earlier 5,000-gallon tenders were replaced by brackets against the spring ends, this modification being ordered after Ashford commenced assembly and the unplugged holes for the hangers remained as evidence of this late decision. The steam carriage-heating pipe was visible below the tank instead of being concealed behind the skirt.

Before the construction of these second series locomotives commenced, Bulleid had drawings prepared for both screw and fine-adjusting steam reversing, but neither proved acceptable and the original steam system with modified hydraulic locking-cylinder was re-used.

Nos. 21C17 to 21C20 entered traffic nameless, but the others carried names from the start, though in several instances these were covered up until official blessing was given. No. 21C12 *United States Lines* was painted malachite green on 6 April 1945, and four days later was the first to be officially named, but it was 13 December 1945, before the last, No. 21C18 *British India Line*, was similarly honoured. Most were painted green before taking part in these ceremonies, but for reasons unknown Nos. 21C11/3/6 were left black. Dates to malachite green for these and the earlier series are as follows:—

Locomotive No.	*Date*
21C1	12/1945
21C2	7/1946
21C3	11/1945
21C4	4/1946
21C5	1/1946
21C6	9/1946
21C7	7/1947
21C8	8/1947
21C9	11/1946
21C10	3/1947
21C11	1/1947
21C12	4/1945
21C13	11/1946
21C14	11/1945
21C15	9/1945
21C16	1/1947
21C17	10/1945
21C18	8/1945
21C19	9/1945
21C20	7/1945

Nos. 21C11 to 21C20 were run-in on the Southampton-Bournemouth stopping trains, the Salisbury goods, and van trains to London before being despatched to Nine Elms for regular service. Usually this commenced with the 9.54 a.m. Waterloo-Basingstoke and other semi-fast duties before graduating to the 9.30 a.m. Waterloo-Bournemouth West. Their arrival at Nine Elms left Lord Nelsons Nos. 862 to 865 without regular work and they were transferred to Bournemouth, thereby presenting that shed with the opportunity of rostering six-coupled locomotives for all its Waterloo services. When new, the availability of Nos. 21C1 to 21C10 seldom exceeded 25 per cent, but the second series proved more reliable, although at 55 per cent their availability remained far below that of the Stanier and Gresley pacifics.

Once hostilities ceased in Europe, the Southern Railway made immense efforts to improve its passenger services and public image, both of which had suffered badly during the latter stages of the war, when too much had often to be attempted with inadequate resources. Little in the way of acceleration was possible until the backlog of track maintenance and renewal had been overcome, but by the autumn a noticeable number of malachite green locomotives, new and re-painted coaches, and refurbished stations offered travellers a more promising future.

On 14, 15 and 16 August 1945, a series of test runs were made by No. 21C2 *Union Castle* on the Eastern Section between Victoria and Dover Marine. Two return journeys were worked daily loaded to ten Pullmans and two bogie vans, and operating, as far as possible, to pre-war schedules. To give Battersea crews the opportunity of familiarising themselves with the class before trials, use was made of No. 21C1 *Channel Packet* for eight days on the 8.35 a.m. Victoria-Ramsgate and other Kent coast expresses. A careful check was made of the speeds and sectional timings of the test trains, and to ensure that all permanent way and other restrictions were punctiliously observed, a speedometer had been fitted at Eastleigh Works on 10 July 1945. Unfortunately, this foresight was ill-rewarded for, following complaints of inaccuracy at the end of the test period, it was found to record 9 m.p.h. below the true speed at 60 m.p.h.

These trials were followed on 23 October 1945 by the resumption of the Eastern Section continental expresses with Nos. 21C17 *Belgian Marine* in immaculate malachite green heading the inaugural train out of Victoria. The load of six coaches, three Pullmans and two vans hardly warranted such motive power and, once the ceremonial occasion was concluded, the services were delegated to King Arthurs Nos. 768/70/8/9/80/1/8. The next milestone of post-war rehabilitation was reached on 15 April 1946, when No. 21C1 *Channel Packet* headed the "Golden Arrow" out of Victoria. No. 21C1 had been specially prepared by Eastleigh Works earlier in the month when, in addition to a fresh coat of malachite green, it was fitted with a circular plaque on the smokebox door which was lettered "Golden Arrow" and crossed diagonally by an arrow. Larger arrows were attached to the side casing above the nameplates and pointing forwards. In preparation for the event, No. 21C1 *Channel Packet* was worked light engine on 11 April between Battersea and Ashford, while on 13 April a trial run was made with the full train from Victoria to Dover Marine and back. The Pullman cars had gold arrows painted under the windows at each end, with the words "Golden Arrow" and "Flèche D'Or" at opposite ends. A small Union Jack was flown on one side of the locomotive above the numberplate, with a French Tricolor on the other. Once again, after a brief stay at Battersea, No. 21C1 *Channel Packet* was returned to the Western Section, leaving this express to be worked for the next few years by the West Country class.

On the Western Section it was the autumn before the "Bournemouth Belle" recommenced running with No. 21C18 *British India Line* having charge of the first train on 7 October 1946. A timing of 87 minutes to Southampton Central was over-generous and early arrivals were common. This was followed on 16 October by a resumption of the Cunard Boat specials, when No. 21C4 *Cunard White Star* headed an all-Pullman express to Southampton Docks for the first passenger voyage of RMS *Queen Elizabeth* to New York. Once again a trial run had been made, thus 4 October was the first visit to the docks of a Merchant Navy.

From the very beginning there had been talk of excessive fuel and water consumption, and this had been proved during the early trial runs of the class and by the shed fuel returns. Bulleid, however, was not fully convinced, and in mid-1946 decided to hold a series of fuel and haulage trials with No. 21C14 *Nederland Line*, Lord Nelson No. 861 *Lord Anson*, and King Arthur No. 789 *Sir Guy* over the West of England main line. All three were stationed at Exmouth Junction for the period of the trials and manned by two experienced crews, one from Nine Elms and the other from Exmouth Junction. Each locomotive in turn worked for five days the 9.00 a.m. Waterloo-Salisbury and the 12.36 p.m. Salisbury-Exeter services, and the 7.30 p.m. Exeter-Waterloo. This was followed by six days with a variety of Salisbury-Exeter trains with loads of twelve, fourteen and sixteen coaches. No. 861 *Lord Anson* on 17 September 1946 acquitted itself well with fourteen coaches on the 10.25 a.m. Exeter-Salisbury and the 2.43 p.m. Salisbury-Exeter expresses, but the next day with two additional coaches it lost two minutes up and six minutes down. No. 789 *Sir Guy* also gave a good account of itself during the following two weeks, but was restricted to fourteen coaches between Exeter and Salisbury on which no loss of time was debited. Uphill, the running was superior to that of the Lord Nelson, although the drain on the boiler frequently reduced the pressure to 125-130 lb./sq. in. No. 21C14 *Nederland Line*, apart from one failure on shed and another on arrival at Salisbury, gave a most impressive performance and gained time west of Salisbury with sixteen-coach trains and toyed with those of normal formation. Coal consumption details are as follows:

Locomotive No.	*Coal burned per train mile*	*Coal burned per d.hp. mile*	*Remarks*
789	46.60 lb.	3.29 lb.	light winds and showers
861	44.89 lb.	3.26 lb.	dry, light westerly wind
21C14	56.70 lb.	3.59 lb.	periods of rain, blustery wind

At the conclusion of the trials a special eighteen-coach train was worked to pre-war timings from Woking to Exeter with stops at Salisbury and Sidmouth Junction. The schedule was kept with ease, but only at a cost of 60.8 lb. of coal per mile. Water consumption was similarly high and, with this in mind and to enable larger tenders to be provided, if necessary, a larger turntable was installed at Exmouth Junction shed in May 1947. The turntable displaced could take the class as built, but with little space to spare.

On 10 June 1947, No. 21C8 *Peninsular & Oriental* had the misfortune to crash into an electric train at Waterloo while running into the terminus with a West of England express. No one was seriously injured and damage to the electric was not excessive, but the fragile outer shell of the pacific suffered out of all proportion to the impact and repairs took from 19 June to 28 August 1947. In the following month No. 21C14 *Nederland Line* received a glancing blow from Adams 0-4-4 tank No. 204 on Nine Elms shed, the latter escaping with sundry scratches, whereas the former lost much of its cab and firebox sheeting. At this period major running sheds such as Exmouth Junction, Nine Elms and Salisbury were regularly undertaking light and heavy intermediate repairs, so the crippled pacific was repaired and partially re-painted at Nine Elms. As late as January 1949 Exmouth Junction gave No. 21C2 *Union Castle* a heavy intermediate repair at 67,254 miles, which accounted for this locomotive not being renumbered into the 35XXX series until January 1950, when Eastleigh Works were visited for a general overhaul. No. 21C1 *Channel Packet*'s renumbering was similarly delayed by repairs at Exmouth Junction in November 1948.

The continuing popularity of the all-Pullman "Bournemouth Belle" suggested that similar patronage was available to and from the West Country, and on 20 June 1947 the "Devon Belle" was introduced. Running on Mondays, Fridays, Saturdays and Sundays, it offered non-stop travel, according to the public timetable, between Waterloo and Sidmouth Junction, although, in actuality, a brief stop was made at Wilton to change locomotives. Connection was offered at Sidmouth Junction to Sidmouth while at Exeter the train divided, the first four Pullmans proceeding to Plymouth and the rear eight, including the observation car, to Ilfracombe. The up train similarly served Plymouth and Ilfracombe, combined at Exeter and made a service stop at Wilton. The inaugural services on 20 June 1947 were worked between Waterloo and Wilton by No. 21C15 *Rotterdam Lloyd*, which carried a special red headboard with yellow lettering and side flashes attached to the smoke-deflector plates. From Wilton to Exeter No. 21C3 *Royal Mail* had charge while No. 21C4 *Cunard White Star* worked the up train to Wilton, both carrying similar headboards and flashes. For a time West Countries Nos. 21C103 *Plymouth* and 21C117 *Ilfracombe* were rostered for the Plymouth and Ilfracombe portions, but later any locomotives were employed.

Until private motoring made severe inroads into West Country travel, the service proved most popular and regularly called for the provision of thirteen or fourteen Pullmans, the extra capacity being for Ilfracombe. Timekeeping was good, and in the up direction Clapham Junction was usually passed several minutes early. Unlike the twelve-car Pullman "Bournemouth Belle", Merchant Navies were always rostered for the workings and were a credit to the Region and the depots concerned. In the winter months there was little demand for such luxurious travel, and on 27 November 1947 Nos. 21C4/18 headed the last up run of the year.

Despite the improved visibility offered by the front-end modifications, many drivers considered that the view ahead of the track and signals was dangerously restricted, and on numerous occasions in 1946-7 expressed themselves forcibly on the subject. As a result, in August 1947 No. 21C8 *Orient Line* was equipped with a wedge-shaped cab front similar to that appearing on the Battle of Britain light pacifics. No change was made to the sidesheets and the two side windows were retained. The lookout ahead was considerably improved, but what was more important was the reduction of glare by day and the absence of false reflections at night. Approval was universal and the modification was applied to the other nineteen locomotives in 1948-53, although in their case new cab panels and three side windows were fitted. No. 35008 *Orient Line* had its cab sides similarly modified in July 1949. Details are as follows:

Locomotive No.	*Date*
35001	12/1950
35002	1/1954
35003	6/1950
35004	10/1950
35005	2/1950
35006	3/1951
35007	3/1950
35008	8/1947, 7/1949
35009	2/1953
35010	11/1949
35011	10/1950
35012	3/1949
35013	12/1952
35014	5/1949
35015	6/1949
35016	6/1949
35017	4/1948
35018	5/1948
35019	4/1948
35020	5/1948

Around the same period, trouble was experienced from sand and other abrasive substances reaching the slide bars of the outside cylinders, causing some overheating and excessive wear. When first built, Nos. 21C1 to 21C10 only had sanding applied to the front of the centre coupled wheels, but experience proved this inadequate and it was extended, first to the leading coupled wheels, and later to the trailing pair, so that by mid-1944 all three sets of driving wheels were equipped for sanding. The containers for the centre and trailing wheels were sited part way up the casing and those for the leading wheels higher still against the rear of the smokebox, where replenishment was a difficult and time-consuming task. Bulleid is reputed to have envisaged refilling sandboxes on his pacifics by means of specially provided overhead flexible piping, and nozzles, but even so the distance above track level and the absence of running plates would still have called for the use of ladders. Nos. 21C11 to 21C20 entered traffic with sanding to all three sets of coupled wheels, although by that date the wisdom of applying it to the leading pair had been questioned. As a result, in September 1948 No. 21C12 *United States Lines* had its leading sand pipes blanked-off, while in 1949-50 Nos. 35001/9/14/5/7/8 had dust covers fitted to their outside slide bars to keep them free of sand. This, unfortunately, gave rise to lubricating problems and the covers were removed when locomotives were next in works. No. 35019 had its sandboxes and piping removed from the leading coupled wheels in June 1951 and, when this gave reasonable satisfaction it became the standard arrangement until rebuilding. In some instances the containers were left in place and only the piping removed, while all had the casing openings plated over.

At nationalisation, all twenty locomotives entered British Railways stock and were renumbered 35001 to 35020, details being:

Locomotive No.	*Date*
35001	10/1949
35002	1/1950
35003	6/1948
35004	4/1948
35005	4/1948
35006	12/1948
35007	12/1948
35008	7/1949
35009	8/1949
35010	12/1948
35011	11/1948
35012	3/1949
35013	8/1948
35014	5/1949
35015	6/1949
35016	10/1948
35017	4/1948
35018	5/1948
35019	4/1948
35020	5/1948

The temporary 'S' prefix was carried by No. 21C5 between 20 March and 8 April 1948.

Just prior to nationalisation, ten more Merchant Navies were ordered from Eastleigh Works at an estimated cost of £25,000 each. To hasten their construction, the boilers and tenders became the responsibility of Brighton, the cylinders and framing that of Ashford, and the remaining parts that of Eastleigh Works. Even so, long delays occurred in collecting the necessary materials, in particular the cylinder castings and steel for the firebox, and assembly had not commenced before the Southern Railway had become the Southern Region of British Railways. Therefore, when they eventually entered traffic between September 1948 and April 1949, it was as Nos. 35021 to 35030, and not Nos. 21C21 to 21C30 as intended by Bulleid. Details are as follows: 1948 Nos. 35021 *New Zealand Line* (September), 35022 *Holland America Line* (October), 35023 *Holland Afrika Line* (November), 35024 *East Asiatic Company* (November), 35025 *Brocklebank Line* (December), 35026 *Lamport & Holt Line*, 35027 *Port Line*, 35028 *Clan Line* (December), and in

1949 Nos. 35029 *Ellerman Lines* (February), 35030 *Elder-Dempster Lines* (April). The cost averaged £31,348, some 25 per cent greater than estimated.

Generally, they followed the 1944-5 series, Nos. 35011 to 35020, but from the outset had wedge-shaped cab fronts and three side windows. Further weight reduction was found possible by a greater use of welding and a scaling down of many unimportant items, and this gave a weight in working order of less than 94 tons.

On Nos. 21C1 to 21C20, the entire frame structure of the trailing truck was formed of one-piece cast steel, but to reduce the weight the new batch had fabricated steel-plate trucks. From mid-1953 they were exchanged in works and could be seen fitted to the earlier locomotives, including No. 35001 *Channel Packet*.

All carried TIA feed water treatment equipment of similar pattern to that fitted to later Battle of Britain locomotives, the initials being the abbreviation of "Traitement Integral Armand". Briefly, the operating procedure was as follows: The chemical fluid required for treating the feed water was contained in a small tank on the tender and displaced automatically into the tender tank in proportion to the quantity added during the turn of duty and the daily analysis of both boiler and tender contents. This maintained the feed water chemically capable of precipitating all the scale-forming constituents in the form of a soft non-adhering mud which could be removed by means of a manually-operated blow-down valve at the base of the firebox. If this were activated for half a minute every hour, it avoided all priming, deposited a high proportion of the precipitate on the track, and made it possible to extend the boiler washout periods from seven to fifty-six days, which conveniently coincided with routine inspection of the firebox plates and stays. At the same time boiler maintenance was reduced, the cracking of throat plates practically eliminated and availability greatly improved. Nos. 35001 to 35020 were similarly modified with equal success in 1949-51. Later, a simpler water treatment using brickettes was substituted without loss of efficiency.

As Brighton failed to complete the tenders to schedule, the first not being despatched until 5 November 1948, resort, in some instances, had to be made to spares in hand for the light pacifics, details being as follows:

Locomotive No.	*Date to traffic*	*Tender No. and type*	*6,000-gallon tender fitted*	*Destination of temporary tender*
35021	11.9.48	3333 Battle of Britain	3342 13.11.48	35024
35022	9.10.48	3335 Battle of Britain	3345 8.1.49	34090
35023	6.11.48	3341 Merchant Navy	when built	
35024	13.11.48	3333 Battle of Britain	3346 12.2.49	34089
35025	27.11.48	3343 Merchant Navy	when built	
35026	4.12.48	3260 West Country	3350 1.7.49	34039
35027	11.12.48	3288 West Country	3349 14.4.49	34060
35028	23.12.48	3344 Merchant Navy	when built	
35029	19.2.49	3347 Merchant Navy	when built	
35030	1.4.49	3348 Merchant Navy	when built	

There were also livery variations, with Nos. 35023/5/8/9/30 entering traffic in lined malachite green, and Nos. 35021/2/4/6/7 painted a plain dull green which rapidly became discoloured and was impossible to keep clean. Nos. 35021/2/4/6/7 were repainted on being attached to their 6,000-gallon tenders, Nos. 35021/2/7 becoming lined malachite green and Nos. 35024/6 dark blue. These last two locomotives, therefore, were the only members of the class never to wear the full malachite livery. Nameplates were fitted when new; these were covered up pending official naming, although as these ceremonies tended to be delayed the covers, in most instances, disappeared in part, if not entirely, before these occasions were reached, the last, No. 35029 *Ellerman Lines* having to wait until 1 March 1951.

The 6,000-gallon tenders had an unequally divided wheelbase of 7ft. 4in. and 7ft. 0in. which gave a total of 14ft. 4in., as against the 13ft. 0in. of the earlier pattern. Officially, the reason for the extra capacity was to ensure that at the height of summer, when delays were inevitable, locomotives had sufficient water to make the non-stop run to Bournemouth. By using more advanced welding techniques, lighter wheels and thinner wash plates, the tare weight was restricted to 21½ tons, which gave the very reasonable figure of 53 tons 6 cwt. fully laden.

Externally the design differed in several respects. The high, curved-topped tank sides and narrow coal bunker were retained to give rearward viewing tunnels and stowage for fire-irons, but the two forward filler holes were omitted, the vacuum brake hose lower with no swan neck and the tank top manhole cover deeper and wider. There were also differences in the positioning and pattern of the rear ladders. Details for the various batches of tenders are as follows:

5,000-gallon: Nos. 21C1/2 when new, footsteps and short handrails.
Nos. 21C3-10 two ladders with loops at top.
Nos. 21C1/2 were subsequently altered to conform.

5,100-gallon: Nos. 21C11-20 two ladders, no loops at top.

6,000-gallon: Nos. 35021-30 two ladders with loops on the inner arms only.

The excessive weight of Nos. 21C1 to 21C10 was still causing concern, and when they passed through Eastleigh Works in 1945-7 the opportunity was taken of removing more of the heavy cast-steel frame stretchers and replacing them by much lighter fabricated plate structures welded to the main frames. Thinner plating was applied in part to the cab and air-smoothed casing, the steel sheet support to the lagging discarded, and any other unnecessarily heavy steel fittings removed or replaced by lighter structures. A new and lighter, but nevertheless stronger, oil-bath was fitted to most locomotives, while heat-resisting steel firebars and C.P. steel tyres offered minor reductions. Nos. 21C1/2 remained slightly heavier, at 94 tons 19 cwt. and 94 tons 11 cwt. respectively, than Nos. 21C3 to 21C10, but after Nationalisation were brought more or less in line. In 1946-7 Nos. 21C11 to 21C20 similarly had weight reductions made and in this modified form became the basis of the final series. 1947-8 working order weights of the three series were as follows:

Locomotive No.	*21C8*	*21C11*	*35021*
Date	8/1947	1/1947	9/1948
Bogie	16 tons 5 cwt.	16 tons 4 cwt.	16 tons 3 cwt.
Leading coupled wheels	20 tons 17 cwt.	20 tons 16 cwt.	20 tons 17 cwt.
Centre coupled wheels	20 tons 17 cwt.	20 tons 17 cwt.	20 tons 17 cwt.
Trailing coupled wheels	20 tons 17 cwt.	20 tons 17 cwt.	20 tons 17 cwt.
Trailing wheels	15 tons 8 cwt.	15 tons 6 cwt.	15 tons 4 cwt.
Total	94 tons 4 cwt.	94 tons 0 cwt.	93 tons 18 cwt.

All were in steam with a light fire and 3in. of water showing in the glass.

Of the final series, Nos. 35021/2/3/4 went new to Exmouth Junction, and Nos. 35025/6/7/8/9/30 to Bournemouth, where they replaced Lord Nelsons on the London expresses. In May 1949 the allocation of the earlier locomotives was as follows: Nine Elms Nos. 35005/11 to 20, Salisbury Nos. 35004/6/7/8/9/10, Exmouth Junction Nos. 35001/2/3. However, the stay of Nos. 35028/9/30 at Bournemouth was brief, for towards the end of September 1949 they were transferred away to Dover as replacements for Battle of Britain Nos. 34071/2/3 on the "Night Ferry" and other Continental expresses. When the "Night Ferry" recommenced running on 15 December 1947, its working was shared by Nos. 21C155/6/7, with L1 class 4-4-0's acting as pilots should the load contain more than three sleeping cars. Later, Nos. 34071/2/3 took over and performed most creditably especially in the summer months when, with steam heating no longer required, four sleeping cars were handled unaided. Tender capacity was the limiting factor, not the power output. It was hoped that the 6,000-gallon tenders of Nos. 35028/9/30 would enable such loads to be accepted all the year round. At Bournemouth the loss of Nos. 35028/9/30 was temporarily filled by Nos. 34054/5 until new Nos. 34093/4/5 became available. In February 1950, further changes saw Battersea gaining No. 35028 from Dover and Nos. 35025/6/7 from Bournemouth where Nos. 34105/6/7/8/9 and later No. 34110 arrived as substitutes. At Battersea Nos. 35025/6/7/8 took over many of the Continental expresses, as well as appearing on some of the Victoria-Ramsgate services. No. 35029 *Ellerman Lines* on the afternoon of 15 February 1950 was derailed whilst running tender-first through the crossover to No. 1 platform road at the west end of London Bridge, the tender keeping the rails, but the locomotive being completely derailed. As only one down road was available between Borough Market Junction and London Bridge, No. 1 platform was completely cut off, and many evening rush-hour services had to be cancelled, causing complete chaos at all stations. Because of the very awkward positioning of the derailment, little could be done until the early hours of the 16th when *Ellerman Lines* was returned to the track and towed away.

In early 1945, Bulleid had thoughts of equipping one of the second series with a mechanical stoker, but delivery proved impossible during the closing months of the war and the scheme had to be deferred until October 1947. In that month a reconditioned Berkley stoker was obtained in Canada and shipped to Southampton for assembly at Eastleigh, but when unpacked, several minor and, unfortunately, essential items were found to be missing, which delayed its installation on No. S21C5 *Canadian Pacific* until March 1948. It was of American design, and consisted of a small reciprocating steam engine in the tender which drove a flexible helical screw within a tubular duct along which coal was fed from a hopper at the base of the coal space to a distribution head in the firebox. Trials commenced locally at Eastleigh on 22 March 1948, but at once trouble was met from coal jamming the hopper entrance and also the duct. This not only radically reduced the firebox intake, but also caused the helical screw to overheat and the steam engine to vibrate itself off the seating. As a result 21C5 re-entered Works on 2 April for adjustments and modifications to be made to the coal space and tubular duct.

These were completed on 8 April 1948, when *Canadian Pacific*, now renumbered 35005, returned to Eastleigh running shed and successfully worked empty stock and slow passenger trains to Bournemouth and Basingstoke before being despatched to Nine Elms for general service. Occasional appearances were then made on the Bournemouth expresses, but mostly it was rostered for the West of England services, including the "Atlantic Coast Express" which, on several occasions, had the load increased to sixteen coaches. Apart from making more smoke and wasting more steam from the safety-valves than hand-fired members of the class, it was difficult to note any change in performance either from the trackside or train, some excellent runs being recorded as well as many of average quality.

The locomotive returned to Eastleigh Works on 25 October 1949 for a heavy intermediate repair (57,886 miles run with stoker) and to be prepared for a visit to the Rugby Testing Plant and road trials with the LMR dynamometer car and mobile test unit between Rugby and Euston. Modifications were also made to the coal hopper to ensure a constant supply of fuel to the firebox and additional greasing points fitted to the helical screw to avoid overheating of the universal joints. It re-entered traffic on 18 February 1950, when vans were worked from Eastleigh to Clapham Junction, and on 26 February No. 35005 *Canadian Pacific* ran light engine to Willesden en route to Rugby. The trials were completed on 15 March and a return made to the Southern Region the following week for a further series of trials with the LMR mobile testing unit between Battersea and Salisbury. These were concluded at the end of the month and on 4 April 1950 Eastleigh commenced removing the stoker to enable comparative tests to be made employing hand firing.

After further modifications the stoker was refitted between 31 May and 16 June 1950, while the steam reversing gear was replaced by an improved pattern capable of fine adjustment and not subject to creep. Regular service was resumed from Nine Elms towards the end of the month when, unlike the previous year, most of the work was performed on the Bournemouth expresses, especially the 8.30 a.m. and 10.30 a.m. ex-Waterloo. It was while heading the 8.30 a.m. Bournemouth near Raynes Park on 15 September 1950 that the chain gear parted at speed and completely wrecked the oil-bath and motion. H16 4-6-2 tank No. 30516 had to be summoned hurriedly from Wimbledon to haul both train and locomotive to Surbiton, where No. 34054 *Lord Beaverbrook* took over, some eighty-one minutes late. As a result, No. 35005 again entered Eastleigh Works on 6 October for repairs and the fitting of LMR self-cleaning equipment to the smokebox. Commencing on 17 November a further series of test runs were made on the Bournemouth expresses as well as on several of the Southampton Docks-Nine Elms fitted freights. Although much of the manual work in clearing the smokebox of ash was avoided, the steaming suffered badly, especially in the late stages of a long journey or with poor-quality coal.

The mechanical stoker episode was concluded on 16 April 1951, after 77,338 miles had been run, most in general service from Nine Elms. Hand firing was reintroduced on 27 April when No. 35005 *Canadian Pacific* was out-shopped from Eastleigh. Most crews liked the stoker, although a few drivers regretted the loss of direct fire control and found the noise and dust irritating on long journeys.

Notwithstanding the various front-end modifications made over the years to improve the exhaust clearance and keep the cab windows free of steam, the problem had again to be faced in May 1948 following three instances of overrunning signals on the Eastern Section. At the time, No. 35020 *Bibby Line* was in Eastleigh Works being prepared for the Interchange Trials, and before leaving the Erecting Shop was equipped with smoke-deflector plates extending to a point abreast of the leading coupled axle instead of stopping short at the centre of the slide bars. As anticipated, greater exhaust lift was achieved, but only at the expense of impaired lookout, for the larger deflector plates interfered with the observations of signals. Because of this no other members of the class were similarly modified, but No. 35020 *Bibby Line* was not returned to standard until rebuilding.

The attractive and hard-wearing malachite green remained the standard livery until 12 February 1949, when No. 35024 *East Asiatic Company* left Eastleigh Works painted dark blue with horizontal red bands and hand-painted tender emblem. It was inspected at Brighton six days later by the Railway Executive, having run there from Eastleigh via London because the coast line over Ford Bridge was still subject to severe restrictions. The stay at Brighton was extended until 22 February, then it ran light to Angmering and worked the 5.42 p.m. fruit and perishable vans to Victoria. It appears that the new livery did not receive universal approval, for on 2 March 1949 Eastleigh Works were re-entered to have the cabside numerals painted straw colour instead of yellow, the tender emblem re-positioned to be in line with these figures and the three horizontal red bands replaced by two in black with fine white lining. A further inspection was made outside the Erecting Shop on 29 March, but this, too, failed to please, for on 29 April No. 35024 *East Asiatic Company* was back in shops having the wheels painted black and a narrow black splash skirt added. Authority at Marylebone was appeased, though the result was hardly an improvement on the original theme. The next six Merchant Navy repaints, Nos. 35012/4/5/27/9/30, were malachite green, but commencing with No. 35026 *Lamport & Holt Line* on 1 July 1949 blue became standard, dates for the class being as follows:

Locomotive No.	*Date*
35001	10/1949
35002	1/1950
35003	6/1950
35004	10/1950
35005	2/1950
35006	3/1951
35007	3/1950
35008	7/1949
35009	8/1949
35010	11/1949
35011	—
35012	2/1951
35013	8/1950
35014	—
35015	2/1951
35016	5/1950
35017	7/1949
35018	9/1949
35019	1/1950
35020	5/1950
35021	11/1950
35022	7/1950
35023	—
35024	10/1950*
35025	9/1949
35026	7/1949
35027	4/1950
35028	1/1951
35029	2/1951
35030	5/1950

* No. 35024 was painted in the standard blue livery on this date.
Although Nos. 35011/4/23 were never painted blue, Nos. 35001/17/24/6/9 received two coats of this colour, No. 35029 twice within eight weeks.

On 27 February 1951, No. 35029 was prepared at Eastleigh Works for the official naming ceremony at Southampton Docks on 1 March, while on 25 April the same year it was chosen to haul the royal special conveying the King and Queen of Denmark from Dover Marine to Victoria, and was again painted blue.

By ill-luck all these careful preparations very nearly came to nothing, owing to a hot tender box developing on 7 May, the day before the royal visit, but this was rectified in time and the train worked without mishap. The return to Denmark was made via Liverpool Street and Harwich, with No. 70000 *Britannia* heading the royal special.

The dark blue livery and sombre lining proved a poor substitute for the malachite green, it being more expensive to apply and not long-wearing. This probably applied to the other Regions, for in June 1951 instructions were received to paint all express classes dark green with orange lining, edged in black. By coincidence No. 35024 *East Asiatic Company* was in Eastleigh Works and, when despatched to the nearby running shed on 15 June 1951, it was the first to lose the blue livery for green. Although the change was an improvement the overall effect remained drab for there was little bright work to give relief. Dates to Brunswick green are as follows:

Locomotive No.	*Date*
35001	5/1952
35002	6/1951
35003	8/1953
35004	7/1954
35005	2/1954
35006	9/1953
35007	12/1952
35008	5/1952
35009	2/1953
35010	11/1952
35011	11/1951
35012	7/1952
35013	12/1952
35014	8/1951
35015	6/1953
35016	3/1953
35017	4/1953
35018	7/1951
35019	6/1951
35020	6/1952
35021	2/1952
35022	2/1952
35023	3/1952
35024	6/1951
35025	6/1952
35026	6/1952
35027	11/1953
35028	6/1953
35029	7/1952
35030	5/1953

This remained the standard livery until the class was rebuilt in 1956-9, although changes to the lining were made on those attached to modified (cut-down) tenders. The deep black skirt along the base of the firebox and tender was omitted, while the lining of the cab sides and tenders became rectangular panels instead of straight lines.

Altogether, thirty-five boilers were provided for the class, ten being obtained under contract from the North British Locomotive Company, thirteen being constructed at Eastleigh and the remainder at Brighton.

Boiler No.	*Maker*	*Date built*	*First locomotive*	*Date to traffic*	*Cost*	*New firebox*
1090	NBLC	11/1940	21C1	6/1941	£2,850	1/1948
1091	NBLC	11/1940	21C2	6/1941	£2,850	3/1948
1092	NBLC	11/1940	21C3	9/1941	£2,850	8/1947
1093	NBLC	12/1940	21C4	10/1941	£2,850	9/1946
1094	NBLC	12/1940	21C5	12/1941	£2,850	10/1948
1095	NBLC	1/1941	21C6	12/1941	£2,850	5/1947
1096	NBLC	1/1941	21C7	6/1942	£2,850	11/1947
1097	NBLC	1/1941	21C8	6/1942	£2,850	11/1947
1098	NBLC	2/1941	21C9	6/1942	£2,850	9/1948
1099	NBLC	3/1941	21C10	7/1942	£2,850	10/1948
1100	Eastleigh	10/1944	21C11	12/1944	£3,900	9/1953
1101	Eastleigh	11/1944	21C12	1/1945	£3,900	7/1951
1102	Eastleigh	11/1944	21C20	6/1945	£3,825	1/1950 & 10/1962
1103	Eastleigh	11/1944	21C19	6/1945	£3,825	5/1950
1104	Eastleigh	12/1944	21C13	2/1945	£3,745	9/1950
1105	Eastleigh	12/1944	21C15	3/1945	£3,745	3/1950
1106	Eastleigh	1/1945	21C14	2/1945	£3,745	10/1953
1107	Eastleigh	1/1945	21C16	3/1945	£3,745	8/1951
1108	Eastleigh	2/1945	21C17	4/1945	£3,745	6/1951

Boiler No.	*Maker*	*Date built*	*First locomotive*	*Date to traffic*	*Cost*	*New firebox*
1109	Eastleigh	3/1945	21C18	5/1945	£3,745	7/1951
1110	Eastleigh	4/1946	21C4	4/1946	£4,005	—
1111	Eastleigh	10/1946	21C11	1/1947	£4,005	—
1112	Eastleigh	11/1946	21C16	1/1947	£4,005	—
1113	Brighton	8/1948	35023	11/1948	£4,220	—
1114	Brighton	9/1948	35024	11/1948	£4,220	—
1115	Brighton	9/1948	35025	11/1948	£4,220	—
1116	Brighton	9/1948	35026	12/1948	£4,220	—
1117	Brighton	10/1948	35027	12/1948	£4,220	—
1118	Brighton	11/1948	35028	12/1948	£4,220	—
1119	Brighton	12/1948	35029	2/1949	£4,220	—
1120	Brighton	2/1949	35030	4/1949	£4,220	—
1121	Brighton	4/1949	35015	6/1949	£4,445	—
1122	Brighton	5/1949	35017	7/1949	£4,445	—
1123	Brighton/ Eastleigh	10/1950	35004	10/1950	£4,510	—
1124	Brighton/ Eastleigh	3/1951	35010	5/1951	£4,640	—

NOTES: The order numbers for the various batches of boilers were:

1090–1099	Eastleigh HO 1068, although built by NBLC
1100–1109	Eastleigh HO 1189
1110–1112	Eastleigh HO 2575
1113–1122	Brighton 1456
1123–1124	Brighton 1456 and Eastleigh HO 3407

Boiler numbers 1110/1/2/21/2/3/4 were built as spares, while numbers 1123/4 were commenced at Brighton and completed at Eastleigh. Locomotives Nos. 35021/2 entered traffic new with second-hand boilers Nos. 1098/9 which had been fitted with new fireboxes after removal from Nos. 21C9/10.

The design of the first ten boilers, Nos. 1090 to 1099, differed from the remainder by having the front ring tapering on the underside and the rear ring parallel, the latter having parallel front and tapered rear rings. Bulleid's intention was obviously to save weight both in steel and water content, for there were no changes in the tube or firebox heating surfaces, and thereby the steaming capacity or power output. Nos. 35021/2 of the final series, therefore, entered traffic new with boilers of this non-standard pattern, whereas Nos. 35023 to 35030 carried the final variety. In course of time, boilers of both series were carried indiscriminately by the class, no structural changes of significance being necessary. Boilers of both types remain extant on the four preserved members of the class, details being:

Locomotive No.	*Boiler No.*	*Type of boiler*	*Remarks*
35005	1095	1st series	Steamtown, Carnforth
35009	1108	2nd series	Wessex Railway Society
35028	1121	2nd series	Merchant Navy Locomotive Preservation Society
35029	1103	2nd series	National Railway Museum, York

The ten North British boilers suffered severely from cracking of the firebox throatplate around the thermic syphon connections, and also from surface cracking both around the stay holes and in the backplate below the fire door. The syphon necks were largely at the top of the fire where the heat was fiercest, where scale tended to collect and impair conduction and circulation. It was logical to anticipate trouble developing there, but not at

80,000 to 120,000 miles, or so extensively. As a temporary expedient, two openings were cut in the throat sheet and a separate diaphragm welded around each of the syphon holes, while any leaking by the steel staying was halted by the substitution of Monel metal stays.

Careful and prolonged investigation suggested that the use of untreated feed water was the main culprit, although a contributory factor was the contraction experienced when hot boilers and fireboxes were washed out with cold water before adequate time had elapsed for cooling-off. It was also considered advantageous to eject all hot ash from the grate and ashpans as soon as locomotives were stopped and not to leave some there until lighting up. As a result, strict instructions were sent to all shedmasters insisting that locomotives stood for not less than twelve hours before washout commenced. This, however, came too late to be of assistance to these ten fireboxes, which all required renewal within 6½ years at mileages far less than those attained by the King Arthurs and Lord Nelsons. Details are as follows:

Locomotive No.	*Boiler No.*	*Date firebox condemned*	*Age of firebox*	*Mileage*
21C1	1090	16/7/1947	6 yrs. 1 mth.	213,398
21C2	1091	4/10/1947	6 yrs. 4 mths.	195,499
21C3	1092	21/4/1947	5 yrs. 7 mths.	234,100
21C4	1093	21/2/1946	4 yrs. 4 mths.	151,350
21C5	1094	3/1/1948	6 yrs. 1 mth.	239,559
21C6	1095	12/8/1946	4 yrs. 7 mths.	196,548
21C7	1096	16/1/1947	4 yrs. 7 mths.	194,137
21C8	1097	1/7/1947	5 yrs. 1 mth.	220,933
21C9	1098	14/10/1947	5 yrs. 4 mths.	234,792
21C10	1099	16/10/1947	5 yrs. 2 mths.	225,084

The average life of these fireboxes was 5 years 4 months and the average mileage 210,539. Nos. 21C1 to 21C10 received boilers 1090 to 1099 new and carried them until new fireboxes became necessary. No spare boilers were available until 1946/47.

Boilers Nos. 1100 to 1109, built at Eastleigh for the 1944-5 series, had the advantage of modified thermic syphon seatings and connections, more attention given to places where scale collected, and a stricter washout schedule, but without water treatment this proved insufficient to lengthen their life beyond 1950-3. However, the second steel fireboxes fitted to the early boilers and those carried new by boilers 1110 to 1124 lasted the remaining life of the class, for with the beneficial effects of water treatment only one more renewal became necessary. Indeed, it was seldom the boiler or firebox which caused withdrawal, merely the need of routine repairs.

After Nationalisation, the reduction in working pressure from 280 to 250 lb./sq. in. was probably a contributory factor in prolonging firebox life. This modification had been advocated as long ago as 1946, but no action was taken as far as the Merchant Navies were concerned until 4 July 1952, when No. 35012 *United States Lines* left Eastleigh Works with its safety-valves set to operate at 250 lb./sq. in. A number of test runs were then made on the 11.30 a.m. Waterloo-Bournemouth West and Southampton Docks-Nine Elms fitted freights before it returned to general service from Nine Elms. In October 1952 further trial runs were made on both the "Bournemouth Belle" and the "Atlantic Coast Express" before a report was presented. This suggested that there was no deterioration in power output, performance or steaming, while the coal consumption was fractionally better, and less slipping occurred when starting away. The Eastleigh boilersmith estimated that the reduction in maintenance and wear would add 80,000 miles to the period between successive boiler lifts.

As a result, No. 35024 *East Asiatic Company* had its working pressure similarly reduced in November 1952, and at the same time had the three Ross pop safety-valves re-sited between the firebox and dome, the seatings being housed in a shallow recess. This, too, had been suggested some years earlier to avoid water surging in the boiler during braking being discharged to the atmosphere via the safety-valves. Any observer at Winchester could have vouched for this because down trains stopping there with Merchant Navies in charge before the re-siting invariably showered the platforms with boiling water. Dates of these changes are as follows:

No. 21C1 *Channel Packet*, August 1941, with front numberplate, repositioned route indication lights and disc brackets, right-hand footsteps and foot block, inverted ownership plate and widow's peak (*British Railways*)

No. 35001 *Channel Packet* at Eastleigh, October 1949. BR blue, V-cab, transfer numerals, standard smoke deflectors and "Devon Belle" batons, smokebox door numberplate and front sanding blanked-off (*D. L. Bradley*)

No. 35003 *Royal Mail* at Bournemouth Central, 29 June 1963, with rebuilt 5,250-gallon tender and AWS

The footplate of *Canadian Pacific* showing the mechanical stoker

No. 35005 *Canadian Pacific* heads the up "Devon Belle" into Salisbury, 4 July 1954. BR green livery and later-pattern train headboard (*E. W. Fry*)

No. 21C12 *United States Lines* in shops grey at Eastleigh, 14 January 1945. Sanding to all coupled wheels, short straight smoke deflectors, 5,100-gallon tender, and modified cab front and side valance

No. 35017 *Belgian Marine* leaving Southampton Central with the "Bournemouth Belle", 17 August 1956. BR green with standard lining (*E. W. Fry*)

No. 35028 *Clan Line* heads the down "Bournemouth Belle" away from Southampton Central, 16 April 1960 (*E. W. Fry*)

No. 21C101 *Exeter* on 2 July 1945, with cast nameplates, plaques and scrolls. The gap remains in the centre lining band (*British Railways*)

No. 34011 *Tavistock* on Eastleigh shed, 27 September 1952. BR green with black background to nameplate and lining adjusted to suit modified 4,500-gallon tender. Fitted with V-cab and sanding to centre and coupled wheels, and valance cut away ahead of cylinders (*E. W. Fry*)

No. 34036 *Westward Ho* on Eastleigh shed, 3 September 1960. Modified 4,500-gallon tender, extended valve spindles with smoke-deflector pockets and black background to nameplates (*E. W. Fry*)

No. 34077 *603 Squadron* on the Bournemouth Central turntable, 5 April 1963

No. 21C1 under construction, January 1941. Note slot across smokebox front, coupled wheel splashers and absence of frame lightening holes (*British Railways*)

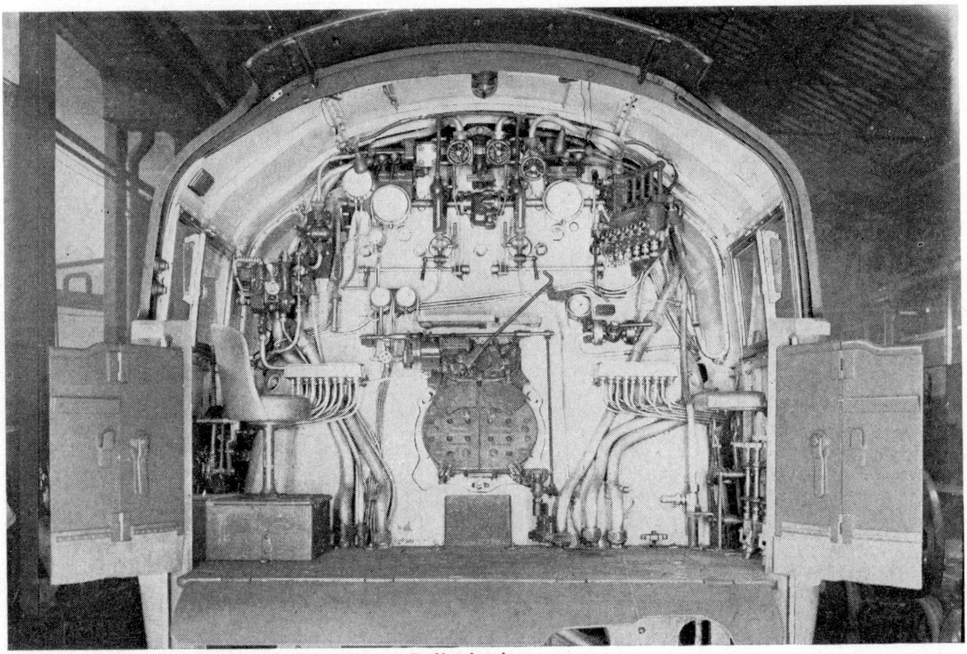
The well-equipped and spacious Bulleid cab

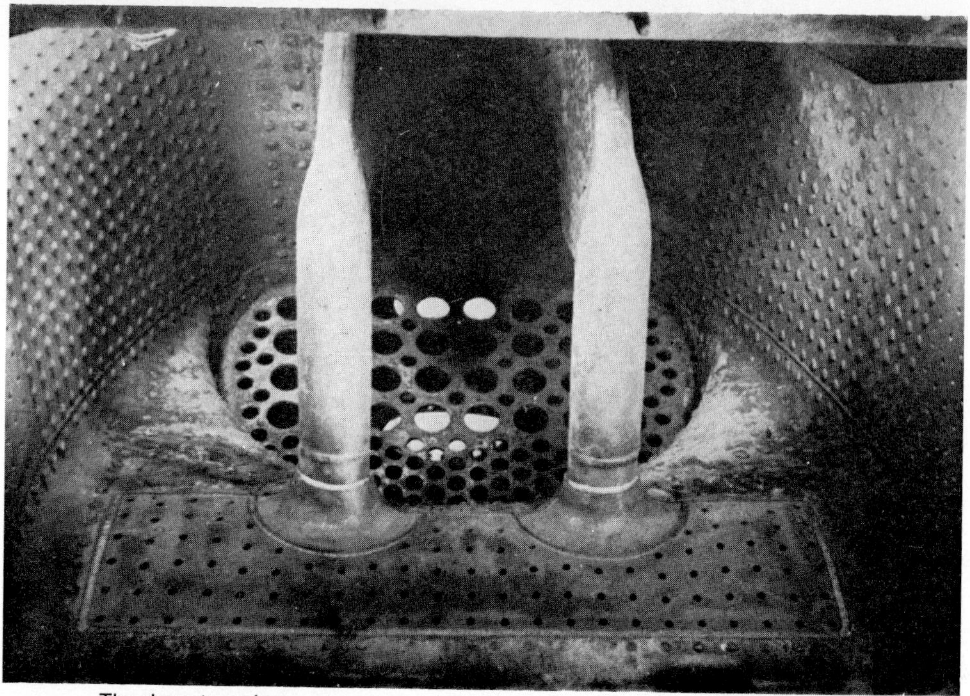

The thermic syphons

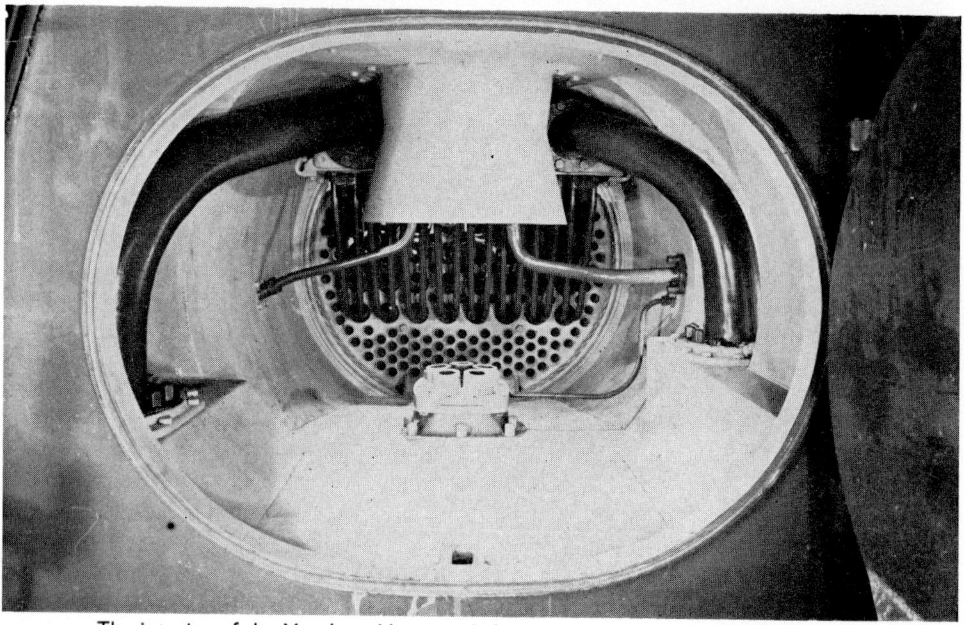

The interior of the Merchant Navy smokebox

No. 21C1 *Channel Packet*, Eastleigh Works, March 1941. Sanding to centre coupled wheels only, single front footstep, numberplate on angled plating, and chimney cover (*Real Photographs Co. Ltd.*)

No. 21C1 *Channel Packet* in charge of the "Golden Arrow" at Bickley Junction, 20 April 1946. Short smoke-deflector plates and original cylinder casing (*LCGB*)

No. 21C1 *Channel Packet* at Exmouth Junction, 29 June 1948. Malachite green, modified top casing and cowl, standard smoke deflectors, sanding to all coupled wheels disc brackets on smokebox door and circular ownership plate (*J. H. Aston*)

No. 35001 *Channel Packet* with modified 5,000-gallon tender, 20 July 1957 (*D. L. Bradley*)

Locomotive No.	*250 lb./sq. in. working pressure*	*Safety-valves re-sited*
35001	3/1955	6/1956
35002	9/1954	8/1955
35003	3/1955	3/1955
35004	6/1954	10/1955
35005	2/1954	2/1954
35006	9/1953	7/1955
35007	6/1955	6/1955
35008	10/1953	10/1953
35009	6/1954	—
35010	5/1954	1/1957
35011	6/1954	—
35012	7/1952	—
35013	10/1954	—
35014	11/1953	11/1953
35015	4/1954	4/1954
35016	8/1954	8/1954
35017	7/1954	7/1954
35018	8/1954	—
35019	9/1954	10/1955
35020	5/1954	5/1954
35021	6/1954	10/1954
35022	2/1955	6/1956
35023	5/1954	10/1954
35024	11/1952	11/1952
35025	5/1954	—
35026	1/1955	1/1955
35027	11/1954	11/1954
35028	12/1954	12/1954
35029	12/1954	12/1954
35030	10/1954	10/1954

As mentioned previously, when describing the construction of the various batches of locomotives, there were three types of tender supplied to the class, details being as follows:

Locomotive No.	*Tender Nos.*	*Capacity (gallons)*	*Weight fully laden*	*Wheelbase*
21C1–21C10 (35001–35010)	3111–3120	5,000	47 tons 16 cwt.	6′ 6″+6′ 6″=13′ 0″
21C11–21C20 (35011–35020)	3121/2/3/4/6 3125/7, 3129, 3128/30	5,100	50 tons 2 cwt.	6′ 6″+6′ 6″=13′ 0″
35021–35030	3342/5, 3341/6, 3343/50, 3349, 3344/7/8	6,000	53 tons 6 cwt.	7′ 4″+7′ 0″=14′ 4″

Before 1952, apart from the temporary use of LMS pattern in 1948, tender changes were few, and those which did occur were confined to locomotives of the same series and maintained the capacity differentials. In May 1952, however, it was decided to equip one of the 6,000-gallon variety for self-weighing to facilitate fuel and water consumption trials. At the time, No. 35025 *Brocklebank Line* was under repair at Eastleigh and advantage was taken of this to commandeer its tender (T3343) for modification and to replace it by T3350, previously attached to No. 35026 *Lamport & Holt Line*. The latter, in due course, left shops coupled to 5,100-gallon tender T3130 off No. 35020 *Bibby Line*, which in turn led to further exchanges.

During modification, tender T3343 had much of its top plating cut away, although not in the fashion used on other Merchant Navy tenders, to make replenishing easier. When ready for service this tender was temporarily attached to No. 35012 *United States Lines* for an official photograph and several trial weighings with varying quantities of water and coal. It entered traffic with No. 35018 *British India Line* on 11 July 1952. At Nine Elms this engine was regularly rostered for the 10.30 a.m. Waterloo-Bournemouth express until returned to Eastleigh Works on 28 September 1952, where the tender was removed and, after adjustments to the draw gear and springing and minor modifications to the self-weighing equipment, transferred to No. 35014 *Nederland Line* on 8 November 1952. This locomotive carried the boiler without thermic syphons (No. 1107) and as such was of particular interest to the trials staff. Over the next few months it was worked extensively on both the Bournemouth and West of England expresses, as well as the Nine Elms-Southampton Docks fitted freights. When these trials were completed tender T3343 remained until No. 35014 *Nederland Line* entered Eastleigh Works for rebuilding on 18 May 1956. It reappeared behind No. 35015 *Rotterdam Lloyd* on 6 July 1956, was removed on 1 May 1958, and ran attached to No. 35024 *East Asiatic Company* from 14 May 1958 until 20 December 1961, when the self-weighing equipment was removed and the tender re-bodied.

Apart from riding well, and in the two later series offering an unobstructed view rearwards, the Bulleid tenders had little to endear them to the men, for the high sides made watering and coaling unusually tedious and frustrating, as well as blasting the footplates with coal dust. Corrosion and ease of damage also proved failings, but whereas they remained so to the end, replenishment was simplified by removing much of the plating above tank level to give a profile with a drop of some 21in. at mid-length. No. 35021 *New Zealand Line* (T3342) was the first, on 29 February 1952, to receive a modified tender. Prior to the 1956-9 rebuilding, only six other tenders were similarly modified, details being:

Tender No.	*Attached to locomotive No.*	*Date modified*
T3111	35001	6/1956
T3114	35007	9/1956
T3121	35011	8/1957
T3122	35012	7/1952
T3124	35013	12/1952
T3347	35020	6/1953

The self-weighing tender which had partially cut-away side sheeting saw service with Nos. 35014/5/8/24 before they were rebuilt.

On rebuilding, all locomotives received modified tenders, although No. 35020 *Bibby Line* between 25 May and 11 July 1956, ran with unmodified tender T3345 while engaged on dynamometer car trials between Waterloo and Exeter, it having been found that the necessary cables from the locomotive to the recording instruments could be more readily fitted and supported by one of the high-sided tenders. To match the lining of *Bibby Line*'s cab, the sides of the tender were repainted with lowered panelling and emblem and a black top to the side sheeting. When the trials were concluded, this tender was transferred to No. 35028 *Clan Line* without any changes being made to the painting.

The provision of the self-weighing tender of necessity led to a chain of exchanges, and by 30 June 1954 the position was as follows:

Tender capacity (gallons)	*Locomotive Nos.*	*Tender Nos.*
5,000	35001–35010	T3111/2/7, 3113/5/6, 3114/8/9/20
5,100	35011/2/3/5/6/7/9/24/6/9	T3121/2/4/6, 3125/7/8, 3123/30, 3129
6,000	35014/8/20/1/2/3/5/7/8/30	T3343/6/7, 3342/5, 3341/50, 3349, 3344/8

At this period the tenders attached to Nos. 35012/3/20/1 were modified and that with No. 35014 was self-weighing. It will be noted that the 5,000-gallon tenders were restricted to the first series, Nos. 35001 to 35010.

Six of the 5,000-gallon tenders (T3113/4/6/8/9/20) were partially renewed in 1945-7, but advantage was not taken either to increase the tank capacity or to modify the design to correspond with the 5,100-gallon series attached to Nos. 21C11 to 21C20. Externally, there was no apparent difference, the changes being entirely concerned with strengthening the coal space and tank plating, and making good the considerable inroads caused by corrosion and rough usage.

Five of these small-capacity tenders were subsequently rebuilt in 1959-63 with entirely new tops constructed at Ashford Works. According to the official drawings they then held 5,250 gallons, but when filled from a metered supply at Eastleigh in August 1959, tender T3117 was found to hold no less than 5,308 gallons at 56° F. These tenders were readily recognisable by the divided handrailing at the cab entrance, the higher side plating which obscured more of the coal space than on the modified variety, rectangular manhole covers, BR-pattern lockers and more robust rear-end ladders. The original underframing, wheels, braking gear, etc., was re-used with some strengthening pieces welded in the corners and around the drawgear.

On 20 December 1961 the self-weighing tender was declared surplus to requirements and on removal from No. 35024 *East Asiatic Company* was similarly rebuilt at Eastleigh. Its capacity, however, remained at 6,000 gallons and the special equipment was removed. The locomotives involved with these six rebuilt tenders were as follows:

Tender No.	Locomotive No.	Date ex-Eastleigh after rebuilding	Remarks
3111	35001	2/2/1963	Tender to 35026 10/4/1965
3112	35002	9/4/1960	Kept to withdrawal
3115	35005	30/5/1959	Tender to 35014 10/9/1965
3117	35003	29/8/1959	Kept to withdrawal
3118	35018	13/1/1962	Tender to 35008 17/10/1964
3343	35008	3/2/1962	Tender to 35018 17/10/1964 for scrapping

The fully-laden weights of the rebuilt tenders were:

Tender No.	T3117	T3343
Date	8/1959	2/1964
Leading wheels	16 tons 18 cwt.	17 tons 16 cwt.
Centre wheels	14 tons 8 cwt.	17 tons 6 cwt.
Trailing wheels	18 tons 5 cwt.	18 tons 6 cwt.
TOTAL	49 tons 11 cwt.	53 tons 8 cwt.

At nationalisation, LMS No. 10000 was the only express diesel locomotive at work in the country and very few others were planned, while those favouring large-scale main-line electrification had suffered a severe setback in the recently-published Government White Paper on capital investment. Of necessity, any new locomotive construction, except for shunting, had to be steam, but little agreement existed as to the design or type. Many in authority considered that the answer lay in widespread adoption of LMS classes, but in fairness to the other three pre-nationalisation companies, a series of trials was ordered to record the leading features of performance and efficiency of the principal existing modern locomotives over the lines of all six Regions. At the same time a Locomotive Standards Committee was to examine and select a limited range of existing or planned modern classes of all types for construction until the new standard classes could be developed, built and set to work.

Fortunately, the running of the Interchange Trials alone concerns us here. These were organised during the spring of 1948 and directly concerned five express passenger, four mixed-traffic and five heavy goods classes of LMS, LNER, Great Western, Southern and War Department design. All the trial runs were to be made in revenue-earning service to the best current schedules and with maximum loads over a number of carefully-selected routes. The express classes chosen consisted of the LMS Duchess and Royal Scot, the Great Western King, LNER A4 and Southern Merchant Navy, three being pacifics and two 4-6-0's. Since potential universal service was the issue, a single type of coal, best Midland hards, was provided throughout the trials with no attempt to ensure the quality or size, other than that normally found at the depot where replenishing occurred, but locomotives were operated by footplate crews from the owning Regions, assisted, when necessary, by conductors from the home line.

The Southern Region prepared four Merchant Navies as its contribution to the express locomotive trials, their details being as follows:

Locomotive No.	Mileage since general repair	LMR 4,000-gallon tender	From Works	Area of trials
35017	34,409	10123	17.4.48	Kings Cross-Leeds Euston-Carlisle
35018	43,789	—	22.5.48	Waterloo-Exeter
35019	23,356	10219	13.4.48	Paddington-Plymouth
35020	34,061	10373	8.5.48	Spare engine, not required

All were given light repairs and fitted with speed recorders, heat-resisting steel firebars, Aiton's bellow-joint exhaust steampipes and V-front cabs, while No. 35020, in addition, received extra-long smoke-deflector plates. Nos. 35017/9/20 were exceptionally well cleaned when despatched from Eastleigh Works, which made the failure to paint the borrowed tenders malachite green difficult to comprehend. Their use instead of the Bulleid variety was necessary because water pick-up gear was called for on the Eastern, London Midland and Western Regions.

The routes selected were Kings Cross-Leeds (Eastern Region), Euston-Carlisle (London Midland Region), Paddington-Plymouth (Western Region) and Waterloo-Exeter (Southern Region). In a preliminary week each foreign crew had the opportunity of working the trains selected for the trials twice in each direction, down on Mondays and Wednesdays and up on Tuesdays and Thursdays, and thereby of learning what they could of each road in such a limited time. In the second week the test runs proper were made with full loads and dynamometer cars, down on Tuesdays and Thursdays and up on Wednesdays and Fridays. In one respect Southern Region crews were at a distinct disadvantage, for their maximum continuous working at the time was over the 142¾ miles between Waterloo and Weymouth, whereas the exchange working involved unbroken journeys of 171¾ to 299 miles.

From a grading point of view, probably the most extreme test was that presented by the Western Region between Newton Abbot and Plymouth, where crews faced gradients of 1 in 36 and 1 in 42. Even with loads restricted to 360 tons, Dainton, Rattery and Hemerdon banks must have appeared awe-inspiring to foreign crews and locomotives, especially the last-mentioned climb, for permanent way works forbade any chance of a run being made at this exceedingly formidable obstacle.

Among other arduous tasks was the long climb at the head of 500 tons to Shap summit on the London Midland line. This was especially onerous when travelling north, when the hard pounding came as the climax of 250 miles more or less continuous collar work. On the Southern Region the easterly ascent of Honiton came as an unwelcome, and possibly unexpected, surprise to northern crews suffering the misapprehension that no real gradients were to be found out of Waterloo. Their task was, to some extent, alleviated by the preliminary descent to Axminster, which offered hard-pressed crews the opportunity of topping up the boiler, tending the fire and raising the speed into the eighties before tackling the climb. With loads of 470 tons, many of the starts coming east from Exeter gave rise to considerable concern, in particular with the pacifics, where adhesion losses demanded enginemanship of the highest order. Across on the Eastern Region the sternest task was undoubtedly that of getting the 500-ton test trains unassisted up the 1 in 105 bank from the Kings Cross start through two greasy-railed, smoke-filled tunnels to Holloway. There were no failures, but No. 35017 *Belgian Marine* on its first preliminary run came within an ace of disaster.

The "Atlantic Coast Express" not unexpectedly offered little difficulty to No. 35018 *British India Line*, although for some reason it was not handled with the verve and joyous exhibition of speed regularly featured by Exmouth Junction and Salisbury crews. Possibly the driver was attempting to economise with fuel and water whenever the opportunity arose and relying on his line knowledge and experience to maintain overall, if not sectional timings. Slipping at all starts, except Axminster, in the up direction, was much less than encountered daily with ordinary services and drivers not possessing the same skill and dedication. This phenomenon was not fully appreciated at the time, and it was only later, when the results of the various trials were analysed, that the effect of first-rate crews was placed in perspective. Coal consumption was as follows:

Locomotive	*Lb. of coal per mile*	*Lb. of coal per drawbar h.p.-hour*
ER A4	45.57	3.20
LMR Duchess	42.74	3.17
LMR Royal Scot	44.39	3.24
SR Merchant Navy	***50.85***	***3.52***

Of the four test routes, that from Euston to Carlisle proved most frustrating to visiting crews, for, as the returning Merchant Navy men averred, the LMR main line consisted of a long series of temporary speed restrictions interlaced by others of a more enduring nature. Be that as it may, timekeeping was out of the question for the most determined crews, and try the Southern men certainly did.

On one of the preparatory journeys No. 35017 *Belgian Marine* was brought to a halt with the 500-ton down "Royal Scot" on Shap at the 33½ milepost just north of Tebay station. The signal cleared as the train stopped, but too late to assist Driver Swain who fought for 2½ minutes to get a grip, backing and sanding continuously, until a slow but steady re-start was made for the summit. The weather at the time could not have been worse, it being an unpleasant combination of low cloud, mist and drizzle. During the test runs proper, No. 35017 *Belgian Marine* gave a remarkably lively performance north of Crewe and notwithstanding several desperate handicaps, the crew succeeded in regaining 1½ minutes between Crewe and Carlisle. Similar excellent performance was recorded between Penrith and Preston on the up services. Coal consumption was as follows:

Locomotive	Lb. of coal per mile	Lb. of coal per drawbar h.p.-hour
ER A4	41.25	3.00
LMR Duchess	44.09	3.07
LMR Royal Scot	41.42	3.37
SR Merchant Navy	*50.66*	*3.57*

Other than service checks, the Western Region main line between Paddington and Taunton held few serious problems for enginemen of the calibre of those engaged in the trials, but west of Taunton many visiting crews found themselves in deep trouble. On the down journeys with loads of 350 tons the 38-minute allowance for the 30.8 miles to Exeter proved one of the most exacting of all point-to-point bookings and, even apart from checks, all lost time except No. 35019 *French Line CGT*. The main difficulty was the unbroken climb of some nine miles from Norton Fitzwarren to the summit box of Whiteball in the Blackdown Hills, a climb which, after a reasonably gentle beginning, deteriorated into 2½ miles of 1 in 90-86-80 to the mouth of Whitehall Tunnel and then eased to 1 in 127 for the last half mile. No. 35019, with its excellent boiler, was never short of steam, but the fire-throwing was reminiscent of the North Western at the turn of the century. The fireman's efforts appeared to be leaving via the chimney as soon as they entered the firebox.

Similarly, the gradients between Newton Abbot and Plymouth were considerably steeper than visiting crews would have met regularly on their own systems. If this alone was insufficient to douse enthusiasm, then restrictions added their quota, for the up line was so beset that timekeeping, even for Western men accustomed to the vicinity, proved impossible. Once again the Merchant Navy was resolutely and skilfully driven, and with brute force and much slipping gave an excellent account of itself. Its behaviour amazed the pilotmen, but they had to admire its tenacity and strength. Coal consumption was as follows:

Locomotive	Lb. of coal per mile	Lb. of coal per drawbar h.p.-hour
ER A4	42.45	3.19
LMR Duchess	41.67	3.24
LMR Royal Scot	42.76	3.64
WR King	48.82	3.74
SR Merchant Navy	*48.02*	*3.61*

Like the trials run over the Western Region, the Kings Cross-Leeds line had the distinction of entertaining all five competitors, which gave observers the opportunity of sampling the work of two 4-6-0's and three pacifics with 500-ton loads. Northbound, once clear of the sharp and slippery ascent through the tunnels from Kings Cross, the journeys lacked character and suffered badly from over-leisurely schedules. However, in the reverse direction with tighter sectional timings the running reached high standards and proved most interesting. The track compared favourably with that of pre-war and, being free of severe restrictions, offered crews every incentive to gain time and book before-time arrivals at Kings Cross. No. 35017 *Belgian Marine* revelled with these trains and, despite the handicap of an over-anxious pilotman, did Bulleid proud before his late colleagues. Coal consumption details were:

Locomotive	Lb. of coal per mile	Lb. of coal per drawbar h.p.-hour
ER A4	39.08	2.92
LMR Duchess	44.05	3.04
LMR Royal Scot	46.66	3.26
WR King	47.25	3.39
SR Merchant Navy	*49.41*	*3.73*

If all these figures from the Regional trials are collected together and the average values determined, the league table reads as follows:

AVERAGE COAL CONSUMPTION RELATED TO POWER OUTPUT:

Locomotive	Lb. per drawbar h.p.-hour
ER A4	3.06
LMR Duchess..	3.12
LMR Royal Scot	3.38
WR King	3.59
SR Merchant Navy	*3.60*

AVERAGE WATER CONSUMPTION RELATED TO POWER OUTPUT:

Locomotive	Lb. per drawbar h.p.-hour
ER A4	24.32
LMR Royal Scot	25.81
LMR Duchess..	27.08
WR King	28.58
SR Merchant Navy	*30.43*

AVERAGE EVAPORATIVE RATE:

Locomotive	Lb. of water per lb. of coal
SR Merchant Navy	*8.45*
LMR Duchess..	8.67
WR King	8.07
ER A4	7.92
LMR Royal Scot	7.70

In coal and water consumption the Merchant Navies badly tailed the field, although in boiler efficiency the position changed dramatically with only the LMR Duchess pacifics returning better figures. It would appear that the advantages presented by the well-proportioned and excellently-designed Bulleid boilers were more than nullified by the erratically performing front end and the tendency for incomplete combustion. By skilful control there was much less slipping on starting than normally found with less experienced or keen men on Southern Region metals, but at speed, and especially when working hard uphill, all three locomotives showed most effectively their slipping propensity. Much of this resulted from oil-bath leakages, which on the Euston-Carlisle trials were no less than 85 per cent of capacity. On the Western Region the pilotman, after an exceptionally long and severe bout on Rattery bank, found it difficult to believe that No. 35019 *French Line* was unscathed and capable of working the train for the remainder of the journey. Performance-wise the Merchant Navies did the Southern Region proud, but at what a cost!

Many factors limited the scope of these trials; therefore, over the next few years advantage was taken of the Rugby Testing Plant and the LMR Mobile Test Unit to gain a more detailed knowledge of many of the pre-nationalisation locomotives as well as the new British Railways classes. When called upon to provide a Merchant Navy for testing in December 1951, Eastleigh chose No. 35022 *Holland America Line* and took it into works for a light intermediate repair and the addition of various items of specialised equipment. Repair and mileage details are as follows:

To traffic new	9/10/1948
6,000-gallon tender attached	8/1/1949
Heavy intermediate repair	15/5/1950 to 5/7/1950 (92,805 miles)
Light intermediate repair	10/12/1951 to 8/2/1952 (188,928 miles)
Left for Rugby via Willesden	3/3/1952

A mileage of 188,928 for a trials locomotive, without a general repair or boiler lift, was unusually high, and one wonders why this particular locomotive was chosen. If one of the final series were required, then surely the last built, No. 35030 *Elder-Dempster Lines*, with a mileage of 55,000, would have been more suitable. However, if this remains a mystery, it is quite certain that no LMR or BR locomotive would have been presented to Rugby with more than a few thousand miles logged since the last general repair or entry to traffic new.

At Rugby, the stationary plant tests were conducted at constant rates of evaporation and combustion, and at a constant speed. The coal and water rates were established by the summation of increment method and with the aid of the Swindon steam flow meter. The range covered by the tests was from 15 to 85 m.p.h., from 10 to 50 per cent nominal cut-off and from 10,000 to 42,000 lb./hr. of feed water. The majority of the tests were performed with the regulator fully open, whereas in normal service on the Southern Region it was general practice to run with it partially closed and correspondingly longer cut-offs. Indicating was by means of a modified Farnboro recorder, while the equivalent of 10,304 miles were run during the plant tests.

The controlled road trials were undertaken in October and November 1952 using the Midland main line between Durranhill, Carlisle and Skipton with 594-ton trains of twenty-bogie coaches. For the schedules involved these were the heaviest expresses worked over the route and were 42 per cent greater than the tare loadings normally entrusted to LMR Class 7 4-6-0's. 3,838 miles were run without loss of time or undue trouble, except for a failure with buckled coupling-rods after a particularly vicious bout of slipping at speed.

By adjustment the steam reversing gear could not be prevented from creeping; the actual degree was slight and probably insufficient to affect seriously the running in traffic, but it prevented testing under the uniform conditions of the plant. To overcome this, a number of distance pieces were prepared which ensured that the gear could be secured in a definitely fixed position. However, as these pieces could only be inserted while the locomotive was stationary, it was impossible to adjust the cut-off once a test commenced. For the road testing, the reversing gear was modified to accept fine adjustment, but the creep remained because of the necessity of continually altering the cut-off to cover the speed and power requirements of the undulating Carlisle-Skipton line.

The propensity for slipping at speed, as opposed to slipping at starting, was ascribed to No. 35022 *Holland America Line* proving incapable of running for any length of time without copiously lubricating the coupled wheel treads and, on the Test Plant the rollers, with oil from the bath. A thorough cleaning before every test and the wiping of the rollers at frequent intervals were necessary if any of the high-power tests were to be completed without wrecking the locomotive and, possibly, the plant also. Nevertheless, on several occasions the coupling-rods buckled and it was thought prudent not to attempt to ascertain the true front-end limit.

In conclusion, it was considered that the Merchant Navy locomotives as designed were most effective and capable, but relatively uneconomical. If operated, as they would be frequently in general service, with the reversing gear in a relatively long cut-off and the regulator partly open, they would be even less economical, though from the mechanical point of view as well as power output, the performance would be more reliable. The vibration, associated with full regulator and short cut-off working, would also be avoided.

In spite of the free draught provided by the multiple-jet blastpipe, the combustion was poor, particularly with low-grade coal. The draughting arrangement could almost certainly be improved by some re-design of the chimney, for the actual choke was located 7in. above the effective choke, where the vacuum was highest. Similar thoughts had been expressed some years earlier and No. 35019 *French Line* was fitted experimentally with a single blastpipe and chimney in June 1951.

Trials were run from Eastleigh shed, but steaming proved so poor that on 17 August 1951 the blastpipe diameter was reduced from 17¼in. to 15½in. by inserting a liner. Steaming improved, though remaining erratic, with the result that further blastpipe modifications were made in September 1951 and January 1952, when a 16in. liner was fitted. Steaming now proved acceptable, although below the maximum achieved by the class in regular service, while crews complained that sectional timings could not be maintained with loads of more than eleven coaches, and that slipping on starting and at speed was more pronounced. From the lineside the passage at speed was reminiscent of the Drummond "Paddleboxes" in full cry. Regular traffic from Nine Elms was entered in February 1952 and the multiple blastpipe refitted in September 1954.

To gain a more detailed account of a single blastpipe performance No. 35022 *Holland America Line* was equipped with one in February 1953, and between 9 March and 11 May 1953 engaged on a series of test trials at Rugby. An equivalent of 2,463 miles was run and similar conclusions reached as those gained earlier with No. 35019 *French Line*, details being as follows:

Maximum boiler output	reduced from 34,000 to 31,000 lb./hr.
Boiler efficiency and combustion	unchanged
Smoke emission	marginally less
Ease of firing	more skill required
Fuel consumption	heavier at higher output

Because of loading gauge restrictions an entirely satisfactory single blastpipe could not be fitted, for there was insufficient height available between the inside valve-chest top and the chimney. A longer blastpipe was necessary to gain full efficiency and, if this could have been provided, there would have been no loss of maximum boiler output.

The fitting of thermic syphons to the relatively small British boilers was questioned by many locomotive engineers, for Doncaster had found them ineffective and expensive gimmicks which reduced the firebox life by some 20 per cent. On test at Rugby no firm conclusions were reached, either in favour or against, so a series of trials with a boiler not so equipped was authorised. Eastleigh Works, however, had anticipated this instruction and in May 1951 fitted boiler 1107 with a new steel firebox not having syphons, and on 25 August that year despatched it to general service on No. 35014 *Nederland Line*. Details of this boiler and its movement round the class are as follows:

Built at Eastleigh Works (No. 8 of H.O. 1189)	28/1/1945
Fitted to No. 21C16	14/3/1945
Off at 86,121 miles	22/11/1946
To No. 21C15	22/2/1947
Off at 178,020 miles	13/4/1949
To No. 35001	21/10/1949
Off at 235,229 miles	29/11/1950
New steel firebox with no thermic syphons	
To No. 35014	25/8/1951
Off at 116,005 miles	1/10/1953
To No. 35022	21/11/1953
Off at 233,763 miles	27/4/1956
To No. 35017	30/3/1957
Off at 566,940 miles	5/7/1963
Boiler not re-used, broken up	9/8/1964

When first fitted to No. 35014 *Nederland Line* in August 1951, the steaming proved erratic and trouble was met from clinker; thus after running only 781 miles a new and modified brick arch was substituted with immediate beneficial results as regards steaming, although this still fell below that normally achieved in regular service by standard members of the class. Clinkering remained a problem with poor-quality fuel, while there arose on long journeys a new one in the form of "birds-nesting" of the tubeplate. Further changes were therefore made to the brick arch in May 1952, and again five months later, when a satisfactory steaming rate was gained and the other troubles reduced to manageable levels.

For testing this boiler at Rugby it was decided, in the interests of uniformity, to use No. 35022 *Holland America Line* and on 21 November 1953 this locomotive left Eastleigh Works carrying it. After running-in on the Bournemouth slows and making several appearances on the Waterloo expresses, No. 35022 proceeded via Willesden to Rugby on 8 December 1953. The tests were completed by the end of January 1954, and on 2 February it was turned on the local depot turntable by jacking up the rear wheels of the tender to make this possible and then set off south.

Despite all the facilities available at the Rugby Testing Plant, some doubts still remained as to whether any of the steaming differences observed were caused by the removal of the syphons or the fitting of a non-standard brick arch. Of necessity, this displayed major changes in design, and some test officials considered that this affected the steaming capacity more than the syphons. The report, therefore, was inconclusive, details being as follows:

Maximum boiler output	unchanged
Inlet steam temperature	40°-60° higher
Boiler efficiency	marginally higher
Combustion	unchanged
Smoke emission	no reduction
Clinkering of fire	a major problem with poor fuel
Ease of firing	much more difficult
Fuel consumption	unchanged
Conclusions reached	It would not be economically justified on boiler performance alone to remove the syphons, nor would it be worthwhile fitting them in any British coal-fired locomotive of similar or smaller size than the Merchant Navies

Boiler 1107 remained with No. 35022 *Holland America Line* until 27 April 1956, by which date 117,758 miles had been run, and after repairs was transferred to No. 35017 *Belgian Marine* on 30 March 1957, where it remained until removed for scrap on 5 July 1963. The mileage run with this locomotive was 333,177, which gave a grand total of 566,940 since the firebox renewal in May 1951, this being about average for syphon-equipped fireboxes employing water treatment.

During the spring of 1952 a series of haulage trials was held on the Eastern Section to compare the performance in regular service of the Merchant Navy, West Country, Battle of Britain and Britannia pacifics between Dover Marine and Chislehurst. The trains consisted of thirty laden partially-fitted ferry vehicles and a pair of 25-ton eight-wheeled brake vans, weighing in all some 718 to 733 tons. On the first test run No. 35030 *Elder-Dempster Lines* in the early morning of 17 February had no trouble whatsoever with its train and, despite a bad signal check approaching Tonbridge, climbed the bank up through Hildenborough in great style. Three other runs were made on 18, 20 and 21 February, in which stops were made at Paddock Wood, Tonbridge, Weald Box and before Polhill tunnel, but apart from some slipping, the restarts were made with ease and the tight schedule maintained. Later in the month, No. 34012 *Launceston* worked similar trains, while No. 34073 *249 Squadron* in mid-March and No. 70014 *Iron Duke* on 23 March 1952, were put through their paces. Again, time was kept and the trains handled reasonably easily, although the two Bulleids made poor starts from Weald Box and Polhill in rain, and the Britannia had to be removed from traffic after reaching Chislehurst when the driving wheels were found to have moved on the axle. Repairs could not be undertaken at Eastleigh and the offending parts had to be removed and despatched to Derby for re-centring.

Exactly what was the outcome of these trials is difficult to say, although in the autumn of 1952 there was a rearrangement of the Continental services with some loadings increased and fewer reliefs worked at holiday periods. The Battersea duties were then as follows: Duty 1 (MN) 9.00 Victoria-Dover Marine, 2.25 p.m. Folkestone-Victoria; Duty 2 (MN) 10.00 a.m. Victoria-Dover Marine, 1.30 p.m. Dover Marine-Victoria; Duty 3 (Britannia) up and down "Golden Arrow"; Duty 4 (MN) 1.30 p.m. Victoria-Dover Marine, 6.10 p.m. Dover Marine-Victoria; Duties 5 and 6 (MN or WC) relief boat expresses. The "Night Ferry" was Dover Merchant Navy duty 430, the locomotive of which also worked the 12.30 p.m. Victoria-Folkestone and 5.10 p.m. Dover Marine-Victoria. In the winter months, it was usual for this duty to be shared by two locomotives daily.

On 24 April 1953, No. 35020 *Bibby Line* came close to disaster at Crewkerne with the 4.30 p.m. Exeter-Waterloo express, when the driving axle fractured at speed. By good fortune and prompt action of the crew a serious accident was avoided, but investigation into the cause of failure suggested that other axles might be faulty, and on 12 May 1953 the entire class was withdrawn from traffic pending ultrasonic inspection of all coupled axles. To fill their duties, Britannias, V2's, Class 5's and B1's were transferred from the other Regions, details being as follows: Nine Elms Nos. 45051/61, 45130, 45216/22/3, 45350, 60893/6, 60908/16/7/28, 73003/15/7; Salisbury Nos. 70017/23; Exmouth Junction Nos. 70024/8/9; Dover No. 70030; Battersea Nos. 61015/41/50, 61109/33/8/48/88/92, 61219/73/4, 61329/38/54, 70034. The first recorded "foreign" workings were on 13 May, when No. 70029 *Shooting Star* headed the "Bournemouth Belle", No. 70023 *Venus* the 3.54 p.m. Waterloo-Basingstoke and No. 70024 *Vulcan* the 9.00 p.m. Nine Elms-West of England fitted freight. The first V2 class noted was No. 60928 which took the 10.30 a.m. down to Bournemouth on 14th May and returned with the 5.35 p.m. from Weymouth. Once all the V2's were available, the Britannias were normally rostered for the West of England line and the 2-6-2's for the Bournemouth services. All the latter were in good mechanical order with low mileages and were much appreciated by the men; the Britannias, in contrast, were considered rough riders and erratic steamers by Western Section crews. The LMR Class 5's were also well received, but the BR variation, Nos. 73003/15/7, made few friends. The former were usually rostered for the Waterloo-Salisbury semi-fasts or the Basingstoke commuter services, although use was also made of them to Southampton Docks, Bournemouth and Weymouth. Over on the Eastern Section, No. 70030 *William Wordsworth* appeared regularly on the "Night Ferry" and other Dover boat-train duties, while No. 70034 *Thomas Hardy* took over the 1.30 p.m. Victoria-Dover Marine. Both arrived rusty, covered in grime and without tools, but within twenty-four hours much hard cleaning had transformed them into two immaculate pacifics and a credit to the Southern Region.

All the suspect driving axles were checked with the aid of ultrasonic equipment at Eastleigh Works, although Nos. 35005/10/2/3/4/7/27/9 were actually dismantled at Ashford, some on the shed and others in works, and their axles despatched there by road. The axles of Nos. 35001/12/23/4 proved faulty, while those belonging to Nos. 35025/6 were replaced as a precautionary measure, although no actual fracturing had occurred. The return to traffic commenced on 16 May 1953, when No. 35018 *British India Line* worked the 9.00 a.m. Waterloo-Exeter, No. 35006 *Peninsular & Oriental* the 6.48 p.m. perishables from Templecombe, and No. 35026 *Lamport & Holt Line* the 10.00 a.m. Victoria-Dover Marine. By the following day Nos. 35001/2/3/4/10/1/2/27/9/30 had also become available and the motive power crisis was over without the travelling public being fully aware of the excellent inter-Regional co-operation which kept Southern Region services operational. At the end of May only Nos. 35020/2/8 remained out of traffic, and the task of applying similar checks to West Country and Battle of Britain axles could commence.

At Bournemouth in the autumn of 1953 the hardest London duties were in the hands of light pacifics Nos. 34093/4/5, 34105 to 34110, in preference to the nominally more powerful, but temperamental, Lord Nelsons. Some very fine running was made and only the thirteen-coach "Royal Wessex" taxed these locomotives to the limit, especially in the depths of winter when carriage heating and the bad weather made timekeeping with such a heavy and well-patronised train difficult. As a result, in early February 1954 Nos. 35008/11/12 were transferred to Bournemouth for working this train and the 11.30 a.m. Weymouth-Waterloo, another popular and heavy train.

Once again the reign of the class at Bournemouth was brief, for with the wholesale reorganisation of the locomotive workings on 3 May 1954, many of the almost traditional duties came to an abrupt end. Locomotive changing at Bournemouth Central on the through Weymouth services virtually ceased, while Dorchester received Lord Nelsons Nos. 30864/5 for working two of the Weymouth-Waterloo expresses. The down "Royal Wessex" became part of Nine Elms Duty 36, although the up train, Bournemouth Duty 381, was one of the few workings left unchanged. As a result Nos. 35011/2 were despatched to Nine Elms and No. 35008 to Exmouth Junction, but later Nos. 35014/22 came to Bournemouth as replacements, one invariably taking the up "Royal Wessex" daily. The allocation of the class was then as follows: Nine Elms Nos. 35005/10/1/2/5/6/7/8/9/20/1/5, Exmouth Junction Nos. 35001/2/3/4/8/13/23/4, Salisbury Nos. 35006/7/9, Bournemouth Nos. 35014/22, Battersea Nos. 35026/7/8, Dover Nos. 35029/30.

At the conclusion of these inspections, the Bulleid crank axle received some adverse comment and accordingly in August 1954 a modified, balanced pattern was designed at

Eastleigh and fitted to Nos. 35010 (June 1955), 35011 (February 1955), 35019 (April 1955), 35023 (October 1954), 35026 (January 1955) and 35027 (November 1954). At the same time these locomotives received new steel axleboxes and manganese liners.

Towards the end of the year two mishaps caused lengthy delays in the West Country, the first on 11 November 1954, occurring when No. 35023 *Holland Afrika Line* broke a tender axle near Broad Clyst while heading the up "Atlantic Coast Express". No. 82017, following with the 12.35 p.m. Exeter-Broad Clyst was summoned forward to haul the train back to Pinhoe where No. 35009 *Shaw Savill* was waiting to take it on to Waterloo, wrong-line working being necessary to pass No. 35023 *Holland Afrika Line*. The second incident on 10 December 1954 concerned No. 35025 *Brocklebank Line*, when a coupling-rod broke shortly after passing Honiton with the 9.00 a.m. Waterloo-Exeter express. The casing was severely battered, several windows broken on the train and about 200 yards of track damaged, but fortunately, derailment was avoided and injuries were minor. After standing for a few minutes, oil leaking from the locomotive ignited and set the boiler lagging ablaze, and was only brought under control after the arrival of the fire brigade. King Arthur No. 30449 *Sir Torre* with the slow 11.46 a.m. Templecombe-Exeter was approaching the scene and, after berthing its coaches in a siding, it drew the express back to Honiton, attached to the front, and then proceeded wrong line to Sidmouth Junction, where the down track was regained for the remainder of the delayed journey to Exeter. The 11.46 a.m. Templecombe followed a few minutes later behind Adams 4-4-2 tank No. 30584, which was running light engine from Axminster to Exmouth Junction. Over on the Eastern Section, No. 35030 *Elder-Dempster Lines* coming up from Folkestone with a relief Continental express on Christmas Eve 1954, failed with a broken tender tyre shortly after passing Paddock Wood. C Class No. 31068 hauled the train back to Paddock Wood where U1 class No. 31904, fortuitously present on a van train, was called upon to work it on to Victoria, wrong-line running being necessary to Tonbridge in order to pass the pacific. The latter was eventually towed to Tonbridge and stowed at the rear of the running shed where it resided over the holiday, looking somewhat out of place surrounded by sundry Wainwright 4-4-0's, 0-6-0's and 0-4-4 tanks.

By this date, serious consideration was being given to rebuilding or scrapping the class, although, economy apart, the necessity of either was no longer so urgent as it had been in 1948/1950, for experience and modification had materially increased reliability, eased servicing and lengthened periods between general overhauls, while the use of TIA had transformed boiler performance and maintenance. This improvement is illustrated by the tables that follow.

GENERAL REPAIRS AND MILEAGES 1944 to 1949

Locomotive	*Years and miles run since last General Repair*					
No.	*1944*	*1945*	*1946*	*1947*	*1948*	*1949*
35001	89,995	—	—	123,403	—	106,214
35002	97,212	42,463	—	98,287	—	
35003	—	162,307	—	—	109,660	
35004	—	124,306	—	—	106,115	
35005	—	—	158,606	—	80,953	
35006	100,140	—	96,408	—	108,274	
35007	100,647	—	—	106,304	—	
35008	113,569	—	—	107,364	—	93,085
35009	103,501	—	—	131,291	—	84,270
35010	—	120,033	—	—	105,051	92,988
35011	—	—	—	84,768	84,650	
35012	—	—	—	102,314	—	78,696
35013	—	—	85,747	—	—	80,133
35014	—	—	—	84,493	—	95,444
35015	—	—	—	94,620	—	91,899
35016	—	—	—	86,121	75,447	—
35017	—	—	—	100,809	—	81,327
35018	—	—	—	96,346	—	91,744
35019	—	—	—	106,463	—	—
35020	—	—	—	94,134	—	—

GENERAL REPAIRS AND MILEAGES 1950 to 1955

Locomotive No.	*Years and miles run since last General Repair* 1950	1951	1952	1953	1954	1955
35001	—	—	—	—	—	—
35002	102,322	—	—	—	—	274,531
35003	95,001	—	—	—	—	246,303
35004	115,464	—	—	—	—	248,081
35005	—	—	—	—	165,589	—
35006	—	—	—	256,429	—	—
35007	129,867	—	—	—	—	298,694
35008	—	—	—	251,429	—	—
35009	—	—	—	183,064	—	—
35010	—	74,816	—	—	—	—
35011	—	—	—	—	—	—
35012	—	—	144,506	—	—	—
35013	—	—	181,789	—	—	170,246
35014	—	107,409	—	116,005	—	—
35015	—	—	—	—	229,860	—
35016	—	—	—	—	274,356	—
35017	—	—	—	—	276,989	—
35018	—	90,937	—	—	—	225,873
35019	87,932	75,177	—	—	—	182,950
35020	104,800	—	—	155,573	—	—
35021	—	—	—	—	314,060	—
35022	—	—	—	—	—	—
35023	—	—	—	—	306,965	—
25024	—	—	—	—	289,428	—
35025	110,880	—	—	—	—	—
35026	—	—	—	—	—	245,662
35027	—	—	—	—	238,806	—
35028	—	—	—	—	222,813	—
35029	—	—	—	—	224,999	—
35030	—	—	—	—	207,887	—

If boiler lift mileages and the time between general repairs are added to a summary of the foregoing tables, we have:

Period	*Averages between General Repairs* *Mileages*	*Months*	*Average mileages between boiler liftings*
1944-9	99,036	27.2 months	83,926
1950-5	189,932	47.7 months	189,932

The introduction of TIA and the overcoming of many initial problems became apparent in the 1950-5 repair mileages which were vastly superior to those of the earlier period and compared favourably with other express classes, details of these being as follows:

Class	*To Intermediate Repair after General* *Miles*	*Months*	*Between General Repairs* *Miles*	*Months*	*Between boiler liftings* *Miles*	*Months*
MN	**103,484**	**19·8**	**189,932**	**47.7**	**189,932**	**47.7**
Duchess	96,650	17.2	209,620	34.5	209,620	34.5
Royal Scot	78,615	15.6	151,930	28.6	151,930	29.7
A1	73,489	13.2	115,259	19.0	115,259	19.0
King	88,353	19.9	160,717	36.2	110,751	24.1
Britannia	108,498	19.7	184,817	27.0	184,817	27.0

If general repair and boiler lift mileages alone were the criteria, then the Merchant Navies in 1955/6 could withstand comparison with the best express locomotives running on the other Regions, but unfortunately there were other equally important factors which weighed heavily against the class, in particular, repair costs and coal consumption. Details are as follows:

Repair costs per mile

Class	*Year*	*Locomotive*	*Boiler*	*Total locomotive and tender*
MN	**1955**	**5.06p**	**0.24p**	**5.98p**
Duchess	1955	3.85p	1.12p	5.29p
Royal Scot	1955	3.48p	0.54p	4.75p
A1	1954/5	2.87p	0.39p	3.55p
King	1953/4	3.43p	0.91p	4.94p
Britannia	1955	2.97p	0.39p	3.66p

Class	*Coal burnt per train mile*	*Class*	*Coal burnt per train mile*
MN	**50.6 lb.**	A1	44.2 lb.
Duchess	43.9 lb.	King	43.8 lb.
Royal Scot	42.8 lb.	Britannia	42.3 lb.

The introduction of TIA undoubtedly revolutionised Merchant Navy boiler maintenance, but since other repairs remained expensive and coal consumption high, the class cost £93,000 more per annum to operate than a similar number of Britannias. All agreed that action was necessary to remove this drain on Southern Region finances, though opinions differed as to the means, for two options were available—scrapping and replacement by Britannias or reconstruction to remove the extravagant Bulleid features, the respective costs being estimated as:

Thirty Crewe-built Britannias ..	£633,000
LESS scrap value of Merchant Navies	47,000
TOTAL	£586,000

Reconstructing thirty Merchant Navies	£225,000
LESS scrap value of discarded material	2,500
TOTAL	£222,500

At first sight, rebuilding appeared the answer, although much depended on boiler condition, for new fireboxes or other expensive repairs could radically inflate costs. The Eastleigh boilersmith was asked to report on the life expectancy of the fireboxes and tubeplates, and when this indicated renewal was not anticipated the decision not to scrap was taken. Initially, under order HO 7998, the reconstruction of fifteen locomotives was authorised with the necessary material being assembled at Eastleigh for work to commence in the autumn of 1955. Delays, however, occurred with the new inside cylinder castings and it was 16 November 1955 before No. 35018 *British India Line* (mileage 504,900) could be accepted for reconstruction and a start made on stripping it down to the frames. By the end of the year, only the cylinders were positioned, but thereafter better progress was made, and on 9 February 1956 No. 35019 left the Erecting Shop and positioned for the official photographer. The metamorphosis was absolute, the Bulleid extravaganza and air-smoothed casing being superseded by time-proven mechanics and a startlingly impressive profile.

To the rear of the smokebox the boiler was little changed, although to assist combustion on long journeys and to save time on shed, a rocking grate with moveable sections, six to each side of the centre line, was incorporated. Each section was operated manually, offering a small angular movement for grate clearance while on the road and a larger one when on shed.

The ashpan was entirely new, though like the Bulleid pattern it was divided into three sections, one between the frames and two outside, all being of the hopper type and provided with forward-facing damper doors. These were in line and connected to a transverse operating shaft which incorporated a universal joint to ensure that ashpan distortion did not adversely affect tightness or operation. A similar arrangement was applied to the hopper doors which were sited at the bottom and opened from track level by a short lever. The damper doors, a feature not considered necessary by Bulleid and, therefore, not present on the class as built, had single-screw control on the footplate. The working pressure remained at 250 lb./sq. in., and the three Ross pop safety-valves were mounted on the barrel top to the rear of the dome, where they had been sited to avoid water being drawn through them to the atmosphere when braking.

The lightly-fabricated and irregular-shaped smokebox, which had proved so difficult to maintain airtight, was completely discarded and replaced by a robust cylindrical pattern supported by a built-up saddle fashioned in part by the upper section of the new inside cylinder and a new fabricated saddle stretcher. By bolting the latter to the front of the cylinder casting as well as to the frames, greater rigidity was given to the front end. A new superheater header was provided, with new and direct steam passages to the cylinders, those coming from the outside cylinders passing through the smokebox sides. The superheating surface was reduced from 822 to 612 sq. ft. The interior of the smokebox was unusually free of obstructions and being 1ft. $7\frac{1}{2}$in. longer at 9ft. $8\frac{3}{4}$in. was more spacious for cleaning and maintenance. The Bulleid oval-shaped door was refitted to save expense.

The Lemaître multiple-jet blastpipe with its five circular converging $2\frac{5}{8}$in. diameter nozzles had given excellent service and was retained, though major changes were made to the draughting. The height of the chimney choke above the blastpipe orifices was reduced by 7in. to 2ft. $7\frac{5}{8}$in., and the diameter at the choke by $1\frac{1}{2}$in. to 1ft. $11\frac{1}{2}$in., with a corresponding increase of 7in. in the height from the choke to the chimney top, now 2ft. 2in. The chimney diameter remained 2ft. 5in., but the original stovepipe was replaced by a flared cast-iron pattern of similar style to that of the Lord Nelsons.

The much-disliked air-smoothed casing was discarded to gain readier access for servicing and was replaced by normal boiler clothing. Large smoke-deflector plates were fitted alongside the smokebox and secured to a running plate provided above the wheels and of generally similar pattern to that found on the BR Class 7 Britannia pacifics. The cab side panels followed those of Nos. 35021 to 35030 as built, but a foothole was cut to aid movement from the footplate to the running plate. The sliding roof ventilator was replaced by one supported on brackets which gave improved ventilation and was less difficult to manipulate from the footplate.

No change was made to the cylinder layout, the diameter and stroke remaining at 18in. and 24in. respectively, and the diameter of the piston valves at 11in. The two outside cylinders were re-used, but a new inside one was necessary and this, in common with current practice, had inside admission. The outside cylinders in the original design had valves driven indirectly by rocking shafts off the valve-gear and of necessity had outside admission, while the steam chests were placed in the same vertical centre line as the cylinders. To avoid the expense of replacing them, this feature and the outside admission was retained, which necessitated the provision of a high-pressure gland for the valve spindle and special measures to translate movement from the valve-gear plane to steam chest centre line.

The chain gear, oil-bath, etc., were discarded in favour of three independent sets of Walschaerts valve-gear requiring normal attention for lubrication, examination and maintenance. The outside valve-gear, because of the outside admission, transmitted the motion to the valve spindle from the top of the combination, but because of the offset between the centre line of the valve-gear and the steam chest axis, a suspension link was necessary. As this bore the weight of the valve-gear, the provision of normal valve spindle guides was avoided. A short link connected the suspension link to the valve spindle crosshead. The piston valves had a nominal maximum travel of $6\frac{3}{4}$in. and each head was fitted with four narrow rings, while the return crank rod was attached to the return crank by means of an SKF self-aligning roller bearing. The inside valve-gear, being of orthodox design with inside admission, was driven by an eccentric mounted on the right-hand crank web of the driving axle, the maximum travel being about $6\frac{5}{16}$in.

The much-disliked and troublesome steam reversing gear was replaced by a hand screw system on the left-hand side. It was of the revolving shaft variety with universal joints, which had been introduced in 1951 with the Class 7 Britannia pacifics and had given excellent service. The screw was positioned between the centre and rear coupled wheels, while the reversing handle in the cab was face on to the driver with a clearly marked drum-type cut-off indicator. With multi-cylinder engines having independent sets of valve-gear it is usually necessary to provide an auxiliary reversing shaft for the inside motion; Brighton, however, found it possible to employ a single shaft for all three gears. The lifting of the radius rods was achieved by an ingenious arrangement in which a slide block worked in a slot in the radius rod, the former being attached directly to the reversing shaft arm.

Manganese steel liners were introduced between the guides and the coupled axle-boxes, these being of steel instead of solid gunmetal. Plain rectangular-section coupling-rods took the place of the original I-section in an attempt to avoid buckling should severe slipping occur. Although the BFB coupled wheels remained, outside rim balance weights were introduced.

The mechanical lubricators for the cylinders and valve chests were removed from their awkward and ash-collecting location below the smokebox frontplate, and remounted on the running plate above the leading coupled wheels, two on the left side and one on the right. A fourth lubricator was added on the right side to supply oil to the slide bars and coupled axle-boxes; this replaced the multi-feed cab oil boxes. All four were driven off the expansion links of the outside valve motion. Grease lubrication was provided for the rubbing blocks, the pony truck, the bogie and pony truck springing, the spring links and hanger pins.

The steam sanding was modified to return forward application to the leading coupled wheels, the boxes being sited above the running plate to the rear of the smokebox. The forward sanding to the centre coupled wheels was unaltered, but the pipes previously giving delivery in front of the rear coupled wheels had their ends adjusted to provide rearward application for the centre coupled wheels and made the retention of the gravity feed tender sand containers unnecessary. The boxes supplying the centre coupled wheels were sited between the frames on either side of the locomotive, one being ahead of the crank axle and the other to the rear. The filler pipes were extended upwards and stood well clear of the running plate, making replenishing reasonably easy.

Modifications were also made to the intermediate drawgear between the locomotive and tender so that the drawbar was pin-jointed to the tender by means of a plunger sliding freely in guides and controlled by the intermediate drawbar rubber spring which cushioned the pull.

The high side-plating of the tender was cut away to make coaling and replenishing the water supply simpler and less tedious. It also removed a large expanse of thin steel plating which suffered readily from corrosion and damage in service. Nos. 35001/7/11/2/3/20/1 ran at various periods before rebuilding with similarly cut-down or modified tenders, but the remaining twenty members of the class had to await this event.

Another feature not retained was the controversial steam-powered firedoor which, in theory, was operated by means of a pedal on the footplate as the fireman swung his shovel. Bulleid intended that this feature should lessen the physical effort of continuous firing, but only a handful of interested men made efficient use of it, mainly because operation was restricted to the fully open or closed positions. If, for example, the firedoor was partly open, the pedal was incapable of enlarging the aperture, and men accustomed to working with the door always partly open found it difficult to depend on the door air holes for combustion and to leave the door firmly closed when not actually firing. Many crews insisted that the class steamed poorly if the firedoor was left closed for lengthy periods, but on test at Rugby the steaming proved better with the door opened only when coal was actually being fed into the firebox. Another disadvantage was the overheating of the mechanism's lubricating system which filled the cabs with pungent fumes. These mingled with coal dust swirling off the tender, and on a hot day made the footplate on occasions almost uninhabitable.

On 9 February 1956, No. 35018 *British India Line* was hauled out of the Erecting Shop by Adams 0-6-0 No. 30566 and positioned in the works yard for the official photographer before being steamed in preparation for a trial run to Botley and back the following morning. Some minor overheating occurred and, after this had been remedied, further runs were made to Brockenhurst and Basingstoke before departing light engine for Nine Elms on 12 February in readiness for inspection the next day by Sir Brian Robertson at Waterloo. It returned to Eastleigh on the 14th, and on the 17th was rostered for its first passenger duties, taking over a slow to Southampton Central and there relieving the locomotive of the 1.29 p.m. Fareham-Bournemouth West. All went well until approaching Christchurch, when the coupled box lubrication failed and, after attention on Bournemouth shed, it had to return to Eastleigh towed by M7 0-4-4 tank No. 30376. Back in traffic on 20 February, a further trial run was made to Botley, followed by vans to Basingstoke, and then it was set to work on Eastleigh's Waterloo-Bournemouth expresses. However, on 27 February, near Farnborough when heading the 7.20 a.m. Eastleigh-Waterloo, the radius rod fractured causing complete failure and the hurried commandeering of H15 4-6-0 No. 30491 from a stock train to take over for the remainder of the journey. Waterloo was eventually reached seventy minutes late.

After attention in Eastleigh Works, service was again resumed on 28 February with a nine-coach train to Weymouth and back, while on 2 March fifteen coaches were worked to Waterloo and back to Southampton Central. Then followed three weeks on Eastleigh's Waterloo duties before No. 35018 *British India Line* was despatched to Nine Elms and regular service on the "Bournemouth Belle", until stopped for minor attention at Eastleigh Works on 16 April 1956. A return was made to this express on 19 April, while in the following week it had charge of the 9.00 a.m. Waterloo-Exeter and the 4.30 p.m. return to London, the loading being augmented to fifteen coaches.

Some concern was expressed at the high cost of the first rebuild, but the transformation was so obvious and, with the promise that all expense would be recovered within three years, authorisation was granted for the entire class to be similarly modified, details being as follows:

Order 7998

35008	5/1957
35009	3/1957
35010	1/1957
35912	2/1957
35013	5/1956
35014	7/1956
35016	4/1957
35017	3/1957
35018	2/1956
35020	4/1956
35022	6/1956
35023	2/1957
35025	12/1956
35026	1/1957
35027	5/1957

Order 9199

35001	8/1959
35002	5/1958
35003	8/1959
35004	7/1958
35005	5/1959
35006	10/1959
35007	5/1958
35011	7/1959
35015	6/1958
35019	5/1959
35021	6/1959
35024	4/1959
35028	10/1959
35029	9/1959
35030	4/1958

As rebuilding progressed, so minor differences developed, with probably the most interesting concerning the outside valve spindles which, on Nos. 35002/4/7/8/9/10/2/3/4/5/6/7/8/20/2/3/5/6/7/30 had normal blind guides. In service they proved troublesome and in Nos. 35019/24 in April and May 1959 the valve spindles were extended and given open-ended guides which necessitated piercing the sloping sections of the running plate to provide clearance for the leading ends of the spindles. This satisfactorily solved the problem, although at the same time created another by leaving the spindles vulnerable to the introduction of ash and other foreign bodies when engines were being serviced on shed, or at work on the road. Therefore, with Nos. 35001/3/5/6/11/21/8/9, small pockets were inserted in the smoke-deflector plates to enclose the spindles. In course of time the others were similarly modified.

No. 35018 *British India Line* differed from the other rebuilds by having the front sand boxes fitted higher and equipped with tall filler-pipes. In regular service these boxes proved inconvenient to replenish as well as giving rise to considerable spillage over the motion, and in later rebuilds they were lowered and provided with shorter and more efficient necks. No. 35018 was not modified to conform, despite a statement to this effect in its record folder for March 1957.

The weight in working order was around 97 tons, but the three series still showed surprising divergency, details being as follows:

	Nos. 35001 to 35010	*Nos. 35011 to 35020*	*Nos. 35021 to 35030*
Bogie	18 tons 0 cwt.	17 tons 10 cwt.	16 tons 16 cwt.
Leading coupled wheels ..	21 tons 8 cwt.	21 tons 2 cwt.	21 tons 0 cwt.
Centre coupled wheels ..	21 tons 12 cwt.	21 tons 12 cwt.	21 tons 11 cwt.
Trailing coupled wheels ..	21 tons 4 cwt.	21 tons 5 cwt.	20 tons 18 cwt.
Pony truck	15 tons 12 cwt.	15 tons 16 cwt.	15 tons 16 cwt.
Total	97 tons 16 cwt.	97 tons 5 cwt.	96 tons 1 cwt.

Mileages to rebuilding were:

Locomotive No.	*Miles run*
35001	807,318
35002	776,797
35003	859,784
35004	750,880
35005	632,322
35006	862,757
35007	799,299
35008	730,712
35009	684,482
35010	663,174
35011	670,782
35012	564,821
35013	517,915
35014	516,811
35015	549,700
35016	467,091
35017	594,522
35018	504,900
35019	617,368
35020	507,958
35021	575,993
35022	329,083
35023	433,833
35024	552,053
35025	419,374
35026	311,063
35027	363,351
35028	401,005
35029	428,621
35030	351,234

It seldom causes harm, and invariably clears the air, if an author makes a declaration of interest at the outset. Therefore, let me begin by stating, before further discussion of the Merchant Navy rebuilds, that they were the finest express locomotives to work in the country. Just as the BR Class 9 2-10-0's stood head and shoulders above all other freight classes, so did the rebuilds in the ranks of pacifics. This had been my considered and often-stated opinion since No. 35018 *British India Line* returned to traffic rejuvenated in early 1956.

Such forthrightness not only calls for amplification, but positively demands it. There was one other class which ran a very close second—I am referring, of course, to the Gresley A4's, which daily performed work of equivalent calibre. However, much was the result of the magnificent *esprit de corps* developed by top-link Eastern Region men over a line renowned for fast running since the days of Patrick Stirling. On the Southern Region there existed no such deep feelings or veneration for any particular express class or locomotive engineer, while many crews thought themselves badly let down by Bulleid. Because of this the first rebuilds were accepted with some misgivings, but once finding that they were the tools for the job the crews set to work, proving that fine fast-running pacifics were not the prerogative of Doncaster. Therefore, in evaluating the daily work of the two classes, pride of place must go to the Merchant Navy rebuilds, for their excellence was all of their own making.

As built by Bulleid, No. 35018 *British India Line* was not considered a good member of the class, and when the time came to prepare a rebuild for comparative trials in May 1956, Eastleigh passed it over in favour of No. 35020 *Bibby Line*. On 25 May this locomotive, the second rebuild, was taken into the Erecting Shop to have its modified tender exchanged for one retaining the high side-sheeting, for it had been found that this pattern simplified the attachment of the dynamometer car cables and gave better protection to the coal space where, on occasions, a member of the test staff travelled. To match the lining of the locomotive cab, the borrowed tender (T3345, 6,000 gallons) was repainted with the panelling and emblem lowered, while a broad band of black was added along the top of the side sheeting. Incidentally, when discarded at the termination of the trials, this tender was not repainted before being transferred to non-rebuild No. 35028 *Clan Line*, the result being macabre, for the locomotive retained its lining bands, while the tender was panelled and had its emblem out of line with the cab numerals.

No. 35020 *Bibby Line* commenced the trials with a series of controlled road tests run over the West of England main line between Salisbury and Exeter, where delays or interference by other traffic were minimal. The highest rate of working recorded was over 32,000 lb. of steam per hour with a coal rate of 4,780 lb./hr., the only apparent limiting factor being that imposed by the capacity of the tender to provide for minimum test and warming-up periods. The tests were planned in great detail and consisted of special trains booked reasonably fast and integrated with the normal services. The programme was completed without incident or time debited against the locomotive.

To follow these controlled road tests, it was arranged for certain representative service trains to be worked, including the "Atlantic Coast Express", "Royal Wessex" and "Bournemouth Belle". Once again, the programme was successfully fulfilled with no time booked against No. 35020, although on one occasion after arrival at Exeter a tender axlebox was found hot, and this had to be hurriedly attended to before the return journey. On starting, slipping was noticeably less, while at speed little could be detected from the footplate. The valve-gear proved flexible and trouble-free, the boiler steamed freely and the combustion was excellent, with no smokebox carbon monoxide except when the fire was being built up in anticipation of high power output. Ash deposited in the smokebox was moderate and necessitated no action during the working day, while no complaints were received or evidence observed of lineside fires. Details of the coal consumption were as follows:

		Coal burnt			
Date	*Journey*	*lb. per mile*		*THP–HR*	
25/6/1956	12.30 p.m. Exeter-Salisbury	45.52	41.33	3.80	3.51
25/6/1956	2.15 p.m. Salisbury-Waterloo	37.14		3.21	
26/6/1956	3.00 p.m. Waterloo-Salisbury	48.49	49.37	3.29	3.44
26/6/1956	4.47 p.m. Salisbury-Exeter	50.26		3.60	

Coal: Bedwas grade 2A

Train loadings were as follows:

Exeter-Salisbury	400 tons
Salisbury-Waterloo	471 tons
Waterloo-Salisbury	500 tons
Salisbury-Exeter	395 tons

At this period, loads and schedules on the West of England and Bournemouth lines had outstripped those of the Eastern Section Continentals, and because of this it became policy to retain the rebuilds at Western Section sheds. As a result, for the summer services of 1957 Battersea had the use of original Bulleids Nos. 35001/15/28, whereas Bournemouth had rebuilds Nos. 35010/22/5/6/7. The latter were required for the two-hour schedules, inclusive of a Southampton stop, introduced on 17 June, which gave a welcome and long-overdue acceleration of services over the Bournemouth line. On Mondays to Fridays seven such expresses were run, at 8.20 a.m., 10.30 a.m. and 6.30 p.m. ex-Waterloo, and at 12.40, 2.40, 6.40 and 7.40 p.m. ex-Bournemouth Central. Similar but less startling improvements were made to the West of England services, especially the 4.30 p.m. Exeter-Waterloo, which had nineteen minutes cut from the running time, which gave a start-to-stop booking of fifty-four minutes between Exeter and Yeovil Junction (49 miles).

The full allocation was as follows:

Nine Elms	Nos. 35005/12/4/6/7/8/9/20/9/30
Bournemouth	Nos. 35010/21/2/5/6/7
Exmouth Jct.	Nos. 35002/3/8/9/11/3/23/4
Salisbury	Nos. 35004/6/7
Battersea	Nos. 35001/15/28

On 16 June 1957, No. 35017 *Belgian Marine* broke new ground by working the 6.40 p.m. Newhaven Harbour-Victoria Continental, following a failure of an electric locomotive. For several weeks it had been engaged with Nos. 10203 and 20003 on a comprehensive series of track and vehicle tests on the main line between Redhill and Three Bridges, the object being to compare the effect on the track of varying types of vehicle at different speeds. In the course of the proceedings No. 35017 *Belgian Marine* was recorded at 98 m.p.h. by the Horley measuring point. When the Newhaven emergency arose it was at Redhill shed in preparation for returning to Nine Elms and, fortunately, was in steam. This, however, was not the first appearance of a rebuild on the Central Section, for No. 35018 *British India Line* ran light from Nine Elms to Brighton Works on 21 September 1956, supposedly for valve and piston examination, but it also offered staff concerned in planning the reconstruction the opportunity to view the result of their labours. A return was made to London on 10 October 1956 with empty coaching stock from Hassocks to Selhurst. Incidentally, apart from Redhill, the only Central Section turntable capable of accepting the class was at Norwood.

Failures in traffic with the rebuilds were few and far between, although when they did occur it was usually total and necessitated a replacement. Non-rebuilds, however, often managed to keep going at reduced power until assistance was to hand. One persistent source of trouble with the rebuilds concerned the eccentric straps, which at Nine Elms caused 65 per cent of failures in 1957/58. Bournemouth suffered similarly and the author vividly recalls the night of 12 December 1957, when No. 35025 *Brocklebank Line* came to grief at Waltham box with the 9.30 p.m. Waterloo-Bournemouth Central. Before the train could be moved, fitters had to attend the locomotive which then, complete with train, was propelled to Micheldever by No. 30790 *Sir Villiars*. There the King Arthur ran round the train and hauled it to Eastleigh where the failed pacific was removed to the shed, and thereafter took the train on to Bournemouth Central, some 205 minutes late. Commencing with No. 35030 *Elder-Dempster Lines* in April 1958, the eccentric straps were strengthened and modified, and failures from this cause showed a significant reduction. Throughout the summer of 1958, the Western Section on Saturdays suffered an acute shortage of powerful express locomotives, but by the autumn the growing number of West Country rebuilds and slackening in demand had materially eased the position. Rebuild No. 34045 *Ottery St. Mary* was regularly being rostered by Bournemouth for the "Royal Wessex" and No. 34047 *Callington* by Nine Elms for the 9.30 a.m. Waterloo-Bournemouth, both difficult trains to work. Nevertheless, the twenty-seven Merchant Navies at Nine Elms, Bournemouth, Salisbury and Exmouth Junction remained the Western Section's major source of express power, and most ably did they perform. On the Eastern Section Nos. 35001/15/28, not yet rebuilt, lived a generally much quieter existence and, except at holiday periods, seldom earned their keep. No. 35015 *Rotterdam Lloyd* in June 1958 was the first to be rebuilt, but the other two soldiered on until Stage 1 of the Kent Coast electrification in the following summer. Both then succumbed to modernisation and joined No. 35015 *Rotterdam Lloyd* at Nine Elms, the Eastern Section no longer demanding their presence. No. 35028 *Clan Line* was the last of the thirty Merchant Navy reconstructions.

No. 35004 *Cunard White Star* on the evening of 6 January 1959 was particularly fortuitous, for as it approached Porton Station with the 5.15 p.m. Salisbury-Waterloo, several hundred tons of waterlogged earth suddenly crashed down across the track, and a serious accident was only avoided by the chance presence of a ganger who, knowing the train was due, managed to warn the signalman. One track was cleared reasonably quickly, but despite the use of earth-moving equipment, it was 6.45 a.m. on 8 January before the obstruction was finally cleared and the second track repaired.

Equally fortunate were the crew of No. 35024 *East Asiatic Company* on 28 January 1959 when heading the 10.30 p.m. Waterloo-Weymouth in dense, freezing fog. Near Esher the driver misread the signals and overtook on the same line the slowly-moving 10.15 p.m. Nine Elms-West of England fitted goods hauled by No. 35008 *Orient Line*. The impact was reasonably light and after inspection and improved visibility both locomotives and trains were able to proceed.

Automatic train control, intended to avoid such episodes, commenced being fitted at Eastleigh in April 1959, although it was the following August before the first Merchant Navy, No. 35001 *Channel Packet*, was equipped. Other modification around this period included the addition of garlic or aniseed-scented detectors to the big-ends, Britannia-type coupled wheel springs to No. 35016 *Elders Fyffes* in November 1959, and nylon tubing sections in the coupled axlebox guide face oilpipes of No. 35023 *Holland Afrika Line* in February 1959. The last-mentioned feature was intended to eliminate fractures caused by excessive vibration, but at first the inserts proved too weak, and it was not until ICI produced special piping that the modification became general. The Britannia springing also appeared on Nos. 35002/7/10/6/20/7/30 in 1960/61, and was much disliked by the men, who considered the riding much harsher.

Mention has often been made of the fine performance given by the Eastern Region's Norwich-based Britannias, Nos. 70006 to 70013 between 1951 and 1961, in particular the high mileages run. Details are as follows:

Locomotive No.	*Mileage*
70006	737,716
70007	690,932
70008	706,852
70009	661,181
70010	718,686
70011	675,303
70012	717,621
70013	698,458

Similar mention has not been accorded to the Merchant Navies, although in reality their mileages compared most favourably, and for much of the period they were running in Bulleid condition, since rebuilding did not commence until 1956. Their details are:

Locomotive No.	Mileage
35001	671,375
35002	644,350
35003	632,588
35007	647,863
35010	638,098
35012	631,716
35021	674,093
35024	665,917

If the different traffic pattern of the Southern Region is taken into account, then these, too, are excellent figures and equally worthy of note. Also noteworthy are the mileages recorded between rebuilding and general repairs, these being the equal of any express class in the country, details being as follows:

Locomotive No.	*Rebuilding to 1st Intermediate Repair*		*1st to 2nd Intermediate Repair*		*Rebuilding to General Repair*	
	Miles	*Months*	*Miles*	*Months*	*Miles*	*Months*
35003	139,772	24	—	—	228,110	44
35004	104,647	17	81,296	15	272,537	56
35008	119,725	18	89,491	15	314,700	54
35009	110,012	17	91,466	17	296,641	52
35010	95,363	16	85,290	14	337,822	57
35012	115,336	22	113,048	20	315,907	61
35013	116,228	22	121,653	19	325,057	58
35014	131,041	23	105,039	15	375,945	66
35017	163,007	30	80,716	16	333,177	78
35018	139,582	27	90,713	20	329,263	69
35020	109,801	23	82,138	15	289,003	59
35022	118,896	18	91,337	14	397,016	71
35023	149,929	24	91,501	19	339,225	67
35025	125,944	24	84,110	16	310,948	60
35026	126,624	19	173,229	28	387,171	67
35027	119,059	20	172,393	33	375,836	75
35028	94,908	20	95,093	20	210,376	49
35029	96,837	20	—	—	208,458	48
35030	133,410	25		—	230,583	46

Average general repair mileage: 309,409
Average time to general repair: $59\frac{3}{4}$ months

A change of boundaries on 30 December 1963 saw responsibility for the Southern Region lines and services in the West Country passing to the Western Region. This included the transfer of some 150 locomotives, including Merchant Navies Nos. 35003/9/10/3/22/5/6, and the motive power depots of Exmouth Junction, Yeovil Town, Barnstaple and Wadebridge. Locomotive repairs, however, remained the responsibility of Eastleigh Works.

Severe blizzards swept Southern England in the New Year and on 2 January 1963 many services out of Waterloo had to be cancelled. On the Bournemouth line the 8.30 a.m., 10.30 a.m., "Bournemouth Belle", and 3.20 p.m. departures, together with the 9.33 a.m., 11.49 a.m., 2.40 p.m. and 6.46 p.m. arrivals, all failed to run, while those that did were restricted to eight coaches and in some instances double-headed. The West of England services were not so badly affected, although on 3 January No. 35025 *Brocklebank Line*, after battling against a storm-force wind and heavy snow reached Waterloo $3\frac{1}{2}$ hours late with the "Atlantic Coast Express"; no carriage heating had been available since Sidmouth Junction. However, this was by no means the worst delay of the winter, for the Channel Islands service of 18 January did not reach Waterloo behind No. 35012 *United States Lines* until 11.20 p.m. on Sunday the 20th. As the elements relented a full main-line service was attempted, but almost every day this was thwarted by power cuts, track faults, depots running out of coal and failures of both electric and steam trains. A resemblance of normality only returned to the Region in late February 1963, although even then there was a shortage of main-line passenger locomotives, for the wholesale withdrawals of December 1962 had left the Bulleid pacifics and Class 5 4-6-0's virtually the only steam locomotives working passenger services into Waterloo. Class 4 4-6-0's were rarely seen, while appearances of the S15's and Maunsell 2-6-0's were spasmodic.

At this period the "Atlantic Coast Express" with its mile-a-minute bookings each way between Salisbury and Sidmouth Junction probably ranked as the hardest steam passenger duty in the country. Much hard and fast running was necessary if time was to be kept, especially with the up trains, for Exeter appeared unable to complete the necessary marshalling and other activities without the loss of at least two minutes. An instance on 30 March 1963 saw No. 35013 *Blue Funnel* departing 2¾ minutes late, yet making a correct-time arrival at Salisbury despite a severe permanent way slack near Axminster and signals at Wilton. Speed exceeded 84 m.p.h. on three occasions and Honiton Bank was climbed in great style. Unlike Exeter, Salisbury always had a good reputation for getting trains away smartly, and even on summer Saturdays seldom lost more than the odd minute or two.

With the commencement of the summer timetable, the "Bournemouth Belle", except on Saturdays, was accelerated to offer a two-hour service, and this, too, became a difficult assignment and one calling for much hard collar work.

In anticipation of electrification and the provision of main-line diesel locomotives, no general repairs were permitted after August 1964, the last being No. 35007 *Aberdeen Commonwealth*. As a result of this decision, Nos. 35001/2/5/6/11/5/9/21/4 were not given general repairs after rebuilding; when this became necessary they were taken out of traffic. The others received their final general repair in 1961 Nos. 35009/10/3/20, in 1962 Nos. 35008/12/4/6/8/22/3/5/6/30, in 1963 Nos. 35003/4/17/27/9 and in 1964 Nos. 35007/28. Mileages run at this period were very high, as will be noted from the table which follows:

Locomotive No.	*Intermediate Repair*		*General Repair*	
	Date	*Mileage*	*Date*	*Mileage*
35004	1/1960	104,647	4/1963	272,537
35007	4/1961	182,382	8/1964	383,358
35008	4/1960	209,216	2/1962	314,700
35009	9/1958	110,012	9/1961	296,641
35010	8/1959	180,653	11/1961	337,822
35012	9/1960	228,384	4/1962	315,907
35017	10/1959	163,007	9/1963	333,177
35022	4/1959	210,233	7/1962	397,016
35026	4/1961	205,051	10/1962	387,171
35028	9/1962	152,100	2/1964	210,376

Because of this policy, withdrawal commenced in February 1964 with Nos. 35002/15, while before the end of the year the same fate had befallen Nos. 35001/6/9/18/25.

On 24 April 1964, Gresley A4 No. 60008 *Dwight D. Eisenhower* arrived under tow at Eastleigh, and after being photographed was despatched to Southampton Docks behind No. 35012 *United States Lines* for shipment to the American Railroad Museum at Green Bay, Wisconsin, by USS *American Planter*. Before departure on 27 April, Dr. Beeching, representatives of the Museum, invited guests and the press travelled down from Waterloo in a special train headed most appropriately by the gleaming No. 35012. In his speech of thanks, the Museum's President made it known that on withdrawal this locomotive, too, would be a very welcome addition to their locomotive display. Unfortunately, this request fell on deaf ears and *United States Lines* was scrapped by J. Cashmore at Newport in 1967.

The 13 June 1964 once again found a Merchant Navy at work on the London Midland Region, when No. 35012 *United States Lines*, freshly out of Eastleigh Works, headed the "Solway Ranger" rail tour out of Leeds punctually at 8.43 a.m., bound for Penrith via Keighley, Skipton, Hellifield, Wennington, Carnforth and Shap. At Penrith it was the turn of Ivatt 2-6-0's Nos. 46426 and 46458 to haul the special over the heavily-graded CKPR line to Workington and thence via Keswick and Penrith to Carlisle. There, a return journey was made to Silloth behind GNSR 4-4-0 No. 49 *Gordon Highlander* and Caledonian single No. 123 before setting off for Leeds City, some twenty minutes late, in charge of No. 35012 *United States Lines*. Driver Hooker of Nine Elms, aided and abetted by the LMR pilotman, at once set to work removing this stigma and passed Armathwaite in 15.17 minutes at 70 m.p.h. A "yellow" was sighted at Culgaith and speed fell to 23 m.p.h., while a permanent way slack at Long Martin again saw speed reduced, but by Appleby, passed in 42.02 minutes, it had risen to 54 m.p.h. Then followed one of the most dramatic events ever experienced on the line, with the 17.45 miles to Ais Gill, mostly at 1 in 100, being reeled off in 17.41 minutes at an average speed of 59½ m.p.h. and Settle Junction reached in 83.04 minutes from Carlisle. The concluding run through Hellifield and along the Aire Valley was more sedate, but No. 35012 had proved yet again what magnificent express locomotives the Southern Region possessed in the rebuilt Merchant Navies.

For some months threats had emanated from Swindon that dieselisation of the Exeter-Waterloo line was imminent, and on 17 August 1964 the axe finally fell with Western Region Warships taking over the 7.30 a.m., 12.30 p.m. and 5.54 p.m. up services and the 1.15 a.m., 1.30 p.m. and 7.00 p.m. departures from Waterloo. At first, failures were frequent and the standby steam locomotives called upon to deputise, on one memorable day for all six trains, but in course of time when crews became more accustomed to the new motive power there was a marked improvement and the diesels could be relied upon to complete a roster efficiently, if with little enterprise.

These changes and the withdrawal of Nos. 35001/2/6/9/15/8/25 led to a major rearrangement of express steam power in the autumn of 1964, when the Merchant Navies were shared between Bournemouth (Nos. 35003/4/8/10/1/3/21/3/7), Salisbury (No. 35007) and Weymouth (Nos. 35005/12/4/6/7/9/20/4/6/8/9/30). These transfers left Nine Elms with only nine Class 5's available for express duties, although two Merchant Navies and a West Country were stabled there at night. At Weymouth, use was made of the facilities and staff of the erstwhile Great Western running shed. Towards the end of the year, with the Warships performing reasonably well, Salisbury had no need of No. 35007 *Aberdeen Commonwealth* and it, too, was transferred to Weymouth. The last down "Atlantic Coast Express" with its tight 83-minutes Waterloo-Salisbury timing ran on 4 September 1964, and for this nostalgic occasion Nine Elms provided No. 35022 *Holland America Line* immaculately cleaned and complete with train headboard, an item which had been sadly missed during the last year or so. Several minutes were lost to signals in the London area, but thereafter the running was excellent with the loss regained before Salisbury where a right-time arrival and departure was booked. The remainder of the journey was similarly exhilarating and a fitting end to West of England steam.

The new diesel-operated service replacing the ACE commenced on 7 September 1964, but despite the employment of more modern motive power the Western Region saw fit to provide recovery time between Exeter and Salisbury, a feature never tolerated by the Southern Railway or Region. In addition, diesel failures caused much late running and restrictions on loading to overcrowding of trains. Once again, some improvement followed the initial teething problems, but it is doubtful whether regular patrons of the Waterloo-Salisbury-Exeter route to the West Country ever again enjoyed the standard of service and comfort once offered by steam.

A series of mishaps on 1 January 1965 led to the 10.08 a.m. York-Bournemouth West through train reaching Bournemouth Central 82 minutes late behind no less than three locomotives, a Merchant Navy, Hall and Class 4 2-6-0. The train locomotive, No. 6996 *Blackwell Hall*, ran short of steam at Sway and requested assistance from New Milton. No. 76012 was despatched from Bournemouth shed to assist and duly did so until Christchurch, where the Hall became a total failure, and when the 2-6-0 was unable to restart both it and the train, the arrival of No. 35029 *Ellerman Lines* from Bournemouth had to be awaited. The cavalcade eventually ran into the Central station with the pacific apparently providing most of the motive power, knowledgeable travellers having wisely removed themselves at Christchurch and made their way home by other means. After removal to the shed, the smokebox door of No. 6996 *Blackwell Hall* was opened to show ash up to the blastpipe; it had done well to get so far.

During the early months of 1965, following the introduction of diesel services between Reading and Tonbridge, Redhill shed had a full complement of fitters and few steam locomotives to maintain. To provide employment until redeployment could be made, various Western Section locomotives were sent there for casual repairs, tender exchanges and the fitting of AWS, water treatment or exhaust injectors. Two Merchant Navies were involved, No. 35014 *Nederland Line* in April and No. 35030 *Elder-Dempster Lines* in March 1965. The latter worked a heavy permanent-way train from Redhill to Tonbridge on the night of 27 March and then returned light engine early the following morning. Further withdrawals in 1965 saw Nos. 35004/5/16/9/20/1/4 taken out of stock, usually when stopped for heavy repairs, although No. 35004 *Cunard White Star* was far from run-down when condemned on 31 October 1965. It had been repaired and weighed at Eastleigh Works between 26 August and 14 October, and had its mileage extended for a further 10,000 miles, but then had the mischance to slip severely near Hook whilst in charge of the 7.24 a.m. Bournemouth Central-Waterloo on 28 October and subsequently to fail with broken and buckled coupling-rods. Otherwise, damage was minor, but such was official policy regarding steam stock that repairs were not authorised. Final mileages of the 1964/65 withdrawals varied, as might be expected, with the time spent in service, all the first series except No. 35005 *Canadian Pacific* covering more than a million miles. Details are as follows:

35001	*Channel Packet*	1,095,884
35002	*Union Castle*	1,101,914
35004	*Cunard White Star*	1,131,793
35005	*Canadian Pacific*	976,806
35006	*Peninsular & Oriental SN Co.*	1,134,319
35009	*Shaw Savill*	1,127,452
35015	*Rotterdam Lloyd*	813,950
35016	*Elders Fyffes*	900,637
35018	*British India Line*	956,544
35020	*Bibby Line*	981,479
35021	*New Zealand Line*	859,661
35024	*East Asiatic Company*	839,415
35025	*Brocklebank Line*	884,081

Throughout 1965/66 the Bournemouth line services were bedevilled by engineering works of varying magnitude as preparations for electrification gathered momentum. Lengthy slacks, single-line working and diversions were commonplace and the daily duties of train crews became more and more frustrating and tedious. Very seldom was it possible for time lost early in a journey to be regained by fast running during the later stages, while adding to the difficulties were the poor maintenance and low-quality coal. Nevertheless, many crews gave of their best and obtained surprisingly high speeds and performance from their frequently dirty and apparently decrepit locomotives. To their credit, Salisbury men to the end found time to clean their locomotives, and these were a pleasure to behold. Some easement of restrictions came in time for the summer services, while the arrival of Type 3 (Class 33) diesel locomotives at Eastleigh made it possible on Sundays to operate most main-line trains without having to resort to steam. Later in the year, however, when cold weather returned and carriage heating was necessary, steam once more came into demand.

West Countries, both as built and as modified, regularly worked over the Somerset & Dorset lines, but because of their weight the Merchant Navies were prohibited. But by 1966 with closure imminent, nothing so mundane mattered and no objections were raised when Nos. 35011/23/8 were proposed for rail tours. The intention was to effect closure on 2 January 1966, and farewell journeys were organised on both the 1st and the 2nd using No. 35011 *General Steam Navigation*, leaving Waterloo at the head of ten coaches in fine style for Broadstone, which was reached only five minutes late despite an unscheduled water stop at Southampton Central and single-line working from New Milton to Hinton Admiral. At Broadstone, No. 34015 *Exmouth* and 2-6-0 No. 31639 came on for the onward journey to Bath, where they handed over to Class 8F 2-8-0 No. 48309 for passage to Highbridge via Mangotsfield, Bristol (Temple Meads) and Weston-super-Mare. There, a further change of motive power saw 2-6-2 tanks Nos. 41283 and 41307 working the special to Templecombe, where No. 35011 *General Steam Navigation* was waiting for the run in darkness over the West of England main line to Waterloo. Advantage was taken of the postponed closure date by the RCTS to promote a further rail tour on Sunday 6 March 1966, which was headed by No. 35028 *Clan Line* via Twickenham, Staines Central, Virginia Water, Woking and the heavily-graded Aldershot and Alton Line to Winchester City and thence through to Southampton Central and Bournemouth Central to Templecombe Junction. There, *Clan Line* came off and was replaced by 2-6-2 tanks Nos. 41249 and 41283 for the run to Highbridge, where at the GW station they gave way to No. 34013 *Okehampton* for the short journey through Weston-super-Mare and Bristol to Mangotsfield North Junction. Diesel D7014 then came on to the rear of the train to haul it over the ten miles to Bath Green Park. For the run over the Somerset & Dorset main line No. 34057 *Biggin Hill* came on as pilot for No. 34013 *Okehampton*, and together they tackled Masbury summit and the other gradients in fine style with an unforgettable firework display before stopping at Templecombe for No. 35028 *Clan Line* to take over for the journey back to Waterloo, on which 5½ minutes were gained.

Inevitably, more withdrawals occurred in 1966 with Nos. 35010/1/7/22/7/9 being laid aside and sold for scrap during the year. This left ten, Nos. 35003/7/8/12/3/4/23/6/8/30 in service, and of these, Nos. 35012/4/26 were badly run down and only gave assistance until the spring; the others worked until the end of steam, except for No. 35013 which was retired a week early.

Extraordinary measures were necessary to keep them serviceable, measures, which a few years earlier, would not have been tolerated. No. 35007 *Aberdeen Commonwealth* had its tyres condemned on 8 August 1966, and a hunt commenced among condemned stock for replacements. Those carried by No. 35022

Holland America Line were found equally worn and were rejected in favour of the set belonging to No. 35017 *Belgian Marine*. These measured $2\frac{3}{16}$in. and proved acceptable, although the examiners' remarks of "right driving tyre has moved $\frac{9}{16}$in. and left leading tyre $\frac{11}{16}$in., but believed sound" could hardly have created confidence. However, by good fortune or judgment, these tyres safely carried *Belgian Marine* until electrification. Tenders, cylinders, motion and other parts were similarly exchanged, frequently without records being kept.

On 2 January 1967, electric services commenced between Waterloo and Basingstoke, and Woking and Basingstoke, the last-mentioned trains replacing the unpopular Western Region d.m.u.'s. Three months later, on 3 April, some of the Bournemouth services were also electrified which, together with Type 3 (Class 33) and Type 4 diesels (Class 47), left only a handful of trains rostered for steam haulage. Of these, only three of the Basingstoke commuter services and the 11.18 a.m. Weymouth-Waterloo fell to the Merchant Navies, although trouble with the new electric stock and diesel failures frequently made it necessary to summon assistance from the standby steam locomotives.

By this date, with most of the engineering works completed and speed restrictions removed, many crews accepted the opportunity of proving that steam might be superannuated, but far from moribund. Much of the running was good, some excellent, and of an order not surpassed in the palmy days of steam locomotion. Instances were as follows: No. 35013 *Blue Funnel* with 380 tons ran from Southampton to Bournemouth Central in $29\frac{1}{2}$ minutes, breasting Pokesdown bank at 62 m.p.h., while No. 35028 *Clan Line*, after signals at Shawford, accelerated up the bank through Winchester to pass Roundwood at 66 m.p.h., and followed this with a sparkling display after Basingstoke, to reach Waterloo $13\frac{3}{4}$ minutes early in a net time of $75\frac{1}{2}$ minutes from Southampton. No. 35013 *Blue Funnel* again, on 28 April, left Waterloo fourteen minutes late with twelve coaches and a van, and reached Winchester one minute early. Incidentally, the speed recorder on this locomotive was firmly jammed at 104 m.p.h.

The RCTS ran their "Farewell to Southern Steam" tour on Sunday 18 June 1967, with Nos. 73029 and No. 34023 *Blackmore Vale* having charge to Fareham, where No. 34089 *602 Squadron* took over for the journey to Wareham, assistance being given from Southampton Central by No. 34108 *Wincanton*. At Wareham the pilot came off to run light engine to Weymouth, while 2-6-4 tank No. 80146 was attached to the rear of the train for the trip over the Swanage branch. On the return to Wareham No. 34089 *602 Squadron* hauled the train unaided to Weymouth, with a stop at Radipole Halt to set down those visiting the locomotive depot. In the evening Nos. 34023 *Blackmore Vale* and 34108 *Wincanton* worked the special through the New Forest to Salisbury, where No. 35013 *Blue Funnel* was waiting for the dash to Waterloo. As expected, the running was of the highest order, with speeds of 82 m.p.h. at Red Post Junction, 85 m.p.h. at Fleet and 75 m.p.h. at Walton, New Malden being reached seven minutes inside even time, and Waterloo in 75 minutes net.

The official Southern Region "Farewell to Steam" specials were run on Sunday 2 July 1967, but the response was much smaller than anticipated and only two trains were required, No. 35008 *Orient Line* with eleven coaches running to Weymouth and No. 35028 *Clan Line* with ten to Bournemouth. Both locomotives were well burnished and in good mechanical order, and for the occasion had their nameplates restored. Latterly, such locomotives had run nameless to ensure that these highly-prized and expensive items were not mislaid or otherwise lost before withdrawal. On the return from Weymouth No. 35008 *Orient Line* was piloted as far as Bournemouth Central by No. 35007 *Aberdeen Commonwealth*.

For the next week occasional steam workings occurred, with Nos. 35003/7/8/13/28 appearing on boat or van trains from Southampton Docks and Nos. 35007/30 on the 5.30 p.m. Weymouth-Waterloo. No. 35023 *Holland Afrika Line* with the 8.30 a.m. Waterloo-Weymouth on 8 July reached Bournemouth $7\frac{3}{4}$ minutes early despite signal delays en route, while No. 35007 *Aberdeen Commonwealth* two days earlier attained 98 m.p.h. near Bramshot with the 5.30 p.m. Weymouth-Waterloo. No. 35028 *Clan Line* similarly had a final fling with a Docks special, passing Basingstoke $4\frac{1}{2}$ minutes early and Woking with another $1\frac{1}{2}$ in hand. The last steam workings all came on Sunday 9 July 1967, when the honour of heading the last steam train into Waterloo fell to No. 35030 *Elder-Dempster Lines* with the 2.11 p.m. from Weymouth. The redundant and now suddenly lifeless steam locomotives were gathered at Salisbury, Weymouth and Nine Elms to await disposal for scrap or, in a few instances for preservation. The position regarding the Merchant Navies on 27 July 1967 was Nos. 35007/8/13/23/8/30 at Nine Elms and Nos. 35003/14/26 at Weymouth.

The nameplates from Nos. 35004 *Cunard White Star* and 35005 *Canadian Pacific* were presented by the Southern Region to the Canadian Railroad Historical Society in March 1966 for display in the Delson Museum.

Prior to steam operation ceasing on the Southern Region, No. 35028 *Clan Line* had been inspected by the Merchant Navy Locomotive Preservation Society, and on being found mechanically sound was purchased on 10 July 1967 for £2,200. After a brief spell of storage at Nine Elms, it was transferred to Longmoor where, after eighteen months of strenuous effort by members of the Society, steaming was successfully achieved in October 1970. Unfortunately, by this date the security of tenure at Longmoor was uncertain, for with the closure of the Military Railway, funds had to be found to establish the Longmoor Steam Railway and to purchase the land, track and buildings. For a time prospects appeared good, but later, objections by wealthy and influential residents and the failure to gain long-term planning permission caused the scheme to be abandoned. A fresh home had to be found for *Clan Line* and an offer by the South Eastern Steam Society to accommodate it at their depot in the running shed at Ashford was gratefully accepted. There, restoration proceeded apace, and in 1973 all concerned in the project had the pleasure of finding British Rail willing to accept its use on steam rail tours. The first of these, on 27 April 1974 between Basingstoke and Westbury, proved a great attraction and an eminent success. In the following year it appeared at Shildon in the Rail 150 Cavalcade and changed its place of residence to Bulmers at Hereford.

The other twenty-nine members of the class were not so fortunate and were disposed of as follows:

Broken-up by the Southern Region Nos. 35004/20, the former on Eastleigh Shed in February 1966 and the latter in Eastleigh Works in March 1965. Sold for breaking-up to: J. Buttigieg, Newport, Nos. 35007/8/13/7/23/30; Birds Commercial Motors, Bridgend, No. 35016; Birds Commercial Motors, Morriston, Nos. 35001/21; Slag Reduction Company, Rotherham, Nos. 35002/15; J. Cashmore, Newport, Nos. 35003/12/4/9/26; Woodfield, Newport, No. 35024. All were scrapped reasonably quickly, with many of the tenders being cut down to the framing for service in the South Wales steel plants. Ten more, Nos. 35005/6/9/10/1/8/22/5/7/9, were purchased by Woodham Bros., Barry, but not immediately broken-up. Indeed, by mid-1974 only Nos. 35022/7 had reached the steel furnaces, Nos. 35006/9/10/1/8/25 remained more or less intact with No. 35009 reserved for the Wessex Railway Society, while No. 35005 had been purchased in 1974 by Steamtown, Carnforth, and No. 35029 for sectionalised display at the National Railway Museum, York.

So ends the history of one of the most interesting and controversial steam locomotive classes to run in this country. From the very outset contention arose as to how, in the midst of the greatest war ever known to man, Bulleid was able to convince the Ministry of Transport that the construction of such obviously express passenger locomotives could materially assist the war effort, and again, after the eccentricities of the original series had become widely publicised, how was authority gained not only for the provision of ten more in 1944/45, but also for a final batch after Nationalisation.

In regular service their hearty appetite for coal, leakage of oil, violent slipping, while self-ignition formed a ready source of nightmares and the inaccessibility of those parts most-likely to require attention had to be seen to be believed. Yet to their credit, they steamed and rode well, and had a remarkable turn of speed. Some crews liked them, as many hated them; there were no half measures. After Nationalisation and the Exchange Trials prompt remedial action was confidently expected, but for some reason this took long to materialise and even then only after Rugby had confirmed what was already widely known.

Rebuilding may have been overlong delayed, but when this finally occurred, transformation was absolute. No longer was the Southern Region plagued with thirty slab-sided supporters of the National Coal Board, but became the proud owners of a class unsurpassed in performance, economy and speed. Just as the BR Class 9 2-10-0's proved the ultimate in British heavy freight locomotives, so did the rebuilds among express classes.

Boiler diameter ..	5′ 9¾″ to 6′ 3½″
Boiler length ..	16′ 9½″
Firebox length ..	6′ 11″
Heating surfaces:	
Tubes (112×2¼″)	1,121 sq. ft.
Flues (32×5¼″)	748 sq. ft.
Firebox and thermic syphons..	253 sq. ft.
Total evaporative	2,122 sq. ft.
Superheater ..	545 sq. ft.
Combined total	2,667 sq. ft.
Grate area ..	38¼ sq. ft.
Working pressure	280 lb./sq. in.
Weight in working order:	
Bogie	15T 10C
Leading coupled wheels ..	18T 15C
Centre coupled wheels ..	18T 15C
Trailing coupled wheels ..	18T 15C
Pony truck ..	14T 5C
Locomotive total	86T 0C
Tender (4,500 gallons)	42T 12C
	128T 12C

All the principal Merchant Navy features were present, including the oil-bath enclosed valve-gear, BFB wheels, wide Belpaire firebox and inner all-welded steel box, thermic syphons, 280 lb./sq. in. working pressure, Lemaître blastpipe, electric lighting and air-smoothed casing. Like the later Merchant Navy boilers, the front ring of the barrel was parallel and the rear ring tapered along the base to reduce water content and weight. For the Southern Railway an innovation was the rocker grate which was generally similar to the pattern fitted to the LNER A2/1 pacifics Nos. 3696 to 3699 of 1944/45. To avoid burning of the grate firebars, no front dampers were provided, the hopper ash containers being open at the top. Sanding was applied to the front of all three pairs of coupled wheels with rearward running being catered for by containers on the tender, the former having steam application and the latter gravity. To permit passage over routes where hitherto the Maunsell 2-6-0's were the largest permissible class, the boiler, firebox, cylinders and other parts were smaller than those of the Merchant Navies, although this was not readily apparent from side or three-quarter views unless resort was made to the shape and size of the nameplate.

No. 21C101, in malachite green and nameless, was posed outside Brighton Works on 7 May 1945 for inspection by the directors and to have official photographs taken, but, because of a boiler defect, the proposed trial run to Worthing had to be postponed and a return made to the Erecting Shop. Unfortunately, the remedial measures failed and boiler 1261 had to be discarded and replaced by 1266 which was to hand for No. 21C106. At the same time inspection of the cylinders, supplied under contract by Kitsons and machined at Eastleigh, indicated cracking around the ports and these, too, had to be removed and a set from a later locomotive substituted. By early June No. 21C101 was once more available for trials, and on the 5th these were successfully completed, while on the two following days it ran light engine to Tunbridge Wells West, turning on the Groombridge triangle before making the return journey to Brighton. On 14 June, in the full malachite green livery with the name *Exeter*, the city's coat of arms and a scroll recording the class painted on the right side of the air-smoothed casing over the centre coupled wheels, it was once more positioned in the works yard for the company's photographer. The general effect, however, was disappointing for the painted name, coat of arms and class scroll failed to stand out clearly and were lost in the vast expanse of malachite green. Fortunately, this was only a temporary measure, for by the time revenue-earning service was entered on 21 June 1945, cast nameplates, scrolls and shields containing enamelled coats of arms had been fitted.

On that day the 8.00 a.m. Brighton-Victoria via Uckfield and Eridge was successfully worked, as was the return 12.03 p.m. from Victoria which reached Brighton via East Grinstead and Sheffield Park. The class was provisionally granted route availability compatible with the Maunsell N 2-6-0's, but later, when detailed restrictions were published, passage over the Bluebell line was prohibited between Horsted Keynes and Culver Junction, and some eight years were to pass before Sheffield Park again saw a pacific.

In the course of the next few months, most of the early members of the class were worked round to Eastbourne for the taking of official photographs in the shed yard. Several assumed false identities for the occasion; a well-known photograph of No. 21C105 in works grey with white bands was in reality No. 21C107 suitably renumbered and named *Barnstaple*. No. 21C102 was similarly represented by No. 21C103, while in October 1948 No. 21C112 on successive days assumed the identity of Nos.

21C108/9. A photograph also exists of *Bodmin* numbered 21C115 instead of 21C116, the paint shop apparently having become confused and forgotten either to change the nameplate or the cabside numerals.

For most of 1945 the trial runs were generally to Worthing or Angmering, but in the New Year the usual procedure was to work along the coast to Eastbourne, rest on the shed there for an hour or so, then run tender-first to Pevensey and forward via Stone Cross and Polegate to Brighton. After painting, it similarly became standard practice to run-in locomotives on the easily-timed 9.41 a.m. Brighton-Redhill vans. At first the return was made on the 1.47 p.m. vans to Brighton, but before long the duty was extended to cover the 7.05 p.m. goods to Norwood Junction, thence light engine to London Bridge for the 10.35 p.m. mail to Brighton. Should further gentle exercise be considered necessary, then use was made of the class on the 4.18 p.m. Brighton-Eastbourne vans and the 7.05 p.m. Eastbourne-Brighton goods.

On 30 June 1945, Nos. 21C101/3 passed through Salisbury on their way to Exmouth Junction while No. 21C102 was named that morning at Salisbury and travelled on west the following day. Nos. 21C104/5 left Brighton on 2 August and with Nos. 21C101/2/3 relieved T9's and N's on most of the Ilfracombe services, but it was October 1945 before Plymouth came within the scope of their activities. Use was also made of them instead of M7's on the early-morning 6.40 Exeter-Axminster and the 7.55 a.m. return to Queen Street, the lengthy tender-first running not being considered a deterrent in view of the excellent footplate protection and visibility.

In October 1945 the class showed itself for the first time in Kent, when No. 21C111 *Tavistock* ran via Hastings and Rye with a new Bulleid coach for exhibition at Ashford during the town's Thanksgiving Week. At night it was floodlit and made an impressive sight from passing trains. No. 21C114 *Budleigh Salterton* was similarly displayed, together with a Romney, Hythe & Dymchurch pacific, at New Romney. It, too, was floodlit after dark the first evening, but then fell into disgrace when the lights overpowered and burnt out the local sub-station, placing the town in darkness until after midnight.

At the end of the month and for most of November No. 21C110 *Sidmouth* was stationed at Redhill and worked Maunsell 2-6-0 duties over the Reading line. A careful check was made of the coal and water consumption, a notice being attached to the tender front warning crews that water could only be obtained from metered supplies at Redhill and Reading, and coal from special wagons at Redhill. No. 21C110 normally had charge of the 7.43 a.m. Redhill-Reading, the 12.17 p.m. Reading-Redhill, the 5.36 p.m. back to Reading and the 9.34 p.m. home. No attempt was made to increase the loadings until the last week, when services were variously augmented by five or seven empty corridor coaches to offer a reasonably heavy task over such a difficult road. Goods trains were also worked, but after two failures with broken couplings, further such tests were cancelled.

It was not long before minor differences commenced appearing: No. 21C107 *Wadebridge* was the first to carry glass windows in place of the wartime plywood sheeting, while No. 21C108 *Padstow* had the removable panels in the casing and cabsides modified to give easier access to the washout plugs at the base of the firebox. On No. 21C109 *Lyme Regis* the train indicator brackets were removed from the wingplates and repositioned on the smokebox door where the discs would no longer project outside the casing. This became standard for the class with No. 21C118 *Axminster*, although some earlier-built locomotives, for a time, carried brackets on both wingplates and smokebox doors. During the Redhill trials, No. 21C110 *Sidmouth* was experimentally equipped with piping feeding the exhaust discharge of the vacuum ejector and turbo-generator into the firebox above the door. The idea was sound, but, unfortunately, in practice the noise in the cab was deafening whenever the ejector was used, and after modifications failed to offer any improvement the fittings were removed.

The first appearance of the class at Eastleigh was on 30 November 1945, when Nos. 21C110/5 worked troop specials from Hove to Southampton via Netley, and later ran coupled together to Eastleigh shed for servicing. Later in the day the former worked forward with the 10.05 p.m. Salisbury goods while the latter headed another troop special from Southampton to Exeter. In the same month use began to be made of the class on the Exeter-Salisbury expresses and in the following month on the 11.30 a.m. Brighton-Plymouth through train.

The intention was to allocate the first twenty to Exmouth Junction, but the continued deterioration of Eastern Section services in December 1945 necessitated a fresh appraisal of new construction being made. As a result, Nos. 21C119/20 had no sooner reached the West Country than both were ordered to Ramsgate, while No. 21C121's loan to Nine Elms for trials on the Waterloo-Basingstoke-Salisbury slows and semi-fasts was hurriedly concluded so that it, too, could go to Ramsgate.

By the middle of February 1946 Nos. 21C119/20/1/2/3/4/5 were all at work on the Ramsgate-London expresses with No. 21C117 following in March. More new ground was covered on 4 April 1946, when No. 21C122 took a directors' special from Brighton to Victoria via Steyning and Dorking, and on Derby Day when No. 21C129 had charge of the Royal train from Victoria to Tattenham Corner.

After No. 21C1 *Channel Packet* had made the initial runs of the reintroduced "Golden Arrow", its working became the responsibility of Nos. 21C117/9/20/5, which were transferred to Battersea for that purpose. They also appeared on the other Continental services as well as on some of Battersea's Chatham line commuter trains. At Ramsgate the arrival of Nos. 21C126 to 21C130 new from Brighton Works replaced those transferred away.

Before the last of this batch entered traffic a further fifteen were commenced at Brighton Works under order 2885 and entered traffic between June and October 1946, details being as follows: Nos. 21C131 *Torrington*, 21C132 *Camelford* (June), 21C133 *Chard*, 21C134 *Honiton*, 21C135 *Shaftesbury*, 21C136 *Westward Ho* (July), 21C137 *Clovelly* (August), 21C139 *Boscastle*, 21C140 *Crewkerne* (September), 21C141 *Wilton*, 21C142 *Dorchester*, 21C143 *Combe Martin*, 21C144 *Woolacombe*, 21C145 *Ottery St. Mary* (October). A number of minor, but interesting changes, also occurred with this series, including a modified regulator intended to give smoother and more sensitive control, a protecting panel under the sliding roof, a Firthag steel chimney and LMS-type buffers. The last-mentioned had parallel casings instead of the standard Southern Railway pattern where the casing increased in diameter towards the base. Tenders attached to Nos. 21C129/30 had the new-style buffers, though the locomotives carried the original pattern. Less obvious to the casual observer was the re-siting of the coupling-rod knuckle-pin joints ahead of the crankpins on the driving wheels.

The entry to service of these locomotives permitted the transfer of Nos. 21C117/9/20 back to the Western Section with Nos. 21C117/20 going to Exmouth Junction, while No. 21C119 joined No. 21C114 on loan to Salisbury for use on the London expresses in the same link as Merchant Navies. For a week or so the sharply-curved start going eastwards from Salisbury gave local crews considerable trouble and on at least two occasions necessitated a push from behind by the station pilot. The allocation on 1 January 1947 was Exmouth Junction Nos. 21C101 to 21C120, 21C141 to 21C145, Ramsgate Nos. 21C121 to 21C132 and Battersea Nos. 21C133 to 21C140. On most days the "Golden Arrow" was worked by No. 21C135, the relief when unavailable being No. 21C133, while other regular West Country workings over the Kent Coast line were: 6.06 a.m., 6.29 a.m. and 7.20 a.m. Ramsgate-Victoria, 7.30 a.m. Margate-Charing Cross via Dover, 5.15 p.m. and 5.45 p.m. Cannon Street-Ramsgate and 9.35 p.m. Victoria-Ramsgate. In addition, one occasionally headed the 9.40 a.m. Margate-Charing Cross via Dover, usually taking over from a Faversham D1 or D 4-4-0 at Ramsgate. In the West Country, Nos. 21C105/6 were outstationed at Barnstaple in place of N's Nos. 1836/42, while use was being made regularly of the class on the Salisbury expresses as well as in charge of the services west of Exeter. For several months to balance workings the 11.05 a.m. Plymouth Friary-Exeter slow consisting of three coaches was double-headed.

During the third week of January 1947, Nos. 21C140, 21C13 *Blue Funnel* and electric locomotive CC1 were engaged in a series of haulage and braking trials on the Central Section between Norwood and Brighton with trains of fifteen and eighteen Bulleid corridor coaches. The acceleration of No. CC1 was noticeably swifter than the two pacifics, but once well under way the Merchant Navy in particular made better time and reached higher speeds. On most journeys use was made of the LMS dynamometer car, for the Southern possessed no such vehicle, although the drawings for one had been completed in 1945 and authorisation for its construction granted in November 1946.

Once again, as assembly of this series drew to a close, Brighton commenced work on twenty-five more under order 3213. The intention was to perpetuate the West Country nomenclature and a list of names was drawn up for consideration by the Directors, details being as follows: *Appledore*, *Bere Alston*, *Blandford*, *Braunton*, *Brentor*, *Broad Clyst*, *Callington*, *Calstock*, *Crediton*, *Hartland*, *Holsworthy*, *Lapford*, *Lydford*, *Lynmouth*, *Mortehoe*, *Pinhoe*, *Swanage*, *Templecombe*, *Trevone*, *Wells*, *Wenford*, *Weymouth*, *Whimple*, *Wincanton* and *Woodbury*. On hearing that most of the order would be allocated away from the West Country, the directors decided that other names should be found, and at a further meeting agreed that only five should have West Country names, with the remainder having those recalling the 1940 air battles over south-east England when the RAF saved the country from invasion and possible defeat, these locomotives to be known as the Battle of Britain class. Later, the number of West

Countries in the order was reduced to three, while all but four of the discarded names eventually saw service, most with the 1949/50 West Country series. *Whimple* was used to rename No. 21C215 *Rough Tor*, while *Broad Clyst*, *Pinhoe*, *Wenford* and *Woodbury* were not called upon, despite *Saunton*, not on the 1946 list, being allotted to No. 34093.

Dates to service were as follows: West Country class 1946 Nos. 21C146 *Braunton*, 21C147 *Callington*, 21C148 *Crediton* (November). Battle of Britain class 1946 Nos. 21C149 *Anti-Aircraft Command*, 21C150 *Royal Observer Corps*, 21C151 *Winston Churchill*, 21C152 *Lord Dowding* (December). Nos. 21C149/50 were originally intended to be *Holsworthy* and *Lapford* of the West Country class. 1947 Nos. 21C153 *Sir Keith Park*, 21C154 *Lord Beaverbrook* (January), 21C155 *Fighter Pilot*, 21C156 *Croydon* (February), 21C157 *Biggin Hill*, 21C158 *Sir Frederick Pile* (March), 21C159 *Sir Archibald Sinclair*, 21C160 *25 Squadron*, 21C161 *73 Squadron* (April), 21C162 *17 Squadron*, 21C163 *229 Squadron* (May), 21C164 *Fighter Command*, 21C165 *Hurricane* (July), 21C166 *Spitfire*, 21C167 *Tangmere* (September), 21C168 *Kenley*, 21C169 *Hawkinge* (October), 21C170 *Manston* (November). Nos. 21C155/6/7/64/5/6/7/8/9/70 carried Royal Air Force badges below their names, while in addition, at a later date, No. 21C167 *Tangmere* also displayed the station badge on small plaques attached to the cabsides, these having been donated by the Sergeants' Mess. At the naming ceremonies of the three West Countries, as with those built earlier, the person performing the duty was presented with a beautifully-constructed wooden coffee table with the appropriate coat of arms, badge or seal inscribed on the top. These were prepared at Eastleigh Carriage Works and, being highly prized, outlived the locomotives concerned. Indeed, one changed hands at an auction in July 1974 for no less than £320. The Battle of Britains and those West Countries built after Nationalisation by British Railways were not so favoured.

No. 21C164 was officially designated the 1,000th locomotive completed at Brighton Works since construction commenced in May 1852, although this assumed that the twelve B4X 4-4-0's of 1922-4 were rebuilds and not the new locomotives they actually were. On 9 June 1947 it featured in a ceremony to celebrate the occasion, at which the Mayor of Brighton declared it ready for service and duly drove it out of the works yard. Painted grey with white bands and unnamed, it was positioned alongside the Stroudley-liveried Terrier No. 82 *Boxhill* for the company's photographer. Three days later No. 21C164 was again on view, on this occasion for the visit of the Institute of Mechanical Engineers to the works. In the Erecting Shop No. 21C111 *Tavistock* with twenty months' service to its credit was awaiting attention, and to give the visitors a view of the valve-gear the inspection cover was open and provided with electric illumination. All present were immensely impressed by what they saw, every rod, wheel, chain and shaft had the appearance of being made of stainless steel.

From the outset there had been complaints of poor footplate visibility, but no positive action was taken until November 1946 when No. 21C146 entered traffic with a modified vacuum ejector which caused less obstruction to the driver's window. This was a welcome modification, although in itself insufficient significantly to affect the issue, for the combination of the 8ft. 6in. wide cab, narrow lookout windows and soft drifting exhaust made the sighting of signals extremely difficult and, on occasions, brought about potentially dangerous situations. As a result, in late 1946 Nos. 21C137/9/41/2 could be noted running at speed in various locations with lengths of coloured tape attached to the smoke-deflector plates and casing while cameras on the footplate recorded the wind currents and behaviour of the exhaust gases. Inspection of the films and notes compiled by trials staff on the footplate indicated that the smoke-deflector plates were not offering sufficient lift and an increase in size was necessary. To test this theory, No. 21C108 in January 1947 was equipped with a pair of lengthened smoke deflectors and worked for a day up and down the Redhill-Tonbridge line to photograph the wind currents and exhaust gases. Sufficient improvement was noticeable for Nos. 21C122/40 to be similarly modified in February 1947 and, when this was maintained in regular service, the fittings became standard for the class, the first new locomotive fitted being No. 21C158 in March 1947. For a time in May and June 1947 No. 21C162 ran with the leading ends of its deflector plates curved inwards, but when no improvement was achieved the straight ends were replaced. Attention was now given to the cab lookout windows; No. 21C164 after running trials was returned to the Erecting Shop at Brighton and there fitted with a new cab front plate and angled windows. This not only increased the view ahead by 38 per cent, but also reduced reflection after dark. No. 21C165 was similarly equipped before leaving works and like the prototype retained the two cab side windows, whereas Nos. 21C166 to 21C170 received modified cab

No. 21C2 *Union Castle* heading a four-coach special near Merstham, 4 July 1941. Inverted horseshoe ownership plate, front numberplate on vertical section of plating, top of smokebox cut away, and a square aperture around the chimney (*Real Photographs Co. Ltd.*)

No. 21C2 *Union Castle*, June 1947, in malachite livery with circular ownership plate, disc brackets and catch on smokebox door, modified top casing and cowl, standard smoke-deflector plates and sanding to all coupled wheels. Cast number and tender plates retained (*D. L. Bradley*)

The right-hand nameplate of No. 21C2 when new. The sliding cover of the driving wheel sandbox is visible below the centre lining band (*Real Photographs Co. Ltd.*)

No. 35002 *Union Castle* at Waterloo, 11 May 1950. BR blue, transfer numerals, lion-and-wheel totem, smokebox door numberplate and disc brackets, and front sanding discontinued (*J. H. Aston*)

No. 21C3 *Royal Mail* resplendent in malachite green stands on Eastleigh shed, November 1945 (*Real Photographs Co. Ltd.*)

No. 35003 *Royal Mail* in early British Railways malachite green livery in August 1948 (*G. Wheeler*)

No. 21C5 *Canadian Pacific* as built, painted malachite green with yellow bands, gold lettering and numerals, and ribbed Limpet board side casing

No. S21C5 *Canadian Pacific*, 20 March 1948. Malachite green, temporary "S" prefix, and the tender lettered "British Railways". A speedometer and Berkley mechanical stoker fitted

No. 35006 *Peninsular & Oriental S.N. Co.* under general repair at Eastleigh Works, 29 August 1953. Three sand containers, coupled wheel splashers and corrugated steampipes (*E. W. Fry*)

No. 21C7 *Aberdeen Commonwealth* at Eastleigh, 31 May 1947. Retaining black livery, but carrying standard smoke-deflector plates (*J. H. Aston*)

Nearing the end, No. 35007 with nameplates removed approaching Weymouth with the 8.35 a.m. ex-Waterloo, 5 July 1967 (*S. C. Nash*)

No. 21C8 at Salisbury, September 1943. Black, unnamed, circular ownership plate, sanding to leading and centre coupled wheels, and large C to front numerals

No. 21C8 *Orient Line* on West of England express duty, 9 September 1945. Modified top casing and cowl, short smoke-deflector plates and sanding to all coupled wheels (*LCGB*)

No. 21C8 *Orient Line* awaiting repair at Eastleigh Works after the Waterloo accident of 10 June 1947. Lightening holes are visible in the main framing (*British Railways*)

No. 21C8 *Orient Line* at Eastleigh, 2 September 1947. Malachite green and original cab given a V-front (*G. Wheeler*)

No. 35008 *Orient Line* at Southampton Central, 2 July 1967, with rebuilt 5,250-gallon tender (*E. W. Fry*)

No. 21C10 *Blue Star*, June 1946. Small C to front numerals and ribbed Limpet board casing (*D. L. Bradley*)

No. 35012 *United States Lines*, July 1952, with modified 5,100-gallon tender, blanked-off front sanding, smokebox door handle, valance ahead of cylinders cut away, and lining of BR green livery modified to suit tender alterations (*D. L. Bradley*)

No. 21C13 *Blue Funnel* at Nine Elms, September 1946. Second pattern nameplate and black livery

No. 21C14 *Nederland Line* in July 1945, with covered nameplates and route disc brackets not yet resited on the smokebox door (*LCGB*)

No. 21C15 *Rotterdam Lloyd* speeds the "Devon Belle" through West Weybridge, 20 June 1947. Malachite green, disc brackets on smokebox door and train name wings on smoke deflectors (*Real Photographs Co. Ltd.*)

No. 35015 *Rotterdam Lloyd* at Eastleigh, 12 June 1949. Malachite green, unlettered tender, black wheels, standard V-cab and slide-bar dust covers (*W. Gilburt*)

No. 35017 *Belgian Marine* ready to leave Eastleigh Works, 30 March 1957
(*E. W. Fry*)

No. 35018 *British India Line* with speedometer and self-weighing tender, 25 July 1952

The first Merchant Navy rebuild, No. 35018 *British India Line* at Eastleigh, 7 February 1956, with 6,000-gallon modified tender (*L. Elsey*)

No. 35019 *French Line C.G.T.* at Eastleigh, 10 April 1948, fitted with V-cab, speedometer and LMS tender in preparation for the BR Locomotive Trials (*J. H. Aston*)

No. 35020 *Bibby Line* at Waterloo, 16 May 1948, about to leave with the 9.00 a.m. West of England express. Extra-long smoke-deflector plates, standard V-cab and attached to LMS 4,000-gallon tender (*J. H. Aston*)

The cause of the Crewkerne accident of 24 April 1953, the faulty driving axle of No. 35020 *Bibby Line* (*G. Wheeler*)

No. 35020 *Bibby Line* on trial between Salisbury and Exeter with Western Region dynamometer car and unmodified 6,000-gallon tender, 18 June 1956 (*E. W. Fry*)

No. 35024 at Boscombe, 27 November 1948, when new. Painted matt malachite green, attached to Battle of Britain tender (T3333) and without nameplates (*G. O. P. Pearce*)

No. 35024 *East Asiatic Company* outside Eastleigh Works, 10 February 1949, in experimental blue livery with hand-painted BR totem (*D. L. Bradley*)

No. 35024 *East Asiatic Company* working the "Bournemouth Belle" on 7 May 1960. The tender is T3343, rebuilt for self-weighing (*E. W. Fry*)

side sheets with three windows. This became the standard layout and in course of time was applied to Nos. 21C101 to 21C165, the dates being as follows:

Locomotive No.	*V-cab fitted*
21C101	1/1955
21C102	6/1951
21C103	9/1953
21C104	3/1948
21C105	5/1948
21C106	5/1948
21C107	5/1951
21C108	6/1950
21C109	12/1950
21C110	2/1955
21C111	9/1952
21C112	2/1951
21C113	5/1954
21C114	12/1954
21C115	3/1957
21C116	5/1953
21C117	1/1954
21C118	10/1950
21C119	1/1956
21C120	7/1950
21C121	7/1953
21C122	4/1953
21C123	10/1954
21C124	3/1955
21C125	9/1954
21C126	5/1949
21C127	6/1953
21C128	2/1954
21C129	1/1955
21C130	1/1952
21C131	1/1949
21C132	1/1951
21C133	6/1949
21C134	4/1955
21C135	2/1952
21C136	2/1952
21C137	3/1949
21C138	4/1955
21C139	11/1952
21C140	3/1954
21C141	12/1953
21C142	4/1949
21C143	6/1952
21C144	3/1954
21C145	10/1951
21C146	1/1954
21C147	9/1953
21C148	5/1949
21C149	3/1948
21C150	2/1948
21C151	8/1947
21C152	8/1947
21C153	8/1947
21C154	9/1947
21C155	9/1947
21C156	11/1947
21C157	11/1947
21C158	1/1948
21C159	12/1947
21C160	9/1948
21C161	1/1949
21C162	2/1949
21C163	1/1949
21C164	7/1947

No. 21C165, like No. 21C164, entered traffic with two side windows to its V-fronted cab; the standard three-window layout was applied to No. 21C164 in June 1948 and to No. 21C165 in March 1949. The width across the cab had been restricted to 8ft. 6in. when use of the class had been envisaged on the Charing Cross-Hastings services, but when this failed to occur no valid reason remained for its retention and, when forty more were built after Nationalisation, the side sheets were extended to the full 9ft. 0in. with corresponding gain to footplate visibility.

Nos. 21C166 to 21C170 entered traffic equipped with TIA feed water treatment and this subsequently became a feature of the class until the simpler, but equally effective, British Railways system was substituted during the mid-1950's. Like the Merchant Navies, the benefits of longer periods between washouts and greatly reduced boiler maintenance did much to compensate for other extravaganza. The allocation of these twenty-five locomotives was as follows: Exmouth Junction Nos. 21C146/7 (both at first on loan to Salisbury), Salisbury Nos. 21C148/9/50/1/2/3, Battersea Nos. 21C154/5/6/7, Nine Elms Nos. 21C158/9/60/1, Ramsgate Nos. 21C162 to 21C170. The arrival of this series on the Eastern Section permitted the transfer of Nos. 21C122/3 to Nine Elms and Nos. 21C121/4/5/6 to Exmouth Junction with the aim, as far as operating demands allowed, to have the West Countries working from Western Section depots. At Nine Elms Nos. 21C122/3/58/9/60/1 officially replaced N15X class 4-6-0's Nos. 2327 to 2333, but after a brief spell on the Waterloo-Basingstoke-Salisbury semi-fasts, were rostered for top link duties, including the "Bournemouth Belle" and "Atlantic Coast Express". Clearance tests were made in the Old Docks at Southampton early in 1947, but it was 5th July before No. 21C159 made the first appearance on a boat express. It successfully headed the Jersey boat train, but when No. 21C158 attempted to repeat the performance with the 9.00 p.m. Channel Islands boat train on 25th July, it became derailed in the docks and brought all passenger movement to an abrupt halt for several hours. At once all these services returned to 4-6-0 haulage, including the Lord Nelsons, until permanent way work eased two curves and replaced a set of points, at the end of September. Little time was then lost in recalling the class with Nos. 21C158/61 appearing on 4th October 1947, with two of the *Queen Mary* boat trains.

Similar trouble was also met at Dorchester, where use of the shed had to be restricted until the first road could be converted into a loop line. As a result it was 18 August 1947, before the first West Country penetrated beyond Bournemouth West, when No. 21C105 *Barnstaple*, on loan to Nine Elms, worked through to Weymouth on the 1.30 p.m. ex-Waterloo. The return was on the 6.30 p.m. piloted as far as Bournemouth Central by T9 No. 719.

The provision of new and larger turntables at Padstow (65ft.) and Okehampton (70ft.) offered facilities west of Exeter where hitherto such large locomotives could not be accommodated. The former permitted daily workings over the North Cornwall line, including the 5.31 a.m. Exeter-Launceston, a curious train whose formation on leaving Okehampton usually consisted of two coaches, a van or two, a dozen goods wagons and a goods brake. Another duty was the 8.25 a.m. ex-Padstow, the engine for which worked down to Wadebridge with a stopping goods the day before, remained on the shed there overnight and in the morning ran down to Padstow with empty fish vans, turned on the new turntable and took the "Atlantic Coast Express" (8.25 a.m.) as far as Exeter. On Fridays the locomotive ran light to Padstow as soon as it reached Wadebridge, and the following morning had charge of the relief 8.05 a.m. to Exeter. For much of 1947 these duties were shared by four West Countries, two appropriately being Nos. 21C107 *Wadebridge* and 21C108 *Padstow*, while the others were Nos. 21C111 *Tavistock* and 21C120 *Seaton*. On its first appearance at Padstow No. 21C111 blotted its copybook by setting itself on fire during the early hours and having to be attended to by the local fire service. At Okehampton the new turntable permitted the use of S15 4-6-0's and pacifics on the heavy Meldon Quarry ballast trains, hitherto restricted to N class 2-6-0's.

During the Second World War the company's train ferries were commandeered by the Royal Navy, and when hostilities ceased it was two years before they could be recovered, refitted, and returned to civilian service between Dover and Dunkirk. Because of this it was 15 December 1947, before the "Night Ferry" recommenced running, the first down train being worked by No. 21C156 and L1 No. 1757. Both up and down workings, unlike pre-war, became a regular Dover duty for which Nos. 21C156/7 were transferred there from Battersea. At this period, No. 21C155 was the regular "Golden Arrow" locomotive and was kept beautifully cleaned, although it is doubtful whether it surpassed Nos. 21C156/7 once the local cleaners set to work, for not only did the paintwork gleam but also the motion, piping, buffers and wheels.

Light pacifics from time to time had been employed by Brighton on the through services to Bournemouth, Cardiff and Plymouth, but it was April 1947 before the last-mentioned became a regular Salisbury duty. The locomotive stabled at Brighton overnight, worked through to Plymouth, and came back on the following day with the up train. At first, time was regularly lost, mainly because of the poor-quality coal available at Brighton, but later, when a better supply became available and Salisbury regularly exchanged locomotives, so that forty-eight hours was the maximum time any one was off shed, much smart running was recorded. No. 21C153 *Sir Keith Park* appeared on 29 April, but during the summer the task was usually delegated to earlier-built locomotives.

At this period, suitable coal for locomotives was difficult to obtain, while in winter acute shortages of any type of solid fuel occurred. As a result in August 1946 the Government's transport advisers decided to adopt a plan formulated during the war and convert 1,217 locomotives to oil burning, using a heavy oil known as Bunker C, which was unsuitable for compression-ignition vehicles. The Southern Railway's quota was 110 locomotives, consisting of 20 West Countries, 16 N15's and H15's, 34 N's and U's, 10 D15's and 30 T9's and L11's. Unfortunately, the Treasury had not been fully consulted and no sooner had the scheme become operational in 1947/48 than funds to finance the additional purchases of oil could not be made available and locomotives had to be laid aside or returned to coal firing. There was also much opposition from the National Coal Board and the Miners' Union, for both saw the disappearance of a traditional source of revenue and the eventual creation of unemployment in the coal fields. As a result, only two West Countries were actually converted to oil firing, No. 21C119 at Eastleigh Works between 16 June and 26 July 1947, and No. 21C136 at Brighton Works between 9 December 1947, and 28 February 1948. A 1,600-gallon welded fuel tank was positioned in the coal space and the four vacuum brake cylinders re-sited, two on either side of the water tank manhole cover. Tubular ladders were fitted at the rear of the tender to offer easier access for re-fuelling while the rocker grate and ash hoppers were removed.

For a time after conversion No. 21C119 was employed from Eastleigh on local passenger and goods duties, but later graduated to the 6.00 a.m. Southampton-Waterloo and the 11.30 a.m. Waterloo-Bournemouth West services which were the province of King Arthurs. Much trouble, however, was met in maintaining a head of steam, for the thermic syphons severely restricted the efficiency of the burner and on occasions led to the production of dense black clouds of smoke but little heat in the firebox. A second burner was thereupon added with beneficial results, although the steaming remained erratic and it was agreed that the Mexican trough system installed was not entirely suited to the class. Following further trials from Eastleigh and a repositioning of the burners, No. 21C119 was transferred to Exmouth Junction for secondary passenger duties. Reconversion to coal firing took place in September 1948 after 8,220 miles had been run.

In view of the experience with No. 21C119 it was decided to equip No. 21C136 with the more advanced—and it was hoped more suitable—Laidlaw-Drew Swirlyflo system of oil burning at an estimated cost of £640. At this period the short-lived British Railways "S" prefix was in operation and when returned to traffic on 28 February 1948 it was as No. S21C136. Initially the steaming was as poor as No. 21C119 and on several occasions complete failure occurred, but once the teething troubles were overcome excellent service was given with a plentiful supply of steam. Once again local goods and passenger duties were worked around Eastleigh before venturing on to the Waterloo expresses. Later, the "Atlantic Coast Express" was successfully worked as well as other West of England express duties and fitted freights. Various trials were also run including a twenty-coach train between Eastleigh and Weymouth, and a special formed of eighteen new coaches and S15 No. 30510 from Eastleigh to Basingstoke. The 4-6-0 only assisted until a start was made and then became part of the load; passing Winchester No. S21C136 had the safety-valves releasing steam violently and by the Basingstoke stop was showing 265 lb./sq. in. on the pressure gauge. Obviously success had been achieved, but the trials were deliberately prolonged to enable sufficient information to be gained in case oil firing should become necessary in the future; thus it was November 1949 before it reverted to coal firing after 15,044 miles had been run. Despite the failure of the 1946 scheme, it had shown that oil firing offered much improved availability, increased rates of evaporation and reduced the fireman's burden on heavy goods and passenger services. Savings were also possible by the avoidance of coal handling, ash removal and disposal, and the disappearance of the dirt and grime inseparable from the use of coal.

At Nationalisation all forty-eight West Countries and twenty-two Battle of Britains entered British Railways stock to be renumbered 34001 to 34070 as they passed through works for routine attention. The Bulleid-style of numbering had little appeal to the gentlemen heading the Railway Executive. No. 34015 on 7 April 1948, was the first renumbered and No. 34010 the last on 27 January 1950. Prior to April 1948 the Bulleid numbers were prefixed by an "S" to indicate Southern Region, and since a sizeable proportion of the class passed through shops during the opening months of 1948, no less than twenty-two featured this temporary additive, these being Nos. 21C105/6/7/8/9/10/2/6/21/9/31/6/42/6/8/9/50/7/8/9/67/70. The first, No. S21C158, was ex-Brighton Works on 14 January 1948, and is thought also to have been the first in the country to work lettered *British Railways*. A full list of these locomotives follows:

Locomotive No.	*Date 'S' prefix applied*			*Date renumbered to 34xxx series*	
21C105	Eastleigh	30/2/1948	34005	Brighton	28/5/1948
21C106	Eastleigh	16/1/1948	34006	Brighton	27/5/1948
21C107	Eastleigh	29/1/1948	34007	Brighton	25/3/1949
21C108	Eastleigh	7/2/1948	34008	Brighton	12/4/1949
21C109	Eastleigh	19/2/1948	34009	Brighton	6/3/1949
21C110	Eastleigh	27/1/1948	34010	Eastleigh	27/1/1950
21C112	Eastleigh	4/3/1948	34012	Eastleigh	26/6/1948
21C116	Eastleigh	20/3/1948	34016	Eastleigh	3/7/1948
21C121	Eastleigh	12/3/1948	34021	Eastleigh	10/7/1948
21C129	Brighton	14/2/1948	34029	Eastleigh	17/2/1949
21C131	Brighton	28/2/1948	34031	Eastleigh	29/1/1949

Locomotive No.	*Date 'S' prefix applied*			*Date renumbered to 34xxx series*	
21C136	Brighton	10/2/1948	34036	Eastleigh	22/5/1948
21C142	Brighton	1/3/1948	34042	Brighton	5/6/1948
21C146	Brighton	24/1/1948	34046	Eastleigh	22/1/1949
21C148	Eastleigh	14/2/1948	34048	Eastleigh	21/8/1948
21C149	Brighton	13/3/1948	34049	Eastleigh	1/4/1949
21C150	Brighton	5/2/1948	34050	Eastleigh	29/1/1949
21C157	Ashford	23/2/1948	34057	Eastleigh	17/6/1949
21C158	Brighton	14/1/1948	34058	Eastleigh	4/12/1948
21C159	Ashford	21/2/1948	34059	Eastleigh	11/3/1949
21C167	Brighton	11/3/1948	34067	Ashford	20/7/1949
21C170	Ashford	12/3/1948	34070	Ashford	31/3/1949

Some, like Nos. S21C105/6/36, rapidly gained their 34xxx numbers, but others retained the prefix for lengthy periods with the last not becoming 34010 until 27 January 1950. After renumbering and being fitted with smokebox door numberplates, several, including Nos. 34016/21/46, still carried their "S" prefix numbers painted on the front casing, while No. 21C105 became S21C105 on 20 February 1948, 21C105 again at Brighton on 24 March 1948, and 34005 on 28 May 1948. When the "S" prefix was applied, the tender was lettered *British Railways* and this lettering was retained after the prefix had been painted out. Therefore, until the substitution of an LMS tender on 23 March 1948, in preparation for the Interchange Trials, it ran as 21C105 with *British Railways* lettering across the tender. No. 21C104, ex-Brighton Works on 24 March 1948, also ran briefly in this guise, although in its case the "S" prefix was never applied.

The last repaint in Southern Railway livery was No. 21C114 in early January 1948, but the attractive malachite green was not abandoned at once, for it remained standard for the class until mid-1949. At first, tender sides were lettered *British Railways* but from December 1948 they were left blank until supplies of the lion-and-wheel totem became available in late July 1949. Similarly, the front numerals continued to be carried on the casing until June 1948 when the cast smokebox door numberplates came into use and the large circular date plates were removed. Malachite green appeared for the last time on No. 34055 which left Eastleigh Works on 26 July 1949, while No. 34039 on 3 August 1949, was the first to appear in the new British Railways Brunswick green, lined with black-and-orange. Although appearing most attractive on Western Region locomotives where polished brass and copper was to hand to add brightness, on the Bulleid pacifics the general effect was sombre, made more so by the black backing to the nameplates and scrolls. The hard-wearing qualities of the malachite green were well emphasised by its remaining on No. 34070 until March 1953. Dates locomotives became dark green are as follows:

Locomotive No.	*Date*
34001	12/1949
34002	10/1949
34003	3/1952
34004	4/1950
34005	5/1950
34006	7/1950
34007	5/1951
34008	6/1950
34009	12/1950
34010	1/1950
34011	9/1950
34012	2/1951
34013	4/1950
34014	11/1949
34015	1/1950
34016	1/1950
34017	1/1951
34018	10/1950
34019	11/1949
34020	7/1950
34021	6/1950
34022	9/1950
34023	4/1950
34024	12/1951
34025	3/1950
34026	12/1950
34027	12/1951
34028	2/1951
34029	2/1950
34030	3/1950
34031	11/1949
34032	1/1951
34033	12/1951
34034	5/1950
34035	2/1952
34036	2/1952
34037	10/1950
34038	5/1952

Locomotive No.	*Date*
34039	8/1949
34040	8/1950
34041	6/1951
34042	11/1951
34043	9/1950
34044	12/1950
34045	5/1950
34046	8/1950
34047	12/1951
34048	8/1952
34049	6/1951
34050	4/1952
34051	12/1950
34052	8/1952
34053	1/1951
34054	4/1951
34055	5/1951
34056	1/1950
34057	4/1951
34058	2/1951
34059	4/1951
34060	11/1951
34061	10/1949
34062	12/1949
34063	7/1951
34064	6/1950
34065	3/1951
34066	5/1950
34067	4/1951
34068	9/1950
34069	10/1952

Locomotive No.	*Date*
34070	3/1953
34071	2/1952
34072	4/1952
34073	12/1950
34074	6/1950
34075	9/1952
34076	9/1950
34077	8/1951
34078	8/1951
34079	5/1951
34080	8/1951
34081	4/1950
34082	9/1950
34083	9/1952
34084	3/1950
34085	3/1950
34086	10/1950
34087	10/1950
34088	12/1950
34089	6/1952
34090	3/1952

Before selecting the standard liveries for the various categories of locomotives and rolling stock, the Railway Executive gave instructions for a number of locomotives and vehicles to be painted experimentally, both for inspection and use in regular service. The latter included West Country No. 34011 and Battle of Britain Nos. 34056/64/5/86/7/8, their details being as follows:

Locomotive No.	*Experimental livery applied*		*Repainted dark green*	
34011	Eastleigh	26/5/1948	Eastleigh	8/9/1950
34056	Eastleigh	3/6/1948	Eastleigh	19/1/1950
34064	Eastleigh	11/6/1948	Eastleigh	24/6/1950
34065	Eastleigh	12/6/1948	Eastleigh	14/3/1951
34086	Brighton	2/12/1948	Eastleigh	11/10/1950
34087	Brighton	17/12/1948	Eastleigh	25/10/1950
34088	Brighton	22/12/1948	Eastleigh	16/12/1950

All were painted apple green with two widely-spaced cream bands edged with red and grey. The rear of the tenders and all the buffer beams were unlined, while the tender lettering and cabside numerals were unshaded yellow edged in black. No. 34011 retained its circular smokebox door *Southern* plate and had painted front numerals, but the others carried LMR-type numberplates. At Brighton Works in October 1949 No. 34086 had the BR lion-and-wheel emblem applied to its tender sides, and was the only apple green locomotive on the Southern Region to be so adorned. There were, however, three malachite green light pacifics with tender emblems, Nos. 34036/71/9, also the result of visits to Brighton Works.

In time for the 1948 summer services a number of train sets were painted plum-and-spilt-milk or chocolate-and-cream and these, together with the experimentally-painted locomotives, were distributed throughout the country in order that as many people as possible could view them and voice opinions. Nos.

34056/64/5 were paired with chocolate-and-cream Ironclad set 237, restaurant car 7934 and two loose coaches (eleven vehicles) for exclusive use on the following Chatham line services:

7.20 a.m.	Ramsgate-Cannon Street
5.15 p.m. (SX)	Cannon Street-Ramsgate
1.15 p.m. (SO)	Cannon Street-Ramsgate
9.40 a.m. (Suns.)	Ramsgate-Victoria
3.15 p.m. (Suns.)	Victoria-Ramsgate

Only No. 34056 was shedded at Ramsgate, but with Nos. 34064/5 readily available at Battersea there was little difficulty in always providing an apple green locomotive for these trains. By the end of the year the similarly-painted Nos. 34086/7/8 were also at Ramsgate. No. 34011 was a Plymouth locomotive and, apart from displaying the experimental livery in the West Country, was not engaged in these workings, although regular use was made of it on the "Devon Belle" west of Exeter.

On 20 July 1948, No. 34056 caught fire at Rochester while working the 5.15. p.m. Cannon Street-Ramsgate. Oil from the bath set the boiler cladding and the cab floor alight and called for the services of the local fire brigade before the journey could be continued.

Regular travellers took a surprising interest in these experimentally painted locomotives and coaches with no less than 11,408 writing to the Railway Executive giving their views. Possibly less surprising was the preference for the Southern Railway malachite green locomotives and coaches, 82 per cent preferring the old to the new. In regular service the apple green wore badly and quickly lost its pristine freshness, while the cream upper sections of the coaches as rapidly became grime-encrusted and streaky, despite regular cleaning. By mid-1949 all interest had been lost in the experiment and any available locomotive was rostered for the duties worked by the chocolate-and-cream coaches, while the apple green locomotives were repainted dark green as they passed through works in 1950/51.

As might be anticipated from locomotives incorporating so many Merchant Navy features, the West Countries had similar characteristics, some good and others most undesirable. To their credit was the magnificently-steaming boiler, the exceptionally fine riding and free-running downhill and when coasting, the well-appointed footplate, efficient clasp brakes, trouble-free BFB wheels, electric lighting and excellent route availability. Not so satisfactory were the steam reverser, the power-assisted firedoor, the oil leakage and slipping, the siting of the safety-valves, mechanical lubricators and sandbox access, the smokebox and rocker grate design, the front end rigidity and the inaccessibility of most parts requiring regular attention. These failings, and the remedies applied, will now be discussed in detail.

The steam reverser, although a boon on some accounts, was much fiercer and more powerful than the Drummond and Stirling pattern, and tended to unnerve inexperienced drivers by making them close the regulator before notching-up or hesitating to use less than 30 per cent cut-off in case the movement was misjudged and the locomotive suddenly went into reverse, with consequent peril to the train and valve-gear. Experience, unfortunately, did not solve all the problems of the Bulleid reverser for it was heavy in maintenance, incapable of fine adjustment and tended to move on its own. Over the years, various minor modifications were made which greatly improved maintenance and reduced the slipping to a degree not likely to inconvenience most drivers, but the fierce action and lack of fine adjustment remained to the end and over the years must have been a source of much wasted coal.

Fuel consumption returns for Exmouth Junction during the summer of 1946 made no reference to the duties worked, although by deduction much of the mileage must have been performed west of Exeter. Therefore, at 47.9 lb. per mile the average figure for the class was pretty astounding, especially when the ageing Drummond T9's working between Exeter, Plymouth and Ilfracombe undertook similar duties for a mere 32 lb. of coal per mile. Notwithstanding the light loads normally handled in the West Country the power output on the banks was high which, because of the vacuum ejector outlet being sited in the blast-pipe, led to a fall of vacuum and light application of the brakes. Locomotives, therefore, were forced not only to overcome the normal force of gravity, but also the partial retardation of the train. This also had an adverse affect on the amount of coal burnt.

In theory the steam-powered firedoor, operated by a pedal on the cab floor, was an excellent idea, but in practice it proved an embarrassment to most firemen for it could only be actuated from the fully-closed or fully-opened positions. If, for example, the door was left partly open, the pedal would not bring it fully open for the shovel, and firemen accustomed to work with the door always ajar found it difficult to depend on the air holes and to work with a shut door except when actually firing. As a result, few firemen made any attempt to understand the contraption and did their best to forget its presence. Another disadvantage was the firebox heat causing the lubricating oil of the mechanism to burn and fill the cab with noxious fumes which caused coughing and eye-watering.

Like the Merchant Navies, the chain gear, slide bars, crossheads, piston rods, and the 8ft. connecting rod, big-end and webs were enclosed in a vast bath containing forty gallons of oil. At speed on the road immense pressures were created within the bath, whose structure was beset by severe vibration and racking stresses which in time caused distortion and fracturing of the casing. Much oil was also lost through the bath breathers and through axle and plunger seals, while fractures along the bath top gave entry to water dripping off the boiler barrel. Its presence rapidly led to corrosion which became so severe that parts of the valve-gear required renewal at the first general repair. To prevent this, a higher grade of oil was introduced, and when no improvement occurred instructions were issued to running sheds ordering the daily dipping of oil-baths with rods coated with water-detecting paste and the draining off of any water discovered. This, of course, being heavier than oil had settled at the bottom of the bath as soon as the locomotives became stationary.

The provision of improved breather valves and automobile-type seals reduced oil seepage, and the consumption per hundred miles averaged 23.8 pints as against only eight and ten pints respectively for the King Arthurs and Lord Nelsons. Much of the lost lubricant was absorbed by the boiler and firebox lagging, where after 20,000 miles' service it formed an ever-increasing fire hazard and was the cause of numerous conflagrations, mostly of a minor nature. At first sparks from the ashpans were considered the main source of ignition, and in June 1948 No. 34042 was experimentally equipped with steel fire protection sheets along the base of the firebox and barrel, while Nos. 34001/5/61/2 in February 1949 had water sprays fitted to their ashpans to dampen the red-hot ash and clinker. Neither offered a complete answer, but whereas the sprays created other problems and were later discarded, the protective sheeting became a standard feature. Later, when a number of West Countries were transferred to the Somerset & Dorset line, a further and hitherto undetected source of ignition came to notice following the prolonged periods of braking called for by that steeply-graded route over the Mendips. White-hot particles of metal from the brake shoes were found clinging to accumulations of oil and beginning to smoulder; most extinguished themselves without causing serious trouble, but some were fanned into a sizeable blaze in the slipstream. A change of shoe pattern and material offered a quick and simple remedy.

In itself, oil on the wheel treads was a serious disadvantage for any locomotive, but when insensitive regulators and over-flexible springing were also present, then every start was fraught with difficulties and time-wasting slipping. Most drivers found the regulators incapable of smooth and delicate manipulation as well as being awkward to close once slipping commenced. To gain smooth riding Bulleid had sprung the class evenly with the result that on starting away, when maximum adhesion was required, much of the weight was transferred from the coupled wheels to the bogie and pony truck where its presence was useless. Routes over which the class regularly worked were noted for "rail burn" at all difficult—and even not so difficult—getting-away points, and the frequency with which these sections of rail had to be removed and replaced.

In many ways the positioning of the three Ross pop safety-valves on the front ring of the barrel with locomotives having a 280 lb./sq. in. working pressure was a wise decision. Unfortunately, in practice sudden braking caused surging and the discharge of boiling water to the atmosphere via the safety-valves, an unpleasant and potentially dangerous phenomenon in open country and infinitely more so at stations. With down trains, "favoured" locations were Winchester and Exeter. As a result from 1952 safety-valves were resited to the rear of the dome.

Equally unfortunate was the positioning of the mechanical lubricators at the front of the smokebox, where only the casing offered protection from ash being disposed of at the end of the day's work. Some alleviation came with the provision of a common reservoir, but in general the problem remained to the end.

Steam sanding was provided to the front of all coupled wheels with the containers tucked away within the air-smoothed casing. Access for filling was by means of apertures having sliding shutters fitted high up the casing which necessitated the use of a ladder and a small hand hopper, not unlike the domestic coal scuttle. Replenishing was a time-consuming and unpopular task with the result that usually it was slovenly performed with sand from the leading container being spilt over the outside slide bars. To prevent this occurring and causing unnecessary wear, Nos. 34039/42 in June 1948 had dust covers fitted to their outside slide bars and, when these appeared successful, the modification was applied to most of the class, including Nos. 34001/3/4/6/7/8/9/11/2/5/20/9/34/7/40/8/9/51/2/3/4/6/9/61/2/3/4/5/71/7/86/90 and 34091 to 34109. Unfortunately, although the covers excluded the sand, they also obstructed efficient lubrication and by mid-1950 were being removed as locomotives passed through shops. At the same time the leading sand containers were blanked-off, which effectively settled the matter once and for all. Odd locomotives, such as No. 34005, ran for a time with no front sanding, but retaining the slide bar dust covers.

From outside the smokebox had the appearance of being enormous, but internally it was encumbered by the extra steam piping required for the outside admission piston valves, as well as by the large diameter of the steampipes, the blower pipe and the vacuum ejector exhaust pipe. Instead of being circular and supported on a saddle, the structure was fabricated of thin steel sheeting and of irregular shape for the top front was cut away for smoke lifting and the base intruded by the inside valve chamber. Vibration, corrosion from within and without, over-enthusiastic clearing of ash and scouring by the exhaust rapidly caused air leakage at all manner of places. For long journeys when ash tended to accumulate there was insufficient depth below the door.

Much of the front-end vibration was the result of over-light construction introduced to save weight, and this also led to main frame fracturing, loosening of the cylinders and steampipe breakages. To investigate this problem Nos. 21C105/39 were in mid-1947 equipped with inspection shelters in front of the smokebox and employed on a wide range of express and main-line goods services, while No. 21C156 in November 1947 ran a similar series of trial runs between Brighton and Norwood. Evidently the findings were conclusive, for commencing with Nos. 34034/9/42 in May and June 1948 the stretchers at the front end were modified and strengthened to make the frame structure more rigid. At first only partial success was achieved and in June/July 1950 the bogies of Nos. 34008/64 were fitted with strengthened vertical and horizontal stretchers and longer springs, and when this gave better results, similar modifications were made to the remainder of the class. Nevertheless, steampipe fracturing still occurred and, after unsuccessful trials with Bellows-pattern pipes on Nos. 34008/9/34, solid-drawn steel pipes were fitted to No. 34041 in September 1950. These proved less susceptible to breakage and became standard as and when replacements became necessary.

In everyday service the rocker grate proved a doubtful asset, frequently becoming jammed as well as necessitating constant attention by shed staff. The drop section was more successful, although here too care had to be taken to avoid one large piece of clinker becoming caught up and allowing the remainder of the debris to pile up against it. To avoid this occurring, the knowledgeable assiduously broke up all the clinker in the fire, made sure the ashpan was clear and then dropped the grate. The less knowledgeable or impatient failed to do this and thereby found themselves down in the pit scraping and pulling at the clinker, a truly miserable job.

The lack of dampers surprisingly did not cause crews as much trouble as expected, for it was always possible to take a West Country "off the boil" by piling too much coal across the front of the grate. It was also common to stand or run short distances with a hole in the fire in order to control the steaming rate and only have the grate fully covered when commencing a journey or working reasonably hard. Under such treatment the fireboxes could logically be expected to suffer, but this was not the case, probably because of the welded tube ferrules and the use of TIA. Another good trait seldom mentioned was the brick arch which, because of the thermic syphons, was in three sections of three large bricks each. A collapsed arch was virtually unknown, for one brick down, or at most three, was insufficient to impair steaming sufficiently to warrant demanding a replacement locomotive.

Accessibility was a term never mentioned to men having regularly to work on the class, for practically every item requiring regular attention was tucked away inside the air-smoothed casing and impossible to reach without much effort and dexterity. Entry was often via small openings in the casing, some protected by shutters which were of flimsy construction and difficult to manipulate. Despite the introduction of an improved and stronger pattern, it was common to note locomotives running with manifold valve and clack-box shutters open or missing altogether. Similarly, the oil-bath made it difficult for drivers to detect faults in the valve-gear by noise, with the result that the first evidence that anything was wrong frequently took the form of various valve-gear components sailing through the sump, aided and abetted by some forty gallons of oil. Even should faults be noticed in time, access was a nightmare and not recommended for fitters suffering from claustrophobia or inclined to be portly. Invariably the smallest fitter available was conscripted for the task with suitable bribes of overtime offered to fortify his disappearance into the interior of the ailing locomotive. Should his companions wish to make the job even more hair-raising they had only to keep quiet and pretend they had knocked off for a tea break, because it was virtually impossible to extricate oneself without external assistance.

Other modifications made at this period included the fitting of spark-arresters to Nos. 34033/4 in January 1949 and July 1948 respectively. On No. 34034 the equipment was designed at Brighton and performed its intended task with such efficiency that few pieces of partly-consumed coal escaped its clutches, but the steaming was so poor that when rostered for the through Bournemouth train several unscheduled stops were necessary to "brew up". Officially it was carried until October 1948, although inspection of the smokebox in August 1948 suggested that removal had already taken place. Further attempts to find a solution in January 1949 revolved around No. 34033 and an LMR-pattern spark-arrester, but it similarly adversely affected the steaming and was removed in June 1949.

The maximum cut-off in full forward gear was 70 per cent, which with the susceptibility to slipping when starting was probably overgenerous, but No. 34040 in October 1948 and Nos. 34011/5 in December 1948 had their valve-gear adjusted to give a maximum of 77 per cent. No information has been found concerning their performance while modified, although it is probably significant that by September 1950 they had all been returned to the lower figure.

Trouble was also met from hopper doors opening themselves on the road and causing damage to the permanent way. Usually this occurred as the locomotives came to a halt at stations or signals, although it was not unknown for the bump when coupling on to coaches to set the movement in action. No. 34063 welded itself to the third rail at Woking in December 1948, when one of the outside doors released itself while No. 34076 did the same at Brighton during the same month. As a result, modifications were made to the hopper doors of No. 34061 in February 1949 and when these proved successful they were applied to the remainder of the class.

Some concern was also felt because of the lack of dampers, with the result that Nos. 34004/5/6 had them fitted to the inside ashpans in May 1948, while later in the year and in early 1949 similar additions were made to Nos. 34002/11/5/40/56/61/4/76. Apparently few crews made use of them or were even aware of their existence and in most cases they were later removed. No. 34040, however, still retained its damper when working on the Somerset & Dorset line and had the reputation of being the poorest steamer of the batch stationed there. Probably most crews ran with it shut on a line which could well do without such refinements, steam and yet more steam being the criterion for working heavy trains over the Mendips.

The 1948 Exchange trials were very wisely not solely concerned with the performance of express passenger locomotives, but also included a selection of mixed-traffic and heavy freight classes. Officially the West Country pacifics were classified mixed traffic, and so it was that Nos. 34004/5/6 found themselves pitted against LMS Class 5 and LNER B1 4-6-0's over the Perth-Inverness and Manchester-St. Pancras lines and, with the addition of the Great Western Hall class, also between Manchester and Marylebone, and Taunton, Bristol and Plymouth.

Nos. 34004/5/6 had all been through works recently, but nevertheless they were called to Brighton Works in early April 1948 and carefully prepared for the trials as well as being fitted with V-fronted cabs, Flaman speed recorders, inside ashpan dampers, lengthened smoke-deflector plates and modified mechanical lubricators. At the same time the valve-gear was adjusted to give 80 per cent maximum cut-off and the drawgear, drag boxes and footplate altered to accommodate LMS 4,000-gallon tenders (Nos. 10411, 10346 and 10329), their provision being necessary because no water pick-up was carried by the Bulleid pattern and such equipment was essential away from the Southern Region. No. 34004 in addition had an opening cut in the left cab sidesheets and brackets fitted to take the tablet exchange apparatus required in Scotland. The locomotives remained malachite green, the paintwork being touched up as necessary, but following instructions from Headquarters the borrowed tenders had to be left black, a senseless economy considering the overall cost of the trials. Details of the routes worked are as follows:

Locomotive No.	*Period in Brighton Works*		*Route*	*Date LMS tender removed*
34004	2/4 to 26/5/1948		Perth-Inverness	24/7/1948
34005	5/4 to 28/5/1948		Manchester-St. Pancras	9/8/1948
34006	9/4 to 27/5/1948	(i)	Manchester-Marylebone	9/8/1948
		(ii)	Taunton-Bristol-Plymouth	

After a final polish and inspection at Nine Elms on the morning of 2 July 1948, No. 34004 *Yeovil* was worked across London to Willesden and in the evening piloted Royal Scot No. 6159 *The Royal Air Force* out of Euston with the 5.05 p.m. Holyhead express. Coming off at Crewe it proceeded over the West Coast main line to Perth, which in itself must have been an experience for men long-accustomed to the generally easily-graded and straight lines to Bournemouth and Salisbury. Single-track working was equally unfamiliar, and led to Driver Swain being more than usually dependent on the skill and knowledge of his pilotman when operating between Perth and Inverness, while further difficulties arose with the local dialect. However, after several misunderstandings and some speedy cornering, the word for "brake" sank home, and Swain took no chances and treated all slacks with excessive caution. Indeed, such was his reaction that much time and fuel had frequently to be expended in recovering time especially downhill, in contrast to climbing where time was readily gained.

The 4.00 p.m. Perth-Inverness was obviously chosen to test the capacity of locomotives in recovering from frequent stops, and in many instances up steep gradients. With its timing of 4 hours 19 minutes for the 118½ miles, it was no express and, apart from the 23½ mile Perth-Ballinluig section, stops were scheduled for every station except one. The southbound 8.50 a.m. was 50 minutes quicker, although with seven booked and two conditional stops it, too, had few pretensions of a "flyer". Banking assistance was provided from Blair Atholl to Dalnaspidal on the northward journey. Normally this involved the attachment of a pilot locomotive, but for the duration of the trials the test trains were banked, a system much disliked by local men who preferred to see the pilot locomotive and know that it was taking a fair share of the work. Ex-Caledonian Pickersgill 4-4-0's of doubtful mechanical order were usually provided for the task.

The week of preliminary running, therefore, presented Driver Swain and his partner with numerous operating problems, not least the use of the automatic tablet exchanging equipment. Frequently, such as through the loop at Murthly northbound, Swain was over-cautious and let his speed fall to 30 m.p.h. whereas the Class 5's maintained 50 to 55 m.p.h. and gained a useful run at the immediately following 1 in 82 bank to Kingswood. Other passing loops were similarly negotiated with excessive caution, while much of the downhill running fell far short of what was normally achieved. Nevertheless, time overall was maintained and frequently improved upon by hill climbing of a calibre hitherto unknown in the Scottish Highlands. Indeed, this had its amusing moments, especially up "The Hill" where banking assistance proved a doubtful asset on several occasions and on one a definite liability. The continuous ascent from Blair Atholl to Struan, out of which some three miles were at 1 in 80, would hardly suggest that the nine-minute allowance for the 4.4 miles was excessive, but Driver Swain gave every appearance of considering that this might very well be the case.

Coming south from Inverness with the 8.20 a.m., by far the severest test was the start itself, for after a brief spell of level running came the sharp uphill pull to the 105¼ milepost between Daviot and Moy. From post 117 for 2¾ miles this was at 1 in 60, flattening slightly to 1 in 70 to post 111¾, where a downhill "breather" of ¾-mile through Culloden Moor station and over the great viaduct preceded a second stretch of 1 in 60 which was continuous for 3¾ miles from post 111 to 107¼. Then, after a further easing of grade through Daviot station there followed a final 1¾ miles of 1 in 60 to post 105¼ before six miles of easier grades to Slochd Mhuic summit, altitude 1,315ft. The entire climb, therefore, extended over 21½ miles and could hardly be bettered in these islands for testing a boiler's capacity for continuous heavy steaming. After Aviemore, except for the steep 15½ mile climb from Newtonmore up the wild Glen Truim to Druimuachdar summit, the running was considerably easier, yet remaining very different to that found on the Southern Region. Passing loops remained a problem and it was not until the end of the trials that Swain was using his own judgement and taking them at normal speeds with consequent saving of fuel and time.

Despite the many problems No. 34004 *Yeovil* excelled itself on all its trains, although at the expense of enormous coal and oil consumption, strained frames and fractured oil-bath. On 13 July 1948, the climb from Blair Atholl to Struan was attacked with such vigour that not only was a maximum speed of 46 m.p.h. attained, but the 4-4-0 banker was so badly winded that it required all the Struan standing time to raise steam for the ascent to Dalnaspidal. 1¾ minutes were gained to Struan and another 11½ minutes to Dalnaspidal. No less than 1,548 drawbar horsepower was recorded at milepost 44, while for ten miles there was an average running drawbar output of 1,115 with the 1 in 70 climb being surmounted at an average speed of 36.3 m.p.h. Again on 14 and 16 July when starting up the final climb from Dalwhinnie to Druimuachdar drawbar horsepowers of 1,912 and 1,950 were exerted, while for five minutes continuously on 14 July there was an average running horsepower of 1,377 at the drawbar with a cut-off of 30 per cent. With such power at his disposal Swain acquired confidence rapidly and was able to gain time everywhere accept over the sharply booked short runs, of which the timings were observed meticulously despite occasional spells of slipping. Neither the LMS Class 5, nor the LNER B1 was able to generate a similar effort and on occasions both lost time and had difficulty with steaming.

In the report of the exchange trials full credit was awarded to No. 34004 *Yeovil* for its running and steaming, and the fact that the fireman experienced no difficulty in maintaining the full working pressure, but criticism was expressed of the dirty exhaust when coasting or working really hard, denoting incomplete combustion. Details of the average coal consumption and drawbar horsepowers are as follows:

Class	*Lb. of coal per mile*	*Per drawbar horsepower hour*	*Drawbar equivalent horsepower* *Newtonmore to Dalwhinnie*	*Dalwhinnie to Druimuachdar*
WC	**63.24**	**4.77**	**1,790**	**1,950**
5	48.28	3.90	1,130	1,160
B1	49.53	4.01	1,225	1,115

Argument might range at length as to which of the test courses offered the stiffest opposition for the crews and locomotives concerned. To Southern Region men the passing loops, severe gradients and curvature, and mountainous surrounds of the Perth-Inverness line presented much trouble, although relative to the power of the locomotives involved, especially the 4-6-0's, there was nothing harder than the two Manchester routes with the Marylebone-Manchester (London Road) line being marginally the toughest. It involved some 5½ hours of continuous steaming with gross loads of around 400 tons, and took trains over a summit of all but 1,000 feet above sea level, as well as presenting a climb of twenty miles at between 1 in 120 and 1 in 132 without a single "breathing space".

Once again Driver Swain was sent to represent the Southern Region, on this occasion with No. 34006 *Bude*, and again he did remarkably well, for of the four contestants he was the only one who succeeded and bettered the timings with test loads. Some of his starts, especially from Aylesbury going south were scintillating and a quality not equalled in normal service by Eastern Region locomotives. The climbing was of a similar high quality, although once more this, and the acceleration from stops, was gained at the expense of high fuel consumption, but Swain had the distinction of achieving two of the three highest drawbar horsepower figures of any locomotive in the entire series of tests. In running from Leicester to Rugby in 22 minutes 5 seconds start to stop on 11 June 1948, with a sustained 58 m.p.h. up the long 1 in 176 Ashby bank with 395 tons, No. 34006 gave a maximum drawbar horsepower of 2,010. The other occasion occurred three days earlier, when the acceleration from 20 m.p.h. at Hucknall up the 1 in 132 bank to 46 m.p.h. at Annesly gave a figure of 1,962. Passengers are not interested in fuel returns, only in punctuality, and in this *Bude* did Marylebone-Manchester travellers really proud. Fuel and horsepower details were as follows:

Class	*Lb. of coal per mile*	*Per drawbar horsepower hour*	*Drawbar equivalent horsepower* *Whetstone to Ashby Magna*	*Chalfont Bank*
WC	**50.29**	**3.90**	**2,010**	**1,962**
5	40.49	3.29	1,120	998
B1	41.80	3.32	1,102	1,015
Hall	46.75	3.84	1,156	1,262

Performance-wise, No. 34005 *Barnstaple* in the able hands of Driver James gave an equally exhiliarating account of itself between St. Pancras and Manchester where the easier running conditions of the old Midland main line were partially offset by a galaxy of permanent way checks. There was also the climb in either direction to Peak Forest (982ft.) with lengthy approaches of 1 in 100 to 1 in 90, although with loads averaging 330 tons this was considerably less daunting than the banks on the other Manchester route with trains of 380 to 395 tons.

The multitude of slacks south of Leicester invariably caused all locomotives to lose time, but elsewhere the West Country had little trouble with the test trains and gained time easily, in some instances as much as 17 minutes. It was also the fastest runner, both on the Matlock-Derby and Derby-Leicester sections, while 72 m.p.h. was attained at Little Eaton Junction, following the Ambergate slack, and the same speed again at Loughborough, after a stand for signals at Sawley Junction. Details of the coal consumption and horsepower developed were as follows:

Class	Lb. of coal per mile	Per drawbar horsepower hour	Drawbar equivalent horsepower Chinley to Peak Forest	Drawbar equivalent horsepower Market Harborough to Desborough
WC	**43.33**	**3.80**	**1,173**	**1,236**
5	38.15	3.71	1,186	1,138
B1	33.70	3.34	994	1,085

For the Taunton-Bristol-Plymouth test runs No. 34006 *Bude*, fresh from its exploits over the old Great Central main line was made available, in charge of Driver Snell. The Class 5, B1 and Hall proved more than masters of the Western Region schedules while the West Country was able to make light of them and gain time at will. On one journey it was held at Temple Meads West box some eleven minutes ahead of schedule from Taunton, while much of the hill climbing was of a quality expected of the Western Region Kings and Castles.

The main interest of this series of test runs undoubtedly concerned the fact that the five trial express locomotives also traversed the Taunton-Plymouth section of the route and thereby offered a direct comparison with the mixed-traffic classes on the West Country banks. The only concession granted the latter between Newton Abbot and Plymouth was a reduction in load from 350 to 265 tons gross. Related to the loads concerned No. 34006 *Bude* did better in both directions west of Newton Abbot than the Royal Scot, and often it was difficult to recall that the locomotive heading the train was one of Bulleid's light pacifics and not a Merchant Navy. Slipping there might have been, both at speed and when starting, but there was an abundance of steam. Details of the coal consumption and horsepower developed were as follows:

Class	Lb. of coal per mile	Per drawbar horsepower hour	Drawbar equivalent horsepower Wellington Bank (Down)	Drawbar equivalent horsepower Dainton Bank (Down)	Rattery Bank (Down)
WC	**52.97**	**4.28**	**1,450**	**1,452**	**1,426**
5	39.21	3.39	1,281	1,239	1,200
B1	46.92	3.96	1,336	1,250	1,207
Hall	46.91	4.11	1,235	1,130	1,130
MN	—	—	1,427	—	—
Duchess	—	—	—	1,865	1,817
Royal Scot	—	—	—	1,585	1,422
A4	—	—	1,390	1,481	1,728
King	—	—	1,380	1,472	1,371

Average details of the mixed traffic trials related to power output were:

Class	Lb. of coal per drawbar horsepower hour	Average water consumption lb. per drawbar horsepower hour	Average evaporation rate
WC	4.11	32.64	7.94
5	3.54	27.99	7.92
B1	3.57	27.64	7.68
Hall	3.94	29.97	7.69

In performance and boiler capacity the West Countries headed the mixed-traffic field, but the inefficient front end more than nullified any advantage offered by free steaming, and the class was convincingly beaten as regards fuel and water consumption. Lubricating oil also proved an expensive item, it being estimated that for every gallon supplied to an LMS Class 5 4-6-0, no fewer than 7.4 gallons were required by the pacifics.

The policy of transferring the West Country series away from the Eastern Section continued in 1948 with the despatch of Nos. 21C122/7/8/9 to Exmouth Junction in February, which left only Nos. 21C130/1/2 at Ramsgate and Nos. 21C133/4/5/7/8/9/40 at Battersea. No. 21C136 was also a Battersea locomotive, but being engaged in the oil-burning trials was absent on the Western Section. In the summer the seven Battersea locomotives, assisted by Battle of Britains Nos. 21C153/4/7/62/3, formed the mainstay of the Continental services with No. 34039 *Boscastle* in late July, August and September having charge of the Golden Arrow. On West Countries working this express, the large arrows attached to the air-smoothed casing could be accommodated below the nameplates, but this was not possible with the Battle of Britains and before the arrows could be mounted the plaques carrying the coats of arms had to be lowered.

However, the long West Country reign was rapidly drawing to a close, for with the arrival new of Nos. 34073 to 34076 at Battersea, Nos. 21C133, 34034 and 21C135 were transferred away to Brighton and service on the Bournemouth, Cardiff and Plymouth through trains. No. 34034 worked down to Brighton from London on 28 September 1948, with the 4.50 p.m. via Uckfield and was the first pacific to use that route since the initial running in trips of 1945. New Battle of Britains from Brighton Works also made appearances on these through trains, in particular the Bournemouth, but even so failures frequently necessitated the use of Schools.

By November 1948 the "Golden Arrow" was once more being worked by unnamed pacifics, at first Nos. 34074/5/6 and later, Nos. 34083/4 fresh from Brighton Works. The West Country allocation also showed further changes with Nos. 34033/4 and 21C135 moving on to Salisbury; Brighton in exchange receiving Nos. 21C137/8 and 34039/40. No. 34036, the oil-burner, remained working trials from Eastleigh shed.

A second Pullman car express commenced operation on the Eastern Section on 31 May 1948, this being the "Thanet Belle" consisting of first-class cars *Formosa* and *Coral*, and thirds Nos. 11/5/6, 96, 132/3/5/7. Trial runs were made between Waterloo and Basingstoke on 28 May when a series of emergency stops were made at speeds ranging from 45 to 75 m.p.h. and a number of starts made from signals and stations without the use of sanding. No. S21C170 *Manston* worked both up and down trains on the first day. The timing was as follows:

Dep. Victoria	Sundays and weekdays	11.30 a.m.	Saturdays	3.05 p.m.
Arr. Ramsgate	Sundays and weekdays	1.34 p.m.	Saturdays	5.15 p.m.
Dep. Ramsgate	weekdays	5.05 p.m.	Sats./Suns.	6.15 p.m.
Arr. Victoria	weekdays	7.10 p.m.	Sats./Suns.	8.20 p.m.

Stops were booked for Whitstable, Herne Bay, Margate and Broadstairs.

In 1951 the title was changed to "Kentish Belle" and on summer Saturdays four journeys were run. Patronage varied greatly and on occasions was extremely poor, but the service was maintained until electrification. Probably over the years a greater variety of locomotives was involved than with any other Pullman express, for, in addition to the light pacifics, the Merchant Navies, King Arthurs, Schools, Maunsell 2-6-0's and BR Class 5's made regular appearances. C class 0-6-0's from Faversham were also not unknown, in their case as pilots for ailing pacifics.

In the late summer of 1949, pacifics commenced appearing on relief Newhaven Continentals, No. 34038 being noted on the 6.14 p.m. up express on 28 August 1949. About the end of the year, by some extraordinary aberration, authority was granted for the class to enter Newhaven locomotive yard, which was truly astonishing, since the King Arthurs had always been rigidly excluded from traversing the sharp curve into the depot, while the Schools had only been reluctantly accepted in 1948 and only when driven with the utmost caution. However, the traffic department accepted the concession at face value, although at first having no occasion to make use of it, for no relief Continentals were running in mid-winter and electric locomotives were working the main trains. Therefore, it was Easter 1950 before the privilege was tested with Nos. 34083/4/5 all heading specials to Newhaven and grinding their way slowly into the unfamiliar precincts of the motive power depot. On 12 April 1950, the inevitable occurred. No. 34085 left the road at the critical spot and closed the depot for several hours. The ban was immediately re-imposed and the interlude was over for ever.

With the completion in November 1947 of No. 21C170, the intention was to commence construction of a further twenty locomotives at Brighton Works under order 3383. Boilers were available, but delays and difficulties in obtaining steel for the frames, coupled wheels and cylinder castings made it necessary to postpone assembly until the spring of 1948. The tenders were built in the old paint shop at Ashford Works at the rate of four a week and, after being painted malachite green, were sent to Lancing for storage until required by Brighton Works. The cost averaged £1,030, excluding TIA equipment. The locomotive frames were also cut and prepared at Ashford while Eastleigh machined the cylinders and supplied the bogies, motion, brake gear, steam reversers and cabs.

The first six locomotives were commenced as Nos. S21C171 to S21C176, but were changed to 34071 to 34076 as construction progressed, although the motion of Nos. 34071/2/3 retained the Bulleid notation when despatched to traffic. Details are as follows: 1948 Nos. 34071 *601 Squadron*, 34072 *257 Squadron* (April) 34073 *249 Squadron*, 34074 *46 Squadron* (May), 34075 *264 Squadron*, 34076 *41 Squadron* (June), 34077 *603 Squadron*, 34078 *222 Squadron*, 34079 *141 Squadron* (July), 34080 *74 Squadron* (August), 34081 *92 Squadron*, 34082 *615 Squadron* (September), 34083 *605 Squadron* (October), 34084 *253 Squadron*, 34085 *501 Squadron* (November), 34086 *219 Squadron*, 34087 *145 Squadron*, 34088 *213 Squadron*, 34089 *602 Squadron* (December); 1949 No. 34090 *Sir Eustace Missenden, Southern Railway* (February). No. 34071 was originally named *615 Squadron*, but in August 1948 this was changed to *601 Squadron*, the name intended for No. 34090, and as a result of these exchanges No. 34082 became *615 Squadron* instead of *66 Squadron* and the last-mentioned plates were held in reserve until January 1951, when they were issued to the final Bulleid pacific, No. 34110.

Most ran their trials in works grey with small white cabside numerals, the malachite green livery being applied before entry to general service. Nos. 34071 to 34081 had painted front numerals, but from No. 34082 smokebox door numberplates were fitted, in the first instances with painted numerals as well. No. 34090 *Sir Eustace Missenden, Southern Railway* was specially painted for its naming ceremony at Waterloo station on 15 February 1949, the wheels being malachite green instead of black with yellow tyres and the hubs outlined with a narrow yellow line. The tender carried the new British Railways lion-and-wheel emblem, the wheels remaining black, but the tyres were painted yellow to match the locomotive. The nameplates were curved and of the scroll pattern used on the West Country class while the plaques carrying the Southern Railway coat of arms were of Battle of Britain type, although having the longer axis horizontal. Below were curved scrolls lettered *Southern Railway, Battle of Britain Class.*

These twenty locomotives were the first genuine Battle of Britains, being fitted with 9ft.-wide V-fronted cabs and large 5,500-gallon $47\frac{1}{4}$-ton tenders in addition to numerous modifications found necessary through operating experience. These included fire protection plates, ashpan water sprays, flexible main steampipes, long smoke-deflector plates, strengthened smokeboxes and modified front-end stretcher layout. TIA was standard equipment, although delivery delays made it necessary to complete Nos. 34074/5/6 with untreated feed water, the omission being rectified in November 1948. The smokebox top was modified, making the chimney visible from broadside while the large circular ownership-date plates were omitted from the smokebox doors. An additional electric light was provided at the rear of the tender to ease the task of coupling-up in the dark, a fitting much appreciated by firemen, and one which was added in the course of time to many of the 4,500-gallon tenders.

Nos. 34071/82/3 entered traffic with second-hand boilers, these previously having been carried by Nos. 21C124, 21C121 and 21C127 respectively, while No. 34089 from 31 December 1948, to 11 March 1949, ran attached to 4,500-gallon tender T3290. This was the result of delays in constructing the 6,000-gallon tenders for Merchant Navies Nos. 35021 to 35030 and the decision to despatch these locomotives to traffic with borrowed light pacific tenders, details being as follows:

Tender No.	*Type*	*Merchant Navy Class*		*Transferred to*
3260	4,500-gallon	35026	4/12/1948-18/12/1948	34039 5/8/1949
3288	4,500-gallon	35027	11/12/1948-25/3/1949	34060 11/5/1949
3333	5,500-gallon	35021	11/9/1948-13/11/1948	used on MN No. 35024
3333	5,500-gallon	35024	13/11/1948-31/1/1949	34089 11/3/1949
3335	5,500-gallon	35022	9/10/1948-31/12/1948	34090 1/2/1949

Tender T3260 after removal from No. 35026 was damaged in Eastleigh Works yards and was not returned to service until August 1949, a delay of some eight months.

The weight in working order of this series was marginally greater than Nos. 21C101 to 21C170, details being:

Locomotive No.	34075
Date	13/8/1948
Location	Brighton
Condition	3in. water in glass, a light fire, and 190 lb./sq. in. pressure
Bogie	16T 4C
Leading coupled wheels	19T 5C
Centre coupled wheels	19T 16C
Trailing coupled wheels	19T 4C
Trailing wheels	13T 9C
Locomotive	87T 18C
Tender (fully laden)	47T 15C
Locomotive and tender	135T 13C

The same locomotive and 4,500-gallon tender T3290 when weighed at Eastleigh Works in September 1957 gave 88 tons 2 cwt. and 42 tons 14 cwt. respectively.

Nos. 34071/2 went new to Dover where they replaced Nos. 21C156/7 on the Continental services; Nos. 34073 to 34082 and 34086 to 34090 were sent to Ramsgate and Nos. 34083/4/5 to Battersea. Shortly after delivery Nos. 34073/4/5/6 were transferred to Battersea and with Nos. 34083/4/5 took over the Continental expresses, including the "Golden Arrow". As this Pullman express rated a smartly-turned-out locomotive, it was normal practice to reserve one or two Battle of Britains for the duty to ensure the required standard was always maintained, thus it was that this important task befell Nos. 34083/4. Both gave an excellent account of themselves until the evening of 9 December 1949, when No. 34084 at the head of eight Pullmans, a bogie van and a container truck was approaching Victoria station some twelve minutes late. As it traversed the facing cross-over from the up main to up relief line at about 10 m.p.h., it overtook and converged on light engine No. 34085 which was travelling equally slowly along the up relief line. Both crews observed the danger, but unfortunately too late to avoid a collision, which derailed No. 34085 and tilted it over at an angle of 35 degrees towards the down local line along which the 6.40 p.m. Victoria-East Croydon electric was travelling at about 35 m.p.h. The front portion of the latter passed clear, but the rear six coaches fouled the projecting smoke-deflector plate at waist level, smashing thirty-one windows and injuring eight passengers and the guard. The crew of the light engine also suffered injury, but the "Golden Arrow" escaped unscathed. Damage to the two locomotives was as follows: No. 34085 broken right cylinder casting, motion casing fittings and cab side sheeting wrecked, and smokebox pierced; No. 34084 main frames and platework buckled, left-hand cylinder fractured, main steampipe fractured and a mud plug sheared off the firebox, which led to the boiler discharging its contents on to the track and over-heating of the firebox plates. At the subsequent enquiry, it was found that the driver of the light engine had passed signals at danger and was solely to blame for the accident. Apparently he had gained the impression that No. 34085 was running along the up main line and had read the signals accordingly, whereas it was on the up relief line and should have stopped, awaiting the "Golden Arrow's" passage into the terminus. The total damage was estimated at £13,800, including repairs to the track and signalling equipment.

The construction of Nos. 34071 to 34090 in the first year of Nationalisation created little comment or surprise, since much of the material had obviously been ordered by the Southern Railway. However, when authority was granted in March 1949 for a further twenty light pacifics, many eyebrows were raised, partly because few could accept the necessity of 140 pacifics on the Southern Region, but mainly on account of their well-known heavy fuel consumption at a period when every winter brought its coal and energy crisis. Visitors to Devon and Cornwall were well accustomed to seeing West Countries daily traversing the lines to Plymouth, Ilfracombe and Padstow at the head of two or three coaches, while elsewhere most major running sheds for much of the year appeared to have surplus of the class cluttering up the yards. What justification was offered for the construction of more will probably never be known, but it must have been remarkably potent since the decision was reached with the minimum of delay.

Brighton Works was to construct all twenty under order No. 3486, with the frames being cut at Ashford, and the cylinders, bogie, motion and steel fireboxes at Eastleigh. The 5,500-gallon tenders were to be shared by Brighton and Ashford, but in fact all were built at the last-mentioned works and, after storage for a time at the nearby wagon works, were transferred to Lancing to await the call to Brighton. Some left Ashford painted grey and others in the standard dark green.

Some delay was met in obtaining steel for the fireboxes and chains for the valve-gear which was probably as well, for Brighton was heavily engaged at this period with the first three Bulleid Leaders class locomotives. Being of a completely new, unorthodox and highly sophisticated design, the demands on the various departments were great and were not much reduced when the first commenced its lengthy and not particularly successful trials in June 1949. As a result, the frames of Nos. 34091/2/3 were not set up until May 1949, and even then progress was so slow that assistance had to be requested from Eastleigh where the works manager very wisely avoided involvement with the Leaders and restricted his aid to the assembly of the six pacifics, Nos. 34095/7/9/101/2/4. Entry to traffic was therefore protracted, and with modifications planned for No. 34110 adding to the delay, it was January 1951 before all were at work, details being as follows: Brighton Works 1949 Nos. 34091 *Weymouth*, 34092 *Wells*, later *City of Wells* (September), 34093 *Saunton*, 34094 *Mortehoe* (October), 34096 *Trevone* (November), 34098 *Templecombe*, 34100 *Appledore* (December); 1950 Nos. 34103 *Calstock* (February), 34105 *Swanage*, 34106 *Lydford* (*March*), 34107 *Blandford*, later *Blandford Forum*, 34108 *Wincanton* (April), 34109 *Sir Trafford Leigh-Mallory* (May); 1951 No. 34110 *66 Squadron* (January); Eastleigh Works 1949 Nos. 34095 *Brentor* (October), 34097 *Holsworthy* (November), 34099 *Lynmouth* (December); 1950 Nos. 34101 *Hartland* (February), 34102 *Lapford* (March), 34104 *Bere Alston* (April). All were members of the West Country class, except the last two, Nos. 34109/10, which received Battle of Britain names. Like Nos. 34055/6/7/64/5/6/7/8/9/70, No. 34109 *Sir Trafford Leigh-Mallory* carried Royal Air Force badges below its nameplates, but by the time No. 34110 *66 Squadron* entered traffic in early 1951 the contractor providing badges could no longer do so, for the craftsman preparing them had retired and no replacement could be found. As a result nameplates only were carried.

The frames of No. 34110 *66 Squadron* were set up at Brighton in March 1950, but following a directive from Marylebone no further work was undertaken for several months while a number of alternative designs making use of the Bulleid boiler, tender and other major items were investigated. Two proposals are known to have received serious consideration, both having the working pressure reduced to 250 lb., a cylindrical smokebox, single blastpipe and conventional boiler clothing, but differing as regards cylinder and motion layout. The design most favoured envisaged the use of two 20in. by 28in. outside cylinders and standard Walschaerts valve-gear, while the other made use of the Bulleid cylinders and three independent sets of valve-gear. Unlike the Jarvis rebuildings of later years, both proposals necessitated the provision of new frames and because of this were rejected, so No. 34110 *66 Squadron* left Brighton Works on 26 January 1951, a standard member of the Battle of Britain class.

Generally, this final pacific series followed Nos. 34071 to 34090 and included all the modifications experience had proved necessary with the earlier locomotives. No. 34101 had no rocking section to the grate, it being drop only, while Nos. 34093 to 34110 had round, bottom hinged covers to the sand-filler chutes. To close, two screws had to be rotated and, as these were frequently left undone, the covers hung open and in time broke the hinges. As a remedial measure stronger hinges were provided at the top, but this offered no solution and the standard sliding flaps were introduced, these having given reasonably good service on Nos. 34001 to 34092.

The average costs of the various batches were as follows:

Order No.	*Locomotive Nos.*	*Date*	*Cost*
2421/2561	21C101 to 21C130	1945/46	£17,060
2885	21C131 to 21C145	1946	£19,145
3213	21C146 to 21C170	1946/47	£20,220
3383	34071 to 34090	1948/49	£22,108
3486	34091 to 34110	1949/51	£24,784

Comparative costs of British Railways Class 7 4-6-2's and Class 5 4-6-0's were £17,520 and £16,618 respectively.

With the entry to traffic of No. 34109 in May 1950 the allocation became:

Running shed	*West Country Class*	*Battle of Britain Class*
Nine Elms	—	34049 to 34065
Bournemouth	34093/4/5, 34105 to 34108	34109 (also 34110 later)
Exmouth Junction	34001/2/4/5/6/7/8/9/10/14 to 20/4 to 32/44/5/6/7/8	—
Salisbury	34022/3/33/4/42/3	—
Plymouth	34003/11/2/3/21	—
Battersea	34091/2, 34101/2/3/4	34066 to 71/4/5/6/83/4/5
Ramsgate	34096 to 34100	34077 to 34082/6 to 90
Dover	—	34072/3
Brighton	34035 to 34041	—

Two types of tender were built for the light pacifics, details being as follows:

Locomotive Nos.	*Tender Nos.*	*Width*	*Capacity*	*Class*
21C101 to 21C148	3251 to 3298	8ft. 6in.	4,500 galls.	West Country
21C149 to 21C170	3299 to 3320	8ft. 6in.	4,500 galls.	Battle of Britain
34071 to 34090	3321 to 3340	9ft. 0in.	5,500 galls.	Battle of Britain
34091 to 34108	3351 to 3368	9ft. 0in.	5,500 galls.	West Country
34109/10	3369/70	9ft. 0in.	5,500 galls.	Battle of Britain

Tenders were not allotted in strict numerical order while the ten missing numbers, 3341 to 3350, were filled by the 6,000-gallon tenders supplied to Merchant Navies Nos. 35021 to 35030.

All the 4,500-gallon tenders gave considerable trouble, not only from corrosion, but also from split welds, bulging plating and buckled washplates. Most at one time or another were partially renewed, fitted with additional and stronger washplates and otherwise strengthened while three, together with one of 5,500-gallon capacity were completely rebuilt in 1958/60. Their details are:

Tender No.	Date rebuilt	Locomotive No.	Remarks
3261	2/1959	34046	retained until condemned
3273	3/1960	34059	retained until condemned
3313	1/1959	34039	transferred to No. 34104 8/1965
3354	12/1958	34031	transferred to No. 34087 4/1965

The tanks of these four tenders were 9ft. 0in. wide and could readily be recognised from other cut-down tenders by means of the higher side plating, rectangular manhole covers, BR-pattern lockers, more robust rear ladders and the small oval plates denoting the tender numbers sited on the opposite side to those of the genuine Bulleid tenders. The official capacity was 5,250 gallons and the loaded weight 46 tons 16 cwt., but when put to test on 4 December 1958, tender 3354 was found to hold 5,324 gallons and to weigh:

Leading wheels ..	14T 18C
Centre wheels ..	16T 2C
Trailing wheels ..	16T 18C
Total ..	47T 18C

The original intention had been to work the West Country class over the Tonbridge-Hastings line and for this purpose the width of the cab and tender was restricted to 8ft. 6in. to suit the load gauge of that route, but, apart from a brief visit in 1945 no use was made of the facility, and when the Battle of Britain class was introduced in mid-1947, the opportunity was taken, first to widen the cab to 9ft. 0in. and, commencing with No. 34071 the tenders also, which incidentally increased the capacity to 5,500 gallons.

Although tenders were regularly exchanged in works and on the running sheds, it was not until locomotives were rebuilt from 1957 that Nos. 34001 to 34070 could be seen working with large-capacity tenders.

Like the Merchant Navy class the high tender plating proved too restrictive when taking coal and water, and in 1952 three tenders had the raves cut down to give easier access, details being as follows:

Tender No.	*Capacity*	*Date*	*Locomotive No.*
3263	4,500 galls.	9/1952	34011
3280	4,500 galls	11/1952	34065
3310	4,500 galls.	6/1952	34043

Aesthetically the removal of the raves was a disaster, but in practical terms it took away much of the tedium when refuelling which makes it a mystery why no others were similarly modified before 1957. Then, as locomotives were rebuilt, they received cut-down tenders, if possible of the larger 5,500-gallon variety. Around the same time a start was made in cutting-down tenders belonging to unrebuilt locomotives. Eventually 105 tenders were cut-down, leaving only Nos. 34069/72/4/5/8 with the high-sided variety. All were condemned in 1963/64 when the tender from No. 34075 was transferred to No. 34080 in exchange for its modified type.

The allocation of tenders on 30 June 1961, after rebuilding had ceased was as follows:

4,500-gallon	*Rebuilds:* Nos. 34008/9/24/32/4/6/40/56/8/60/2/77/88/9/90/3/6/8, 34100/4/8/9.
	Non-rebuilds: Nos. 34002/6/7/11/5/9/20/3/30/3/5/8/41/3/9/51/4/5/7/61/3/4/5/6/7/8/9/70/2/3/4/5/6/9/80/1/3/4/6/92/4, 34103/5/8/10.
5,250-gallon	*Rebuilds:* Nos. 34031/9/46/59.
5,500-gallon	*Rebuilds:* Nos. 34001/3/4/5/10/2/3/4/6/7/8/21/2/5/6/7/8/9/37/42/4/5/7/8/50/2/3/71/82/5/7/8/95/7, 34101.
	Non-rebuilds: Nos. 34078/91/9, 34102/7.

Altogether one hundred and twenty boilers were provided for the light pacifics, twelve apiece coming from Eastleigh Works and the North British Locomotive Company and ninety-six from Brighton Works. The North British series was ordered (D6917) on 30 January 1946, and on delivery between July 1946 and April 1947 were fitted on Nos. 21C139/41/4/8/50/8/60/2/4/6/7/9, the cost being £3,210 each. The twelve Eastleigh-built boilers came in two batches, ten at £3,480 each in 1945/46 for Nos. 21C101/5/7/9/12/4/6/20/2/35 and two at £3,620 each in 1950 as replacements on Nos. 34055/64. Those built at Brighton ranged in price from £3,140 to £3,575, with an average of £3,360. No. 21C101 when under construction was fitted with Brighton-built boiler 1261, but this developed faults during steaming trials and was replaced by 1266, the first Eastleigh-built boiler. After repairs, boiler 1261 was transferred to No. 21C110, where it remained until December 1947 when the mileage stood at 93,464. Nos. 34071/82/3, were completed with reconditioned boilers which had previously seen service on Nos. 21C124, 21C121 and 21C127 respectively.

By the time that the first West Countries entered service in mid-1945 much experience in the handling of steel firebox boilers had been expensively acquired and this was bestowed to such advantage that only two completely new fireboxes had to be provided before the end of steam locomotion in July 1967. Details of these two boilers are as follows:

Boiler No.	*Date new*	*First locomotive*	*Firebox renewed Date*	*Firebox renewed Mileage*	*To locomotive No.*
1290	5/1946	21C130	7/1960	615,471	34077
1330	4/1947	21C160	9/1954	300,744	34089

From the beginning, adequate time was allowed for cooling before boiler washouts commenced, while the early introduction of TIA and the allocation of so many locomotives to the West Country where soft water was available materially reduced wear and tear and maintenance costs. No. 21C166 in September 1947 was the first new locomotive to carry TIA, and No. S21C131 in February 1948 the first of those in traffic to be equipped. To conserve fireboxes, a policy was introduced of allocating TIA locomotives to areas of hard water, and of transferring those awaiting equipment to Exmouth Junction. In 1955-7 the simpler, but equally effective, British Railways system was substituted. The reduction of working pressure from 280 to 250 lb./sq. in. undoubtedly also played a significant part in this conservation. Trials commenced with No. 34093 in March 1951 and when these disclosed no readily noticeable loss of power or performance, the reduction was applied to Nos. 34011/43/53/65/9 in 1952 and to the remainder during 1953-6.

As built, all boilers carried three safety-valves on the barrel top ahead of the dome, these being sited triangularly with two side-by-side preceding the third. However, commencing with No. 34082 in April 1952, the latter was removed and the other two recessed into the barrel top, while in June 1952 No. 34089 not only lost its apex safety-valve, but had the remaining pair resited on the rear of the barrel where surging caused by braking was less likely to involve any discharge of water to the atmosphere via the safety-valves. This became the standard positioning of safety-valves from February 1953, often in conjunction with the reduction of working pressure to 250 lb./sq. in.

Two West Country boilers were commenced as spares by Eastleigh in May 1951 but not completed until August 1953, when both were installed as stationary boilers at Ashford, one in the Locomotive Works and the other in the Carriage & Wagon Works. By October 1967 both were derelict and by January 1969 had been removed for scrap.

In early 1949, Marylebone became aware that the Southern Region possessed many more pacifics than could be gainfully employed except on summer Saturdays. As a result the transfer of fifteen light pacifics was advocated to the Great Eastern section of the Eastern Region, where use of ex-LNER pacifics was prohibited and expresses had to be entrusted to 4-6-0's of classes B1, B2 and B17. To explore the feasibility of the suggestion, Battle of Britain No. 34059 *Sir Archibald Sinclair* was transferred on loan to Stratford on 27 April 1949, and set to work on the following services:

28 and 29 April	to Witham
2 to 6 May	Norwich via Ipswich (9, 12 and 9 coaches), Yarmouth South Town (9 coaches), Parkeston Quay (13 coaches).
9 to 13 May	Norwich via Ely (8 and 9 coaches), Norwich via Ipswich (12 coaches), empty carriage workings at Liverpool Street, Clacton (12 coaches).
16 to 20 May	Clacton, Norwich via Ipswich (12 coaches) and returning via Ely, the "Norfolkman" (11 coaches), Parkeston Quay (13 coaches), Cambridge.

With the exception of the 18 and 20 May all services were specials and ran from Stratford. The "Norfolkman" shared with the "East Anglian" the fastest current schedules, although these were appreciably slower than the best of 1939. On 18 May No. 34059 reached Ipswich 4½ minutes late on the down run with a load of eleven coaches, three more than standard, and after taking water left seven minutes behind time. Coming back later in the day three minutes were dropped to Norwich and another 2¼ taking water, but smart running thereafter gave a Liverpool Street arrival only 1¾ minutes late. A similarly fast run was made with the 8.20 a.m. to Cambridge on 20 May, when 3½ minutes were made up en route following a severe permanent way slack and adverse signals. Like all foreign locomotives, there were various grumbles by the crews, mainly concerning the severe slipping, insensitive regulator, heavy fuel and water consumption, and poor cab lookout. All appreciated the great reserve of power, smooth riding, free-steaming boiler, excellent turn of speed and, most surprisingly, the steam reversing-gear. No water pick-up was fitted to the tender; if it had, then much of the anxiety concerning water and time spent at stations would have been avoided. No. 34059 was last seen at Liverpool Street on 26 May, and on 30 May 1949 it was back at work on the Waterloo-Bournemouth expresses.

Nothing more was heard of transfers to the Eastern Region until April 1951, when thoughts turned to replacing B1's on many of the secondary express services in East Anglia. As a result, No. 34039 was despatched to Stratford on 8 May 1951, where it was shortly followed by Nos. 34057/65. At first they were employed on the Liverpool Street-Cambridge trains, but later appearances were made on the "Norfolkman" and the Parkeston Quay Continentals. Once again the reception was mixed, with some crews doing well and others equally badly. Parkeston men fully appreciated their free running and probably had a better understanding of the class than crews from other sheds.

Actually, their assignments to the Eastern Region proved unexpectedly fortuitous when on 22 October 1951, all Britannia pacifics were abruptly removed from traffic for inspection following the mechanical failure of No. 70004 *William Shakespeare* at Headcorn with the "Golden Arrow". In batches they were sent away to Crewe for modification, and it was the end of the year before much reliance could be placed on their services, their loss in part being filled by the additional transfer of Nos. 34076/89. During November and December 1951 these regularly appeared on the Cambridge services, but Nos. 34057/65 spent most of their time on the "Day Continental" and the "Scandinavian" as well as other boat expresses. No. 34039 roamed more widely and on one occasion was noted at Doncaster, as well as gaining notoriety for being the first pacific of any variety to visit Bury St. Edmunds. This occurred on 16 July 1951, when it arrived with the 12.45 p.m. local passenger from Ipswich. It was too large for the turntable and, after coaling, had perforce to return tender-first with the 3.05 p.m. No. 34039's appearance was the result of the locomotive rostered for the 10.30 a.m. Liverpool Street-Cromer failing at the last minute and being hurriedly replaced by the West Country which had already worked the 4.30 a.m. newspapers to Ipswich and the 7.50 a.m. back to Liverpool Street. No time was available for coaling so, not unexpectedly, Ipswich was reached with insufficient fuel to continue to Norwich, and B1 No. 61049 had to be substituted. Fortunately, the crew had anticipated this, and by arriving 2¾ minutes early ensured that the exchange could be made without loss of time. The B1 was rostered for the Bury St. Edmunds local train and since no other locomotive could be found, No. 34039 had once again to be commandeered and, after some anxious moments reached its destination with very little coal in the tender. These exploits so amused the Stratford running foreman that he investigated the tonnage of coal burnt and concluded that around 51 lb. per mile had been consumed.

Once all the Britannias had returned to traffic, the Eastern Region expressed no desire to retain the Bulleid pacifics permanently, and No. 34089 was returned to the Southern Region at the end of December 1951 where it was followed by No. 34039 in January, No. 34076 in April, and Nos. 34057/65 in May 1952. Officially the high coal consumption and the retention of non-standard spares was offered as the reason, but the constant shuttling to and fro between Nine Elms and Stratford of boilersmiths and fitters and their dislike by many crews probably had a greater bearing on the rejection.

In 1950 much greater use was made of the class on the Oxted line with frequent appearances being made on the 6.58 a.m. Brighton-Uckfield-London Bridge and the 4.50 p.m. Victoria-Brighton services. Occasional visits were also made to the mid-Sussex line, an instance on Easter Monday being No. 34069 *Hawkinge* with an excursion to Bognor Regis from Leyton. More interesting was the use of No. 34050 *Royal Observer Corps* on 9 August 1950, with the "Devon Belle" Pullman stock and observation car on a sightseeing special from Waterloo to Chichester. Towards the end of the year Brighton pacifics were being rostered for additional night working to London, this being the 12.30 a.m. Brighton-Bricklayers Arms goods and the 5.31 a.m. London Bridge-Brighton vans.

The severe weather of January 1951 saw the country once more engulfed in a fuel shortage and with the three through trains from Brighton to the west being temporarily cancelled, other duties had to be found for the West Countries. Nos. 34035/6 had recently been transferred to Plymouth which left five, Nos. 34037 to 34041, to hand. For a time they were rostered for the 10.18 a.m. Brighton-Victoria via Uckfield and the 3.25 p.m. return service, but later much of their time appeared to be spent around the shed yards or partially dismantled being leisurely repaired. As a result in May 1951 Nos. 34037/8/9 were sent away to Plymouth and Nos. 34040/1 to Bath, and when the through trains were reinstated U1 class 2-6-0's were entrusted with their working until found inadequate, when Brighton received Nos. 34045 to 34048 from Salisbury.

At this period the Southern Region had charge of the running sheds at Bath, Templecombe, Branksome and Highbridge, and was operating the difficult Somerset & Dorset line with a variety of borrowed LMR locomotives, an arrangement fraught with problems and one unlikely to appeal to either participant, which led to No. 34109 *Sir Trafford Leigh-Mallory* complete with tablet exchange gear, being given trials over the line during March 1951. The first week was mainly spent in charge of stopping trains including the 11.40 a.m. Bournemouth West-Bath, but when the "Pines Express" recommenced running on 19 March it was deputed for the task. On the first day, with eleven coaches to Bath and ten back, assistance was given over Masbury Summit and several tablet exchanges were missed, but no time was lost to Bath, while 2½ minutes were gained on the reasonably tight schedule back to Bournemouth West. Later, ten coaches were taken unaided in both directions, although Masbury proved so taxing that a 270 tons restriction was instigated between Evercreech Junction and Bath, this being the same as for the nominally less-powerful Class 5 4-6-0's. No. 34109 was never short of steam, but slipping made it difficult for crews to make use of the power available, especially in bad weather.

Considering the lack of experience with Bulleid pacifics of the men handling No. 34109, the trials were accepted as reasonably successful and in May 1951 Nos. 34040 to 34044 were sent to Bath for the summer services. Various other Bournemouth locomotives also appeared, while No. 34037 was on loan for several weeks. The "Pines Express" was regularly worked, as were most of the other major duties.

Like most foreign locomotives, they were not universally liked, Bath crews hating them while the men at Branksome and Templecombe tolerated them. On the road all agreed their ability and reliability was much inferior to that of the Class 5's, while the totally-enclosed cab was found dirty, noisy and often unbearably hot. Coal also proved a problem, for five tons was totally inadequate to cover the 143 mile return journey between Bath and Bournemouth West, unless the firebox was filled to capacity before leaving the coal road, the tender packed by hand and some five hundredweight extra stacked on the footplate. It was also essential regularly to clean out the coal bunkers to ensure large pockets of compressed dust did not reduce the capacity. Should only five tons of fuel be consumed, then 79 lb. was being fed into the firebox for every mile run; therefore, the remarks of No. 34043's fireman after reaching Bath with the "Pines Express" that 100 lb. of coal had been burnt per mile was probably no great exaggeration. The 4,500-gallon tender capacity also proved less than generous and on summer Saturdays could add greatly to the crews' anxiety.

Before the class reached the Somerset & Dorset, the grapevine had made footplate staff fully aware of the frequent oil fires, and set them on their guard. However, for a time nothing serious occurred, but then came the day when No. 34040 *Crewkerne* had charge of the up "Pines". All went well until Radstock when much of the locomotive and the cab floorboards burst into flame, and assistance had to be summoned from the local fire brigade. In his report the driver suggested that red-hot particles of metal flung off the brake shoes had caused the conflagration by becoming embedded in the oil-encrusted boiler lagging. At first this fresh appraisal of the long-outstanding phenomenon was viewed with scepticism, but further investigation showed that many very small and short-lived fires did follow periods of heavy braking and in favourable circumstances a number combined to create a major outbreak. As a result Eastleigh investigated the efficiency, longevity and spark propensity of LMR and London Transport brake shoes and in course of time introduced a pattern which proved both longer wearing and less liable to disintegrate under severe usage.

At Brighton much trouble was met in maintaining the local batch of West Countries in good mechanical order and available to work the through services to Bournemouth, Cardiff and Plymouth. Indeed, on 1 June 1952, Nos. 34046/7/8 were all stopped, and Schools No. 30922 *Marlborough* had to be borrowed from Battersea to work the Cardiff and Plymouth on 2 and 3 June, while on the two following days it was transferred to the Bournemouth train. Very reluctantly on 6 June it had to be returned to Battersea and took charge of the 5.42 p.m. Angmering-Victoria vans before resuming its relief Newhaven boat train duties. No. 42105 headed the Cardiff on 5 June and No. 42088 on the following day, when Atlantic No. 32421 *South Foreland* was taken out of store, steamed and for the next two weeks set to work on the Bournemouth. During this motive power crisis Nos. 34039/45 had accepted their share of the through services, although No. 34045 was obviously ailing and regularly lost time before finally succumbing with valve gear trouble on the down Plymouth. Thereupon No. 30415, one of the two surviving Drummond L12's, was deputed to complete the duty and such was Brighton's dilemma that it was retained for the Cardiff on 11 June and the Bournemouth on the following day. The final blow occurred on 11 June when the last active pacific, No. 34039, was in collision at Salisbury and retired to Eastleigh Works for attention. To fill the breach Brighton had to call upon the services of No. 34049, U No. 31805, H2's Nos. 32421/5/6 and 2-6-4 tanks Nos. 42903, 80016/37/9.

The same summer saw the class being rostered for the Saturday through trains from Brighton to the London Midland Region, while on 5 November 1952 the 6.10 Victoria-Uckfield was hauled for the first time, with No. 34104 *Bere Alston* heading a strengthened train of ten corridors because of the Edenbridge Bonfire celebrations. Restrictions on the Bluebell line were also lifted and on 22 March 1953 No. 34071 *601 Squadron* was used on an eleven-coach ramblers' excursion from Victoria to Sheffield Park. In course of the next two years other appearances were made on this route, usually with the 11.02 a.m. Brighton-East Grinstead-Victoria on which, for example, No. 34039 *Boscastle* was noted on 6 February 1954. During the summer of 1953 there were fairly regular troop movements between Victoria and Crowborough, at fortnightly intervals, with the usual routine being for a Battersea pacific to work the 5.20 a.m. Victoria-Tunbridge Wells West on Saturday morning, thence to run light to Crowborough to take the special up to Victoria with soldiers leaving the camp. On Sunday the same, or another, pacific would take a fresh load of troops down to Crowborough, run light to Tunbridge Wells West and return home with the 7.45 p.m. Victoria. Amongst others Nos. 34069/89/101/4 were used.

Having at some length mentioned the failings of the Brighton pacifics, it is only fair to place on record that those at Exmouth Junction, Salisbury, Ramsgate and Nine Elms gave infinitely better service, while those at Battersea, after a very mixed beginning, later gave an excellent account of themselves. Yearly mileages on the Southern Region, because of relatively short distances, were seldom as great as those of the other Regions, but nevertheless many of those recorded by individual locomotives in 1952 were most creditable, details being as follows:

Running shed	*Average mileage worked by Light Pacifics*
Ramsgate	51,213
Salisbury	50,489
Exmouth Junction	49,727
Plymouth	49,611
Nine Elms	42,437
Battersea	42,064
Bournemouth	34,586
Brighton	19,618

The moral was obvious, if high yearly mileages were to be achieved, then much time and labour had to be granted the class. This under normal circumstances was only possible at the smaller depots or those fortunately possessing a full quota of fitters.

On 24 April 1954, electric locomotives 20001/2 were under repair and when the third failed at Southeram with the 9.31 a.m. Victoria-Newhaven, Brighton was ordered to provide a substitute. The only West Country available at short notice was No. 34045 *Ottery St. Mary*, and it was despatched to Newhaven in time for the 5.15 p.m. to Victoria, a mammoth sixteen-vehicle train of 535 tons booked at the accelerated electric schedule. Net time was kept, but the crew had to fight furiously throughout the 73-minute journey and left behind them an impressive trail of lineside fires. This locomotive continued to work these services, though on 26 April No. 34017 *Ilfracombe* headed the 5.15 p.m. and No. 34045 *Ottery St. Mary* the 5.48 p.m. relief boat. With enterprising crews some excellent running was made, but time was occasionally lost and on 27 April easier schedules were introduced and the load reduced to 500 tons. No. 20003 returned to traffic on 29 April, but again failed and on 2 May No. 34077 *603 Squadron* was employed. It was in excellent fettle and with a keen crew cut the steam timing by 2¾ minutes, apparently with few of the usual lineside conflagrations.

In preparation for the state visit of Emperor Haile Selassie of Ethiopia a trial special was worked with a light pacific from Portsmouth & Southsea (Low Level) to Victoria (Eastern Section) via the direct line to Guildford and thence by way of Effingham Junction, Leatherhead and Tulse Hill. Proving successful No. 34088 *213 Squadron* was provided on the day itself, 4 October 1954, when the train consisted of Pullmans *Minerva*, *Orion*, *Phoenix*, *Aries* and *Isle of Thanet*, and a vestibuled van. The six-minute late start was easily recouped by Guildford, and thereafter it was a case of spinning out time to ensure an arrival exactly to schedule. In addition to the royal headcode a large headboard was carried with the Union Jack and Ethiopian flag, and the Emperor's royal arms. The visitors' baggage accidentally missed the special and had to be loaded on to two vans and taken on to Waterloo by No. 34071 *601 Squadron*, the Portsmouth standby locomotive. Other standby locomotives were provided at Petersfield (No. 34005 *Barnstaple*), Guildford (No. 34012 *Launceston*) and Epsom (No. 34017 *Ilfracombe*). Emperor Haile Selassie ended his visit on 28 October 1954, and travelled to the Continent from Victoria, again behind No. 34088 *213 Squadron*.

Also of note during 1954 was the arrival of BR Class 5 4-6-0's Nos. 73050/1/2 on the Somerset & Dorset in mid-summer. Throughout the holiday months they shared the heaviest expresses with the LMR Class 5's and Nos. 34040/1/2, but in the early autumn replaced the West Countries at Bath and the latter were transferred to Eastleigh. There they appeared at once on the London turns, hitherto the province of the Lord Nelsons, as well as on the Docks specials and van services.

The allocation at the end of 1954 was as follows:

Nine Elms Nos. 34005/6/7/8/9/10/1/2/8/9/20/63/4; Bournemouth Nos. 34043/4/93/4/5/105/6/7/8/9/10; Eastleigh Nos. 34040/1/2; Brighton Nos. 34039/45/6/7/8; Salisbury Nos. 34049 to 34057; Plymouth Nos. 34035/6/7/8; Exmouth Junction Nos. 34001-4/13-6/21-34/58-62/9; Battersea Nos. 34017/65-8/70/1/87-92, 34101-4; Ramsgate Nos. 34075-86/96-9, 34100; Dover Nos. 34072/3/4.

Returning to the Central Section and to the ASLEF strike of June 1955, No. 34045 *Ottery St. Mary* was Brighton's only pacific at work. Although it had no regular duties, it worked ten-coach trains between Brighton and Victoria or London Bridge on three days, and on another it went to Newhaven and worked the 7.20 a.m. to Victoria and 10.05 a.m. return. These ran for most of the strike period, with an electric locomotive and a Newhaven crew, but on this day these men were having their rest period. The 10.05 a.m. was the boat train, with additional stops introduced for local passengers, while the 7.20 a.m. up was a rather exotic commuter service, formed of fifteen vehicles including first, second and third class accommodation, and having the unusual amenity of a bicycle van. This may not have carried many bicycles, but at least it afforded valuable standing room for travellers from Horley who were unable to force their way into more normal parts of the train. On one occasion 87 passengers and a dog are reputed to have emerged from the said van at Victoria.

On 17 July 1955, a pacific made its first appearance on the Heathfield line, No. 34066 *Spitfire*, working a ramblers' excursion from Victoria to Heathfield, and thence ECS to Polegate. Thereafter they made occasional appearances over the line with excursions and other specials, but not any regularly diagrammed duties north of Hailsham.

Another first on 13 November 1955, was the appearance of No. 34090 *Sir Eustace Missenden* at Weston-super-Mare with an excursion from Brighton. Not only had a pacific never before been seen there, but it was also the first visit of a Southern locomotive since pre-war when Bournemouth T9 4-4-0's worked through regularly with specials via Templecombe and Highbridge.

Although not strictly entitled to such acclaim, Bulganin and Kruschev on 18 May 1956 were accorded all the panoply of royal train operation when they travelled by rail from Portsmouth Harbour to Victoria via Guildford, Epsom, Tulse Hill and Herne Hill. Indeed, the stock provided—seven Pullman cars—was more lavish than normally supplied by the Southern Region for a "royal" over a comparable distance. No. 34092 *City of Wells* had charge with No. 34101 *Hartland* standing at Portsmouth, No. 34019 *Bideford* at Petersfield and No. 34102 *Lapford* at Epsom to cover any emergencies. All were beautifully cleaned, in particular *City of Wells* which carried the spare buffer beam with highly burnished shackles and buffers retained for such duties, it being quicker to exchange buffer beams than to polish the components of the locomotive detailed for royal duty.

The temporary withdrawal from traffic on 12 May 1953 of the Merchant Navy class because of suspect driving axles cast suspicion on those carried by the light pacifics and when the larger locomotives were available again later in the month, a start was made on examining all 110 members of the class with ultrasonic crack detecting equipment at Nine Elms, Battersea, Bricklayers Arms and Exmouth Junction motive power depots in addition to Eastleigh and Ashford Works. In the majority of cases withdrawal of the axle and wheels proved unnecessary and examination was swift, but where doubt existed a second test was given after removal. Altogether eight axles failed to satisfy the examiners, although only two were considered faulty, the others being replaced in the interests of safety. The locomotives concerned were Nos. 34004/24/7/9/33/4/101/7. During the inspection period Battersea had the loan of B1 4-6-0's Nos. 61015/41/50, 61109/33/8/48/88/92, 61219/73/4, 61329/38/54 and Nine Elms Class 5 4-6-0's Nos. 45051/61, 45130, 45216/22/3, 45350, 73003/15/7, while Exmouth Junction had Nos. 34040/1/2 from Bath and Nos. 34069/70/92 from Battersea. Since only a limited number of pacifics were withdrawn from traffic daily not all the B1's were required by Battersea and some were returned to the Eastern Region within a week. Probably Whit-Monday, 25 May, was their busiest day when Nos. 61133/48/88/92, 61273 all reached Ramsgate in the space of a few hours. The previous day two were used on Central Section workings, No. 61273 took over the Leicester-Brighton day excursion at Clapham Junction, while No. 61274 worked the 9.05 a.m. Victoria-Newhaven boat express. By the third week of June all had been sent away.

The whistle gear frequently gave trouble on the earlier West Countries but seldom caused a complete failure on a train such as occurred to No. 34012 *Launceston* with the "Bournemouth Belle' on 13 January 1953. Apparently, the driver sounded his whistle approaching Woking and it remained in full voice until Basingstoke where he stopped for a change of locomotive, but on being offered U class No. 31798 decided to release the whistle mechanism himself. Unfortunately his enthusiasm was ill-rewarded, for he slipped and broke his leg, so a spare driver as well as a locomotive had to be hastily summoned. No. 31798 gave of its best and by fast downhill running reduced the lost time at Southampton Central to 17 minutes, where No. 30852 *Sir Walter Raleigh* took over to Bournemouth Central and No. 30746 *Pendragon* to Bournemouth West. In the evening the Lord Nelson ran the "Belle" up to Waterloo to time. As a result of this accident, all the earlier West Countries had their whistle gear modified to give more positive operation.

Potentially much more serious was the affray between No. 34050 *Royal Observer Corps* and Z class No. 30954 on 4 April 1955. Soon after 11.00 p.m. the former was entering the yards at Exmouth Junction with the 7.45 p.m. goods from Yeovil Junction when it came into violent collision with the yard shunter, No. 30954, which was running slowly along the same line. Both suffered considerable damage to their cylinders and valve-gear, while the casing of the pacific was badly crumpled. Complete re-railing was not effected until late the following day, after they had been towed apart. Meanwhile, up freight trains were dealt with at Exeter Central and the down at Exmouth Junction down sidings, which normally were reserved for departmental wagons. The track was also badly damaged and a temporary length had to be laid down to release the wagons which should have formed the 12.01 a.m. Exmouth Junction-Launceston goods. Nos. 30954 and 34050 required attention at Eastleigh Works, the former being replaced temporarily at Exmouth Junction by No. 30956.

The 1.55 p.m. Meldon Quarry-Salisbury stone train was regularly worked by a light pacific of Salisbury shed, usually without undue trouble, but on 21 November 1956, No. 34049 *Anti-Aircraft Command* stalled in Blackboy Tunnel on the 1 in 100 climb out of Exeter Central to Exmouth Junction. The train consisting of ten bogie hoppers and a brake van, vacuum fitted throughout, ran back and the rear three vehicles derailed at the catch points. This occurred at 3.55 p.m. and single line working was in force until 9.00 a.m. the next day. In his report the driver stated that slipping commenced part way up the bank and became so violent that he lost control of the train and was only regaining it as the slip points were reached. Blame was placed on ineffective sanding, but inspection proved three of the four sand containers to be empty.

No. 34088 *213 Squadron* was involved in an unusual accident at Herne Hill on 30 June 1957, when in charge of the eleven-vehicle 8.55 a.m. Victoria-Dover Marine Continental express. The distant signal was passed at caution and the speed reduced to 30 m.p.h. in preparation for stopping at the home signal, but for some reason the driver failed to do so and a collision occurred with Schools No. 30921 *Shrewsbury* at the country end of the station. No derailment occurred, but the latter was pushed back 300 yards and had its tender badly damaged while No. 34088 received a crushed front end and minor damage to seven coaches. The Schools was running light engine from Battersea MPD to Eardley and was just starting away from Herne Hill along the Tulse Hill line when the fireman saw the express and warned his driver who minimised the collision by opening the regulator fully and attempting to gain speed. Two passengers and the driver of the light engine were injured.

Much more disastrous was the St. John's accident on 4 December 1957, when in fog, No. 34066 *Spitfire* with the delayed 4.56 p.m. Cannon Street-Dover business express ran into the rear of the 5.18 p.m. Charing Cross-Hayes electric at 30 m.p.h. The latter was running late and had been held at Parks Bridge Junction signals to the south of St. John's station for nine minutes when the Dover train crashed into the rear, crushing the cab and guard's compartment, driving the next coach forward into its neighbour, causing some telescoping, breaking of windows and ripping away of the bodywork. The guard was killed instantly, but other casualties were remarkably light and the crash would not have been serious if the pacific's tender and the following carriage had not struck the girders supporting the flyover bridge carrying the electrified tracks of the Nunhead-Lewisham line. These immediately collapsed dropping the bridge across the tender and first two Dover train coaches, crushing them almost to track level as well as removing half the roof of the third coach and superficially damaging the fourth. A third train, the 5.22 p.m. Holborn Viaduct-Dartford electric, was about to pass over the flyover, but was halted in time to prevent it plunging down on to the wreckage. About 770 passengers were aboard the Dover train and some 1,480 on the Hayes electric, and of these 90 were killed and 108 seriously injured; the greater majority in the two crushed coaches.

Rescue operations were badly hampered by fog, darkness and the unsafe condition of the bridge which threatened to collapse further if any movement was made in the vicinity. Indeed, for several hours no clear information was available as to what exactly had happened, and practically all services in North Kent had to be suspended. By 10.45 p.m. all the injured had been removed to hospital, but the last bodies could not be extricated from the wreckage until 12.30 a.m. on 7 December. Emergency breakdown and engineering gangs in attendance came from Nine Elms, Ashford, Hither Green, Bricklayers Arms, Tonbridge and Beddington Lane. During the night of the accident the seven undamaged Dover train coaches were towed clear and the front six Hayes cars removed to Grove Park, while later the seventh electric car was released, and the third and fourth coaches of the Dover train were cut free and also towed away. On the following day, skeleton services were run over most routes, but the Blackheath-Charlton trains remained suspended and shuttle services catered for the Addiscombe, Sanderstead and Bromley North branches.

As far as main-line trains were concerned, the pattern of services resembled those providing during the first few weeks following the Cannon Street signalbox fire. One or two coastal trains terminated at Chatham or Tonbridge in the morning and returned from there in the evening, but the majority of the Charing Cross and Cannon Street business services ran to and from Victoria, including the Hastings line diesel sets. A few departed from Victoria (Central) and travelled via Redhill, one being the "Man of Kent". Some improvement was possible on the 9th, but otherwise these arrangements remained substantially unaltered until the morning of 12 December, when all main lines were re-opened, the wreckage of the flyover having been cut away and removed. Fog, however, still persisted and with the stock completely disorganised it was several days before services approached normal during the morning and evening rush hours. As soon as possible, work was commenced on constructing a temporary flyover at Lewisham, and by shift working and the introduction of labour from throughout the Southern Region it was ready for traffic on 13 January 1958, and enabled the restoration of the North Kent and Holborn Viaduct services.

At the subsequent enquiry it did not take long to discover the cause of the disaster. No. 34066's driver had passed a double yellow signal and then a single yellow before commencing to brake as he picked out the third signal at danger. He thought he was travelling much slower than his actual speed, had worries about the water supply and was driving a locomotive equipped for left-hand operation over a section of line intended for driving from the right-hand side of the footplate. These factors, together with the fog, must have let his mind wander, with the result that he crashed into the rear of the stationary electric train. Driver Trew was judged entirely to blame for the occurrence and later was tried for manslaughter at the Old Bailey, but the jury failed to agree. He was sent for re-trial, although by this time his health and mind were failing rapidly, and after a petition from his home town of Ramsgate the prosecution was dropped.

No. 34066 was not badly damaged, the visual scars being mainly restricted to the motion, front running plate, top cowling, front of the casing and the smoke-deflector plates. The tender, however, was badly crushed and cost £487 to repair. It was returned to service from Eastleigh Works on 22 March 1958.

In early 1956 it was decided to rebuild the light pacifics in a similar manner to Merchant

Navy No. 35018 *British India Line*. Seventy-five locomotives were scheduled for reconstruction, although in view of main line electrification the final total was reduced to sixty, details being as follows:
1957 Nos. 34001/3/5/13/7/22/5/7; 1958 Nos. 34004/12/4/6/8/21/6/8/9/31/7/45/7/50/2/3; 1959 Nos. 34010/39/42/6/8/62; 1960 Nos. 34008/32/4/6/40/4/56/8/9/60/71/7/82/5/7/8/9/90/3/100/1; 1961 Nos. 34009/24/95/6/7/8/104/8/9. The general policy was to transfer the large-capacity 5,500-gallon tenders to the rebuilds and to retain the 4,500-gallon pattern for those not rebuilt on the assumption that their daily work would be less onerous. In time, however, with only forty of the larger variety available, this proved impracticable and the scheme was abandoned, leaving non-rebuilds Nos. 34078/91/9/102/6/7 with their 5,500-gallon tenders.

In 1952, to give easier access for coaling and watering, the tenders of Nos. 34011/43/65 had their raves cut away, but no others were similarly modified before commencement of the locomotive rebuilding scheme in June 1957. From then all rebuilds left Eastleigh Works with cut-away tenders and this modification was also applied from February 1958 to the tenders of those locomotives not rebuilt, although Nos. 34069/72/4/5/8 worked until withdrawal in 1963/64 with high-sided tenders. After being condemned, the tender from No. 34075 was salvaged and transferred to No. 34080 in April 1964 in exchange for its damaged cut-down variety, so it too ended its days with a Bulleid-contoured tender.

The locomotive rebuilding programme did not deter Eastleigh Works from keeping those not so favoured abreast of modern engineering practice provided that this was possible without major modifications or expense. From mid-1959 the advanced warning system was fitted, evidence being displayed by the battery casing below the smokebox door, while in 1959/60 speed recorders appeared on all members of the class, rebuilds and non-rebuilds alike, and in 1960/61 Nos. 34038/61/84/6/92/102 received new pattern pistons and crossheads. A spark arrester was fitted experimentally to No. 34045 in June 1957, but badly affected the steaming and was removed at rebuilding the following year although the scheme was not abandoned, for in modified form the equipment reappeared on No. 34075 in February 1959, was transferred to rebuild No. 34026 in October 1961 and to another rebuild No. 34101 in February 1964. More noticeable in December 1959 were modifications to the draughting of Nos. 34035/49 which involved the removal of the smoke-deflector plates and the joining of the side casing to the top cowling, thereby giving the front end a more rounded appearance. Apparently little was gained, as no others were similarly modified.

In the autumn of 1957 Plymouth lost Nos. 34035/6/7/8 to Exmouth Junction and no longer could provide the motive power for the Brighton train which on summer Saturdays had taken the Plymouth light pacific right through. This was the longest continuous locomotive working on the Southern Region; the 200 miles compared with the other Regions was not remarkable, but lasted six hours, and included twenty intermediate stops and the passage of Meldon, Honiton, and Hewish banks. The load seldom exceeded eight coaches, but water with the 4,500-gallon tenders of Nos. 34035/6/7/8 caused problems at the height of the holiday season when delays were inevitable. Henceforth Exmouth Junction provided the motive power, while in 1959 the Plymouth Friary station closure and the starting of the train from North Road reduced the distance by about three miles.

No. 34066 *Spitfire* on 30 May 1958 worked the first journey of the Glasgow-Eastbourne car sleeper which became a rostered Battersea pacific duty, with Nos. 34067/8/77/87/9/91/2 also taking a turn during the summer. There was a lengthy lay-over at Eastbourne and use was made of this to cover any special requirements locally.

Another new pacific duty commenced on 15 September 1958, this being the 6.10 p.m. Victoria-Uckfield with a long history of "time lost by engine" and the source of more complaint letters than any other train on the Region. At once there was a complete transformation with before-time approaches to Oxted highlighting the shortcomings of the preceding 5.49 p.m. Victoria-East Grinstead-Groombridge which was always late away from Oxted but previously had not inconvenienced the following train. So the 5.49 p.m. took up the mantle of the problem child until two BR Class 4 4-6-0's were sent to Three Bridges to take over its working from the 2-6-4 tanks. The 6.10 p.m. formed part of a Brighton pacific duty which commenced with the 4.55 a.m. Brighton-Eastbourne newspapers, then the 8.16 a.m. Eastbourne-Hailsham and the 8.45 a.m. return, before working back to Brighton at 10.30 a.m. with the through Birkenhead and later taking the 1.55 p.m. to Victoria via Uckfield.

With the start of the 1959 winter service the long-established 3.25 a.m. newspapers and passenger London Bridge to Brighton and Eastbourne was divided into two trains leaving at 3.20 a.m. and 3.27 a.m. respectively.

Both were entrusted to Brighton pacifics, these working up together with the 11.18 p.m. parcels to London Bridge. After arrival at Eastbourne the locomotive off the 3.27 a.m. continued with the 8.16 a.m. Hailsham, etc. Although an impressive sight, the use of two such locomotives on the 11.18 vans was hardly economical and in November 1959 the duties were adjusted so that a Bricklayers Arms West Country rebuild took over the 3.27, including the Hailsham duty, and worked back to London with an evening goods. About the same time, Brighton pacifics commenced working the 5.08 a.m. London Bridge-Brighton via Dorking and Steyning, their first diagrammed duty over that route.

A derailment at Horley on 8 April 1960 caused the diversion of the 4.14 p.m. Newhaven Harbour-Victoria via Uckfield and Oxted and the provision of No. 34008 *Padstow* from Lewes. This was almost its last duty in Bulleid form, as it went into Eastleigh Works shortly afterwards for rebuilding and when returned to traffic in July 1960 was the first of its kind to be stationed at Brighton.

The completion of Stage 1 of the Kent Coast electrification scheme on 18 June 1959 inevitably curtailed steam operation in the South-East, with Ramsgate losing its pacifics and Battersea and Dover most of their main line express duties. Steam remained over the Tonbridge route although there was a gradual change of motive power, and by the summer of 1960 most of the Charing Cross/Cannon Street to Dover/Ramsgate passenger services were being worked by diesel locomotives. Electric and diesel locomotives shared the Chatham line Continentals, leaving those running via Ashford the East Section's last stronghold of express steam. With the return of colder weather and the need for carriage heating in the autumn a greater use was made of steam on the business services, but this was only a final fling, for on 12 June 1961 the completion of Stage 2 saw multiple-units running via Tonbridge and Ashford.

Transfers were numerous, with Dover sending No. 34073 to Nine Elms and Nos. 34061/70/83 to Ashford where few suitable duties could be found, and within days they were on loan to Battersea for service on the Central Section. Bricklayers Arms shed closed in mid-1962 when its duties were shared between Battersea, Norwood and Brighton, while steam virtually ceased on the Central Section in September 1963 when Battersea also closed its doors to steam and Brighton lost its entire pacific allocation.

In addition to the routine oil-bath fires the non-rebuilds were involved in a number of incidents around this period including yet another derailment at St. Denys. On 29 October 1959 No. 34020 *Seaton* was heading the 6.30 p.m. Weymouth-Waterloo express when it overran the up slow home signal and at the sand drag derailed itself, embedding the front end in the ramp of the up main platform. Damage was not serious, although the interference with the point rodding and signal wiring rendered much of the local signalling inoperative and hampered other traffic for some hours. The passengers were detrained remarkably swiftly and transferred to a following partially empty boat train which was rescheduled to stop at stations booked for the unfortunate 6.30 p.m. from Weymouth. The stock was drawn back to Bevois Park sidings to give the Eastleigh crane access to Nos. 34020 but it proved inadequate for the task, and the following night assistance was sought from the Salisbury crane with re-railing finally being accomplished in the early hours of 1 November 1959. Rebuild No. 34022 *Exmoor* came to grief in similar circumstances on 12 December 1960, the driver having also misread the signals and paid the penalty.

A landslide on the Somerset & Dorset line on 5 December 1960, caused the re-routing of the "Pines Express" via Fordingbridge, Salisbury, Bristol and Westerleigh Junction, and the interesting sight of No. 34102 *Lapford* working throughout from Bournemouth West to Birmingham New Street. It stabled overnight at Saltley and returned next morning with the southbound "Pines" using the same route and had to come off at Bournemouth Central, as the last coal had been fired at Highcliffe. The distance of some 182 miles was not excessive despite the heavy load, but undoubtedly the Saltley crew on the first stage of the journey over-fired as LMR crews always appeared to do with the Bulleid pacifics, and little care was taken before leaving the depot to ensure a full load of coal had been placed in the tender. Southern Region men faced with such a task would have hand-packed the last ton or so.

Changes in the regional boundaries were frequent, and those on 30 December 1962 gave control of the depots at Exmouth Junction, Yeovil Town, Barnstaple and Wadebridge to the Western Region, and with them some 160 Southern Region locomotives. These included Nos. 34002/11/5/20/3/30/3/5/63/5/6/9/70/2/4/5/6/8/9/80/1/3/4/6/106/7/10, all at Exmouth Junction. The remaining non-rebuilds were shedded at Nine Elms Nos. 34006/7/64/73/94, Salisbury Nos. 34049/51/4/67/8/91/2/8, Eastleigh Nos. 34038/61, Brighton Nos. 34019/55/7, and Bournemouth Nos. 34041/3/102/3/5.

Over the years the FA Cup caused many

interesting and unusual workings, though seldom to the extent of Southampton's semi-final match with Birmingham City on 27 April 1963, when a veritable armada of specials was necessary to convey fans from various Hampshire stations. Twelve took both varieties of light pacific through to Snow Hill, nine running via Reading, Oxford and Leamington Spa behind Nos. 34028/40/2/5/50/2/88/94/8, and three via Oxford, Worcester and Kidderminster with Nos. 34009/39/46. A thirteenth special was worked throughout by No. 7919 *Runter Hall*, while another ran over the Somerset & Dorset with No. 34067 *Tangmere* as far as Bath, and a final one was taken via Salisbury to Bristol by No. 34041 *Wilton*. As if this was not adequate for a spring Saturday, another more modest football engagement took No. 34017 *Ilfracombe* from Christchurch to Swindon, and the Schoolboys' International at Wembley necessitated yet another special from Poole which ran as far as Watford behind No. 34102 *Lapford*. Despite the strain placed on Southern Region resources all the fans were in their places long before kick-off and returned home within a few minutes of schedule and, what is more, no complaints were received of unseemly behaviour or vandalism, despite the cup-tie result.

As far as the non-rebuilds were concerned, Eastleigh Works ceased giving general repairs at the end of 1962, the last being Nos. 34061 *73 Squadron* 3 November, 34092 *City of Wells* 24 November, and 34007 *Wadebridge* 8 December 1962. Thereafter, most repairs were of a casual or light intermediate category, but the following locomotives received heavy intermediate repairs and a repaint: 1963 Nos. 34006/15/23/30/3/41/54/63/70/2/6/8/84/102/7; 1964 Nos. 34019/38/57/64/9/79/86/103; No. 34019 *Bideford* in October 1964 being the final repaint.

Mileages run between general overhauls in 1954 to 1962 by those in original condition were most impressive and not inferior to the rebuilds, details being as follows:

Locomotive No.	*Period between general repairs and boiler change*	*Mileage run*
34002	7/1956 to 2/1962	287,239
34007	6/1956 to 12/1962	289,698
34023	3/1956 to 2/1962	305,967
34033	1/1957 to 1/1962	236,248
34035	10/1954 to 10/1959	247,047
34054	6/1954 to 9/1959	228,370
34061	12/1955 to 11/1962	299,239
34064	4/1956 to 4/1962	290,622
34091	4/1955 to 6/1961	157,555
34092	10/1955 to 10/1962	203,663
34099	2/1956 to 9/1961	245,861
34103	9/1955 to 10/1961	236,182
34105	3/1956 to 5/1962	254,181
34106	5/1956 to 4/1961	243,025
34107	5/1956 to 5/1961	253,923
34110	9/1955 to 6/1958	147,966

Nevertheless, thought was being given to withdrawal and when No. 34055 *Fighter Pilot* failed with the 11.00 a.m. Brighton-Cardiff near Chichester on 22 April 1963, it was laid aside and later condemned. At the time Nos. 34035/43/63/74/84 were in store at Exmouth Junction and except for Nos. 34063/84 were similarly withdrawn, while Nos. 34011/49/67/8/9/110 followed before the end of the year. Final mileages and disposal were as follows:

Locomotive No.	*Withdrawn*	*Final mileage*	*Disposal*
34011	11/1963	800,455	broken-up Eastleigh Works 4/1964
34035	6/1963	764,306	broken-up Eastleigh Works 4/1964
34043	6/1963	749,112	broken-up Eastleigh Works 9/1963
34049	12/1963	723,947	broken-up Eastleigh Works 6/1964
34055	6/1963	706,607	broken-up Eastleigh Works 5/1964
34067	11/1963	688,269	sold Woodham Bros., Barry; still extant 1974
34068	12/1963	700,417	broken-up Eastleigh Works 3/1964
34069	11/1963	673,643	broken-up Eastleigh Works 5/1964
34074	6/1963	639,592	broken-up Eastleigh Works 5/1964
34110	11/1963	609,147	broken-up Eastleigh Works 3/1964

The record cards of Nos. 34011 *Tavistock* and 34110 *66 Squadron* make interesting and contrasting reading, details being as follows:

No. 34011 *Tavistock*
New — Brighton Works, 13/10/1945
Boiler — No. 1270
Tender — No. 3272

Date to Works	*Works*	*Type of repair*	*Mileage since last general repair*	*Boiler No.*	*Date to traffic*
31/3/1948	Eastleigh	general	103,246	1279	26/5/1948
6/12/1948	Brighton	casual	17,320	1279	30/12/1948
6/1/1950	Exmouth Junction	light casual	68,024	1279	19/1/1950
8/8/1950	Eastleigh	light intermediate	89,683	1279	8/9/1950
12/8/1952	Eastleigh	general	167,832	1267	27/9/1952
31/3/1954	Eastleigh	light intermediate	72,858	1267	30/4/1954
25/8/1955	Eastleigh	light intermediate	143,328	1267	17/9/1955
16/3/1956	Eastleigh	light casual	174,299	1267	31/3/1956
9/10/1956	Eastleigh	weighing	179,663	1267	18/10/1956
5/7/1957	Eastleigh	general	208,577	1371	24/8/1957
6/11/1958	Eastleigh	heavy intermediate	77,429	1371	6/12/1958
24/2/1960	Eastleigh	light intermediate	141,357	1371	26/3/1960
22/1/1962	Eastleigh	light intermediate	239,159	1371	17/2/1962
21/11/1963	Proposed for Works, mileage run since 17/2/1962 81,641.				

Withdrawn 30/11/1963, broken-up 11/4/1964. Total mileage run to 31/10/1963 800,455.

No. 34110 *66 Squadron*
New — Brighton Works, 26/1/1951
Boiler — No. 1379
Tender — No. 3370

Date to Works	*Works*	*Type of repair*	*Mileage since last general repair*	*Boiler No.*	*Date to traffic*
9/11/1951	Eastleigh	light casual	43,894	1379	7/12/1951
20/5/1953	Eastleigh	casual	107,609	1379	20/5/1953
11/6/1953	Eastleigh	heavy intermediate	113,418	1379	31/7/1953
8/6/1954	Brighton	light casual	161,095	1379	16/7/1954
3/8/1955	Eastleigh	general	199,208	1277	17/9/1955
6/12/1955	Eastleigh	light casual	13,368	1277	17/12/1955
5/2/1957	Eastleigh	light intermediate	74,483	1277	23/2/1957
10/6/1958	Eastleigh	general	147,966	1336	2/8/1958
28/12/1959	Eastleigh	heavy intermediate	80,816	1336	23/1/1960
26/10/1961	Eastleigh	light intermediate	173,963	1336	9/12/1961
9/10/1963	Proposed for Works, mileage run since 9/12/1961 88,010.				

To store unserviceable 9/10/1963, withdrawn 22/11/1963, and broken-up 28/3/1964. Total mileage run to 31/8/1963 609,147.

AVERAGE YEARLY MILEAGE:	No. 34011	44,469
	No. 34110	47,478

The lower yearly figure for No. 34011 was probably accounted for by its lengthy stay at Exmouth Junction and Plymouth, whereas No. 34110 spent the majority of its working life at Bournemouth, where the Waterloo expresses offered longer daily mileages.

In September 1963 Battersea ceased operation as a steam depot and Brighton's pacifics departed to Salisbury, while in November the Western Region returned rebuilds Nos. 34024/32/6/56/8/60/108 to the Southern Region in exchange for non-rebuilds Nos. 34049/54/61/7/8/84. Steam operation was rapidly drawing to an end in the West Country and on 7 September 1964 all the Waterloo expresses, the through Brightons, and many of the semi-fasts changed to diesel haulage. For a time most of the freight services remained steam but except for the Bude-Okehampton-Padstow trains, diesel multiple units took the stoppers. As a result the Western Region withdrew Nos. 34020/30/54/78/80/106/7 and transferred Nos. 34002/23/33/76/9/84/6 to Eastleigh and Nos. 34015/66 to Salisbury. Altogether during 1964 twenty non-rebuilds were condemned, Nos. 34020 /30/54/70/8/80/3/106/7 by the Western Region and Nos. 34061/5/72/3/5/81/91/2/4/9/105 by the Southern Region, and this left a mere twenty in service.

Rail tours during 1964 involved several members of the class, including No. 34066 *Spitfire* which on 22 March took over the "Sussex Downsman" at Tunbridge Wells West for the run over the Cuckoo line to Pevensey where it came off and worked light engine to Brighton in preparation for taking the special up to Victoria via Uckfield later in the day, when a maximum of 73 m.p.h. was achieved near Edenbridge.

Another tour, the "Cornubian" of 3 May, commemorated the departure of steam from the main line through Cornwall and took No. 34002 *Salisbury* from Plymouth over the Brunel bridge to Penzance and back while a third on 9 May saw No. 34038 *Lynton* working the "East Midlander" from Didcot to Eastleigh over the DN & SR line. Later it headed the returning 400-ton special as far as Swindon via Romsey, Salisbury, Westbury and Chippenham, and gave participants an exhilarating journey. More sombre was the task that befell No. 34051 *Winston Churchill* on 30 January 1965, when called upon to work the funeral train carrying the renowned wartime leader to his last resting place at Bladon in Oxfordshire. It was immaculately prepared for the duty and with the five Pullmans and a bogie van was a credit to British Railways, and in particular to the Southern Region. No. 34064 *Fighter Command* was standby at Staines Central while No. 34057 *Biggin Hill* stood spare at Nine Elms in case of a last-minute failure at Waterloo. On account of this journey and the interest created it was decided to preserve No. 34051 *Winston Churchill* and when withdrawal occurred with a mileage of 807,496 in September 1965, it was set aside in store pending preservation and display at the new Transport Museum, York. In addition, Nos. 34007/33/63/84/103, were also condemned in the year.

By Easter 1966 the Bournemouth line electrification works were making rapid progress and with the influx of diesel locomotives the number of main-line steam duties had been substantially reduced, especially on Sundays when it was possible to stand at Waterloo and not see or hear a single steam locomotive. Apart from Nos. 34002/38 of Nine Elms which regularly appeared with Ocean Liner expresses, the non-rebuilds were seldom seen in London. Very occasionally one came up from Salisbury with the 7.49 a.m. semi-fast and returned as far as Basingstoke with the 11.54 a.m. slow, and thence with the afternoon goods.

Again in 1966, rail tours made calls on the class, the first on 2 January taking No. 34015 *Exmouth* over the Somerset & Dorset line from Broadstone to Bath. Piloted by poorly-steaming U class No. 31639, the gruelling climb over the Mendips was made in tremendous style with a two minutes early arrival being recorded. This tour was intended as a farewell to Somerset & Dorset steam, but owing to difficulties in providing alternative bus services, trains had to be kept running until the spring when on 6 March, a further tour was run. On this occasion rebuild No. 34013 *Okehampton* took charge at Highbridge for the journey through Weston-super-Mare and Bristol to Mangotsfield North Junction where diesel D7014 attached to the rear to work the ten miles to Bath Green Park. This manoeuvre enabled *Okehampton* to reach Bath the correct way round for the journey over the Somerset & Dorset line in partnership with No. 34057 *Biggin Hill*. At Templecombe they were relieved by Merchant Navy No. 35028 *Clan Line* for the run home to London.

Another tour on 13 August 1966 took No. 34002 *Salisbury* even further afield, from

Waterloo to Nottingham via the N & SWJ line, Neasden and the Great Central main line. At Nottingham it came off and retired to Colwick shed for six hours while the tour travelled on to Penistone and returned via Sheffield Victoria and Staveley. Taking over the special an hour late *Salisbury* ran up the Great Central to Marylebone where the class had not been seen since the locomotive trials of 1948.

Withdrawals in 1966 numbered seven and included No. 34064 *Fighter Command.* This locomotive had been equipped with a Giesl oblong ejector in May 1962, apparently to offset the loss of efficiency caused by the addition of a spark-arrester rather than to evaluate the improvement in fuel consumption. No official trials were run, but correspondence found at Eastleigh Works suggests that the steaming proved erratic and that most crews found the firing more difficult and the slipping more noticeable. To the lineside observer the acceleration from rest appeared poor and the unevenness of the Bulleid valve-gear more pronounced.

As 1967 progressed so came a gradual reduction in steam duties, although No. 34102 remained a favourite for the Channel Islands boat services and No. 34057 *Biggin Hill* came up from Salisbury on several occasions as substitute for ailing Warship diesels. Nos. 34006/19 were condemned in March 1967 and Nos. 34002/15 in the following month, while No. 34057 failed with a fractured middle cylinder in May and was laid aside. This left but Nos. 34023 and 34102 to work on until steam finally bowed out. The latter, however, showed on 18 May that plenty of life remained, for it worked the 385-ton 5.09 p.m. Waterloo-Basingstoke to Woking in 28½ minutes despite a long and severe slack through Clapham Junction, and reached 76 m.p.h. at Byfleet.

At the beginning of June 1967 the restored LNER blue-liveried A4 pacific No. 4498 *Sir Nigel Gresley* visited the Southern Region to feature in a number of rail tours out of Waterloo. On 3 June it visited Bournemouth and later worked the return special as far as Southampton where it handed over to No. 34023 *Blackmore Vale* and ran light engine via Redbridge to Salisbury for servicing before taking over the train once more for the final stage to Waterloo. The West Country reached Salisbury via Eastleigh and Romsey thereby keeping the participants on the move, yet permitting time for *Sir Nigel Gresley's* crew to ensure that all was well for a fast run up the main line. On 4 June a second tour took the A4 to Weymouth and back with No. 34057 *Biggin Hill* standing-by at Southampton in case of need.

Beside its rail tour commitments No. 34023 *Blackmore Vale* remained active on the "Bournemouth Belle" and other main line services to Southampton, Bournemouth and Weymouth, while No. 34102 *Lapford* made several high-speed runs with the 6.38 p.m. Salisbury-Waterloo as well as working the 6.00 p.m. Weymouth Quay-Waterloo via Netley, Havant, Guildford and Claygate on 11 June.

At Waterloo on Sunday 18 June, the scene was familiar to regular rail tour devotees, the weather was bright, an air of anticipation prevailed, and yet there was an odd sense of sadness. It was indeed sobering that this was the last of so many privately-sponsored, steam-hauled specials over the Western Section of the Southern Region. The twelve-coach train arrived smartly behind 2-6-2 tank No. 41298 and left to time hauled by the immaculately-groomed Nos. 73029 and 34023 *Blackmore Vale*. Steady progress was made via Clapham Junction and the East Putney loop while on regaining the main line speed rapidly increased to 65 m.p.h. at Surbiton before slowing for divergence to the new Guildford line at Effingham Junction. Once more progress was smart with a maximum of 75 m.p.h. being recorded at Clandon before catching up the 9.15 a.m. Waterloo-Portsmouth Harbour electric caused delays to Havant, where a conductor was picked up for the journey to Fareham. There the two locomotives were exchanged for No. 34089 *602 Squadron* to Southampton Central where No. 34108 *Wincanton* was attached as pilot to Wareham. The latter then ran light to Weymouth while 2-6-4 tank No. 80146 was coupled to the rear for the trip over the Swanage branch. On returning to the main line No. 34089 *602 Squadron* hauled the special unaided to Weymouth, where the coaches were serviced in preparation for the return to Salisbury via Bournemouth Central behind Nos. 34023 *Blackmore Vale* and 34108 *Wincanton.* There, Merchant Navy No. 35013 *Blue Funnel* was waiting for the final stage at speed to Waterloo.

All steam workings ceased on Sunday 9 July 1967, when No. 34023 *Blackmore Vale*, the most mechanically-sound surviving West Country was purchased for £1,900 by the Bulleid Preservation Society and transported by rail to the Longmoor Military Railway, where undercover storage was available and preservation could commence. Later in October 1971 it was transferred to Sheffield Park and the Bluebell Railway where reconditioning proceeded slowly, but thoroughly, until 15 May 1976, when it returned to traffic. Numbered 21C123, painted malachite green, and attached to high-sided 4,500-gallon tender T3319, it was a joy to see and hear. Much credit is due to all concerned in its preservation.

No. 34051 *Winston Churchill* rusticated for some years before work commenced preparing it for exhibition at the new York Transport Museum. No attempt was made to return it to running order, but otherwise the final result was excellent.

Of the remaining forty-eight members of the class only Nos. 34011/35/43/9/55/68/9/74/110 were broken-up by the Southern Region, the others being sold to the following scrap metal merchants: J. Cashmore, Newport (Mon.), Nos. 34002/6/15/9/38/41/57/76/9 (broken-up by December 1967); J. Buttigieg, Newport (Mon.), Nos. 34033/66/84/6/102/3 (broken-up by mid-1966); P. Ward, Queenborough, Nos. 34061/91 (broken-up by March 1965); Hayes, Bridgend, Nos. 34064/83 (broken-up by December 1966); Birds Commercial Motors, Bridgend, Nos. 34063/75 (broken-up by mid-1966); Birds Commercial Motors, Byrea, Nos. 34020/30/54/65/78/80/106/7 (broken-up by April 1965); Birds Commercial Motors, Morriston, Nos. 34099 (broken-up March 1965); Woodhams Brothers, Barry, Nos. 34007/67/70/2/3/81/92/4/105. Of these, No. 34094 was broken-up in December 1964, Nos. 34007/67/70/2/3/101 remained intact at the time of writing; Nos. 34081/92 had been purchased for preservation and No. 34105 was reserved for the South Western Railway Society. No. 34081 *92 Squadron* was purchased for £3,850 by the Battle of Britain Locomotive Preservation Society in November 1973 and then underwent refurbishing at Norchard. No. 34092 *City of Wells* arrived at Ingrow on the Keighley & Worth Valley Railway in October 1971, to be repaired and repainted at Haworth.

THE LIGHT PACIFIC REBUILDS

The 1954 decision to rebuild the thirty Merchant Navies with Walschaerts valve-gear and other conventional features suggested the same treatment for the smaller, but basically similar West Country and Battle of Britain locomotives. On several occasions during 1955 the suggestion was discussed, though no positive action was authorised until work on No. 35018 *British India Line*, the first Merchant Navy rebuild, was completed in February 1956.

Once again Brighton assumed responsibility for the detailed planning and with the experience gained from the larger class little time was lost in reaching an acceptable compromise between the ideal solution and that possible with the severely restricted budget. Provisional authorisation for fifteen rebuilds was granted in November 1956 and when confirmed in February 1957 this number was increased to thirty. Assembly of the necessary material commenced at once, and when No. 34040 *Crewkerne* entered Eastleigh Works towards the end of April 1957 preparations were set in motion for its reconstruction. However, before work commenced information was received of No. 34005 *Barnstaple* stopped at Nine Elms with badly fractured frames and damaged centre cylinder. As a result, it was towed to Eastleigh and substituted as the first light pacific rebuild, and No. 34040 returned to traffic unmodified.

On 14 May 1957 work began stripping No. 34005 down to the frames and, when these proved badly wasted below the firebox as well as cracked ahead of the leading coupled wheels, they were rejected in favour of a spare set. This, and another set, had been cut at Ashford in September 1950 when front-end vibration tests were being conducted with No. 34041 *Wilton*, but for some reason were not used. By the end of the month little progress had been made apart from setting up the frames and fitting the new centre cylinder, but thereafter reconstruction proceeded apace, and on 26 June 1957 *Barnstaple* was brought out of the Erecting Shop and steamed in the works yard. No nameplates were mounted and some consternation was displayed by observers who imagined the rebuilds were to be nameless. However, such thoughts proved groundless for the following morning brackets were welded on to the running plate and barrel, and the plaques and nameplates fitted. Shortly after reaching the running shed on 28 June No. 34005 *Barnstaple* was worked up to Winchester and back, while at 6.20 a.m. on the 29th it was noted working light engine through Brockenhurst en route to Bournemouth. The first passenger duty was on 4 July, when Eastleigh employed it on part of Nine Elms duty 72, the 11.28 a.m. Eastleigh-Bournemouth Central and the 4.34 p.m. return. On 5 and 6 July and for most of the week ending 13 July Eastleigh duty 252 was worked, this mainly involving cross-country workings over the Netley line and a trip to Reading with the 5.16 p.m. from Portsmouth. Later several appearances were made at Bournemouth with slows from Southampton while on 3 August the 11.40 a.m. Weymouth-Bradford was worked as far as Brent. The following week it was transferred to Battersea, and on 9 August 1957 began working the Eastern Section Continental expresses.

Rearward of the smokebox, in similar fashion to the Merchant Navy rebuilds, the original boiler was retained practically intact, although the unreliable rocking grate was discarded in favour of the type fitted to the BR

No. 35025 *Brocklebank Line* at Eastleigh, 17 September 1949, painted blue for its naming ceremony (*J. H. Aston*)

The right-hand nameplate of rebuilt No. 35026 in May 1961 (*D. L. Bradley*)

No. 35027 *Port Line* at Bournemouth Central, 25 June 1949. Malachite green, cylinders and front casing black, nameplates covered and 6,000-gallon tender
(*D. L. Bradley*)

No. 35030 *Elder-Dempster Lines*, the last Merchant Navy, heading the 6.10 p.m. Dover Marine-Victoria Continental express, 4 August 1951 (*D. L. Bradley*)

No. 35030 *Elder-Dempster Lines* at Waterloo, 8 August 1962, with modified 6,000-gallon tender, speedometer, AWS and extended valve spindles housed in smoke-deflector pockets (*D. L. Bradley*)

No. 21C101 *Exeter* at Brighton, 7 May 1945. Malachite green with short smoke-deflector plates sanding to all coupled wheels, and the name, coat-of-arms and class scroll painted on the casing

No. 34005 *Barnstaple*, 28 May 1950. V-cab, extended smoke-deflector plates, front sanding blanked-off and slide bar dust covers (*W. Gilburt*)

No. 34006 *Bude* at Waterloo, 17 June 1948, waiting to depart with the 8.47 a.m. to Salisbury. Extended smoke-deflector plates, speedometer and LMS tender for the BR Locomotive Trials (*J. H. Aston*)

No. 34006 *Bude* leaving Southampton Central with the "Bournemouth Belle", 19 June 1960. Long smoke-deflector plates, unmodified tender, AWS and speedometer (*E. W. Fry*)

No. S21C107 *Wadebridge* in early British Railways livery with "S" prefix and "Devon Belle" batons, 5 July 1948 (*J. H. Aston*)

No. 21C112 *Launceston*, showing smokebox door handle and disc brackets, and round ownership plate (*LCGB*)

No. 21C119 leaving Victoria on 11 May 1946 with the "Golden Arrow". No embellishment carried on the casing sides (*Photomatic Ltd.*)

No. 34039 *Boscastle* awaiting the "Golden Arrow" 29 August 1948, the arrows being positioned mid-way between the lining bands without need to resite the nameplates (*J. H. Aston*)

The cabside of No. 34044 in March 1955, showing the BR Loading Classification and the three side windows (*E. W. Fry*)

No. 34046 *Braunton* heads the Birkenhead-Bournemouth through train away from Southampton Central, 10 September 1960 *(E. W. Fry)*

The through Brighton-Cardiff train leaving Southampton Central, 5 May 1956, behind No. 34046 *Braunton* *(E. W. Fry)*

No. S21C149 *Anti-Aircraft Command* on Brighton shed 18 March 1948, with name-plates covered and fitted with standard V-cab and smoke-deflector plates
(*Real Photographs Co. Ltd.*)

No. 34049 *Anti-Aircraft Command* under general repair at Eastleigh, 7 November 1959
(*E. W. Fry*)

No. 21C153 *Sir Keith Park* passing Tonbridge with 3.10 p.m. Dover Marine-Victoria Continental express, 10 September 1948. The RAF plaque has been lowered to permit the arrow being carried on the centre band when on "Golden Arrow" duty (*D. L. Bradley*)

No. 21C155 *Fighter Pilot* makes an imposing sight at the head of the "Golden Arrow" (*D. L. Bradley*)

No. S21C157 *Biggin Hill* and the "Thanet Belle", 24 July 1948. Circular ownership plate removed *(Real Photographs Co. Ltd.)*

A rear view of No. 21C159 showing the 4,500-gallon tender with hooped rear ladder *(D. L. Bradley)*

No. 21C160 at Waterloo, 7 July 1947, waiting to depart with the 9.00 a.m. West of England express. Standard-length smoke-deflector plates (*J. H. Aston*)

No. 21C164 painted works grey with grey wheels, standing in the yard at Brighton, 9 June 1947

standard classes. There were two degrees of rock, a small angular movement for cleaning the fire on the road and a larger one for use at the running shed. The triple ashpan concept was also retained, though the pans themselves were new and of hopper pattern with damper doors in line and connected by a transverse operating shaft equipped with a simple universal joint to eliminate the tendency for tightness should the ashpans suffer distortion. A similar arrangement was applied to the hopper butterfly doors which were controlled from ground level by a short lever. The damper doors were opened or closed by a single screw on the footplate, which by virtue of grease lubrication gave easy movement. The working pressure was kept to the 250lb./sq. in. employed latterly on all the Bulleid pacifics, while the boiler centre line was unaltered at 9ft. 5¼in.

The irregularly-shaped and poorly-designed fabricated smokebox was discarded and replaced by a new cylindrical pattern resting on a saddle formed jointly by the new inside cylinder and a stretcher. Extra rigidity was built into the front end by bolting the saddle stretcher to both the cylinder casting and the main frames. The multi-jet blastpipe was again used, but the stark stovepipe chimney gave way to a flared cast-iron pattern similar to that found on the Lord Nelsons. To save expense, the distinctive Bulleid oval smokebox door was re-employed, but the superheater header was new in order to offer more convenient steampipe connections and greater access. The outside cylinder pipes were brought through the smokebox sides.

The slab-sided, all embracing air-smoothed casing was removed to provide ready access to details necessitating frequent attention, and the boiler was provided with orthodox plating mounted on crinolines. Large smoke-deflector plates were placed on either side of the smokebox and secured to a running plate of similar configuration to the BR Britannia pacifics. Few changes were made to the cab, although the sides were brought out to give a width of 9ft. 0in. and an improved ventilator fitted to the roof. The driver's seat was moved back to accommodate the reversing screw handle and gearbox, while the steam-operated firedoor was discarded and replaced by a manual pattern. The Bulleid valve-gear, chains and oil-bath were removed, and three independent sets of Walschaerts motion substituted, two being outside and one inside the frames. The former had the usual return crank drive, but the inside gear included an eccentric on the right-hand crank web. The outside cylinders were re-employed, but the inside cylinder was new with inside admission and the steamchest offset to the right. By using a steel casting with cast-iron liners for the cylinder barrel and steamchest an appreciable saving in weight was achieved. To accommodate the outside admission of the Bulleid cylinders, the valve stem drive of the piston valves was taken off the top, instead of the second pin of the combination lever. This part of the gear was supported by a suspension link in place of the more general valve spindle crosshead. New main crossheads were provided, these being separate from the piston rods where previously these were integral. The erratic and unpopular steam reversing gear was replaced by screw equipment of the type developed at Crewe and first used on Duchess pacific No.6256 *Sir William A. Stanier, F.R.S.* The handle faced the driver with an easily-read drum indicator. The gear itself was sited on the left side of the locomotive between the driving and rear coupled wheels, and by ingenious improvisation operated the three sets of motions from a single shaft.

A pair of mechanical lubricators was positioned on the footplating on either side above the leading coupled wheels and driven off the outside expansion links. Three lubricators, each with six feeds, had been removed from the front of the smokebox and supplied oil to the cylinders and steamchests while the fourth had twelve feeds and catered for the axleboxes, etc. The steamchest lubricant was atomised and introduced into the steampipes of the three cylinders, while non-atomised oil entered the cylinder barrels through the walls at the top and bottom near the vertical centre line.

In accordance with modern practice the solid gunmetal Bulleid coupled axleboxes were abandoned in favour of steel with manganese liners, while the provision of mechanical feed eliminated the large multi-feed oilboxes from the cab. Mechanical feed was also employed for the slide bars and inside valve spindle crosshead guides, but the axlebox guides and inside piston rod swab box were lubricated by trimming feeds in small auxiliary boxes on the footplating. Similar fittings adjacent to the point of application provided for the outside piston swab boxes while much of the valve gear was grease lubricated.

Sanding remained steam-operated and was restored to the front of the leading coupled wheels, while the pipes formerly leading to the trailing coupled wheels were re-adjusted to give sanding for backward running behind the centre coupled wheels. New sandboxes were provided adjacent to the rear of the smokebox for the leading wheels and between the frames for the centre pair of coupled wheels. Gravity feed on the tender for backward running was no longer necessary and was discarded.

The drawgear between the locomotive and tender was modified in accordance with that fitted beneficially to the Merchant Navy rebuilds. This offered greater flexibility and incorporated a plunger sliding in guides within the tender drawbox as well as being pin-jointed to the drawbar itself. The plunger was controlled by a heavy rubber spring drawing the locomotive and tender together, and bringing the curved rubbing blocks into contact. These had manganese steel facings and were shaped to avoid increased loading of the drawbar and springs by lateral movement between the locomotive and tender.

A 5,500-gallon tender, T3358 from No. 34094 *Mortehoe* was attached, the raves being cut away to facilitate replenishment and to remove pockets where surplus coal tended to accumulate. Compartments for the fire irons were provided on each side, while external feed sumps with shut-off valves permitted removal of the sieves for cleaning without the necessity of tank draining. This feature had proved effective in reducing injector trouble, caused either by clogged sieves or by choked annular injector orifices. To give a clear indication of water remaining in the tank a float type gauge was fitted.

The new superheater reduced the heating surface by 57 sq. ft., but otherwise there was no change in boiler capacity or tractive effort. When weighed at Eastleigh Works on 1 August 1957 No. 34005 *Barnstaple* gave the following details:

Bogie	17T 8C
Leading coupled wheels	19T 15C
Centre coupled wheels	20T 18C
Trailing coupled wheels	20T 14C
Trailing wheels ..	12T 18C
Engine total	91T 13C
Condition of engine: ..	steam pressure 145 lb., light fire and 3in. of water in the glass.
Leading wheels ..	15T 16C
Centre wheels ..	15T 18C
Trailing wheels ..	16T 2C
Tender total	47T 16C
Condition of tender: ..	tank full, 5 tons of coal carried and drawbar tight.

No. 34005 *Barnstaple* proved an instant success on the Victoria-Dover/Folkestone Continental expresses and was later joined by the second rebuild, No. 34027 *Taw Valley*, before it was transferred to Bricklayers Arms for the Kent Coast and Business services. Similarly the next thirteen rebuilds were also sent to the Eastern Section where by the spring of 1958 they were stationed as follows: Bricklayers Arms Nos. 34001/3/4/5/12/3/4 and Ramsgate Nos. 34016/7/21/2/5/6/7/37.

The mileages and rebuilding costs were as follows:

Locomotive No.	*Mileage*	*Cost of rebuilding* £
34001	573,593	8,604
34003	543,328	8,765
34004	512,904	8,448
34005	489,808	11,472
34012	500,788	7,646
34013	559,411	8,125
34014	573,677	8,446
34016	554,230	9,018
34017	459,309	10,236
34021	541,097	10,464
34022	527,822	7,963
34025	512,484	8,463
34026	536,491	8,769
34027	503,085	9,803
34037	480,115	8,964

All were attached to cut-down 5,500-gallon tenders transferred from Nos. 34072/4/5/6/7/80/1/8/92/4/6/104/6/8/9, which in exchange received the smaller 4,500-gallon pattern. The extra capacity was considered necessary to cover the heavier express duties which the rebuilds were intended to work, as well as to match their widened cabs.

At Ramsgate a series of comparative trials were held on the Cannon Street business services between Nos. 34026 *Yes Tor* and 34078 *222 Squadron* (a non-rebuild) over both the Chatham and Tonbridge routes. The latter caught fire at Chestfield and Swalecliffe Halt on one of the down trains and failed at Ashford with a jammed whistle on another occasion, but otherwise gave a reasonable account of itself. The results, as anticipated, fully confirmed the economies promised by the advocates of rebuilding, details being as follows:

Locomotive No.	*Type*	*Coal (lb.) per mile*	*per drawbar horsepower hour*
34026	rebuild	41.42	3.38
34078	non-rebuild	50.64	3.51

After completing the fifteenth West Country rebuild, No. 34016 *Bodmin*, in April 1958, Eastleigh turned its attention to the remaining Merchant Navies under order H09199. However, it quickly became apparent that rebuilding further West Countries would prove more advantageous and the last ten Merchant Navies were postponed in their favour. As a result little time was lost in reconstructing the second batch of light pacifics and at two-weekly intervals between mid-August 1958 and early April 1959 they were returned to traffic. All were stationed on the Western Section, Nos. 34028/39/42/5/6/8 at Bournemouth, Nos. 34010/8/29/31/47 at Nine Elms, Nos. 34050/2/3 at Salisbury and No. 34062 at Exmouth Junction, and frequently rostered for express duties hitherto reserved for the larger and more powerful Merchant Navies. It will be noted that earlier members of the Battle of Britain class were included in this series of rebuilds.

No. 34045 *Ottery St. Mary* had a fortunate escape on the night of 28 January 1959, when at the head of the 10.30 p.m. Waterloo-Weymouth in dense fog it ran into the rear of the 10.15 p.m. Nine Elms-Plymouth fitted goods near Esher. The latter in charge of No. 35003 *Royal Mail* was travelling at about 15 m.p.h. after being held at signals, and although pushed violently forward for two hundred yards was not badly damaged, and after inspection and consultation with the nearby signalbox the trains were able to proceed coupled together to Woking. There the goods was provided with another guards van and the express continued its journey to Weymouth.

All tenders attached to this series had the raves cut away, but were not of similar capacity, details being as follows: 5,500-gallons Nos. 34010/8/28/9/42/5/7/8/50/2/3 (tenders obtained from Nos. 34090, 34086/110, 34093, 34083, 34077/101, 34089/98, 34073/103 respectively); 4,500-gallons Nos. 34062; 5,250-gallons Nos. 34031/9/46. The last-mentioned were completely new above the framing, the tank tops having been fabricated in the old Paint Shop at Ashford Works and the reconstruction performed at Eastleigh at the same time as the locomotives were rebuilt. The history of these three tenders is as follows:

Tender No.	*Original capacity (gallons)*	*Original locomotive*	*Transfers before reconstruction 1st*	*2nd*	*After reconstruction to locomotive No.*
3261	4,500	21C119	34044 2/1949	34046 5/1956	34046
3313	4,500	21C162	34005 2/1949	34039 11/1952	34039
3354	5,500	34100	—	—	34031

These were readily recognisable by the side plating being higher than other cut-down tenders and the water tank, except for the sloping top plate, being completely masked. No. 34062 *17 Squadron* was the first light pacific rebuild to run with the narrow 4,500-gallon tender, a feature which marred its otherwise attractive appearance as the cab was appreciably wider than the tender.

As soon as work on No. 34062 *17 Squadron* was under way, the first of the ten postponed Merchant Navy rebuilds, No. 35024 *East Asiatic Company* was called to Eastleigh Works, thus a delay of some ten months occurred before thoughts once more could be turned to the smaller locomotives. Then, commencing with No. 34059 *Sir Archibald Sinclair* in March 1960, the third batch of rebuilds was passed rapidly through works and returned to service. It was no longer possible to provide 5,500-gallon tenders for locomotives possessing the smaller variety, and all retained the type attached on entering shops, except for No. 34059 which received a 5,250-gallon reconstructed tender. All had the raves cut away to give easier access.

No attempt was made to allocate this series to particular depots or duties; thus No. 34008 returned to Brighton where there was little chance of its enhanced capacity being fully exploited. Of the others, Nos. 34034/6/59 went back to Exmouth Junction, Nos. 34040/4 to Bournemouth, Nos. 34071/82 to Dover, Nos. 34077/85/8/100/1 to Battersea and Nos. 34090/3 to Nine Elms.

The cost of rebuilding the second and third series averaged £10,943 and £12,864 respectively while the mileages ranged from a very presentable 597,083 for No. 34008 to a mere 330,106 for No. 34101.

Down to and including No. 34062 *17 Squadron* of April 1959, all rebuilds were fitted with outside valve spindles and blind guides which did not necessitate piercing the running plate ahead of the smokebox. Time, however, proved this to be a design fault, and following several failures with both the light pacifics and the Merchant Navies, a modified layout was introduced. In this the valve spindles were extended and given open-ended guides, the extension passing through the running plate and being housed in pockets let into the smoke-deflector plates. All rebuilds after No. 34062 entered traffic with this modification, while the earlier two series were altered as they received routine repairs.

Hot big-ends, unknown before rebuilding, occasionally caused trouble, and to avoid serious failures locomotives rebuilt in 1960/61 were equipped with garlic or aniseed aromatic heat-detectors. Many earlier rebuilds were similarly fitted, although, for some inexplicable reason, one of the worst offenders, No. 34045 *Ottery St. Mary* was not so favoured.

During 1959 a final total of seventy-five rebuilds was contemplated, but by mid-1960 with electrification progressing rapidly in Kent, a fresh appraisal of the Region's steam requirements suggested that sixty would suffice. Work on the final series of fifteen commenced in October 1960 and ended in the following May. There were no tender capacity changes, Nos. 34009/24/32/56/8/60/89/96/8/104/8/9 having the smaller pattern and Nos. 34087/95/7 the larger. Once again there was no specific attempt to allocate locomotives to particular depots, Nos. 34009/95 returning to Nine Elms, Nos. 34024/32/56/8/60/96/7/8/104/8/9 to Exmouth Junction and Nos. 34087/9 to Battersea. Costs averaged £13,447, while the mileages ranged from 689,964 for No. 34024 to 557,217 for No. 34109.

The dates of rebuilding these sixty were as follows: Order HO8428 (fifteen locomotives) 1957 Nos. 34001/17/25 (November), 34003/27 (September), 34005 (June), 34013 (October), 34022 (December); 1958 Nos. 34004/26 (February), 34012/21 (January), 34014/37 (March), 34016 (April). Order HO9361 (fifteen locomotives) 1958 Nos. 34018/45/7 (October), 34028/50 (August), 34029/31 (December), 34052 (September), 34053 (November), 1959 Nos. 34010/46 (February), 34039/42 (January), 34048 (March), 34062 (April). Order HO9886 (fifteen locomotives) 1960 Nos. 34008/77 (July), 34040 (October), 34034/90 (August), 34036/100/1 (September), 34044/71/93 (May), 34059 (March), 34082/8 (April), 34085 (June). Order HO9903 (fifteen locomotives) 1960 No. 34032 (October), 34056/87 (December), 34058/60/89 (November), 1961 Nos. 34009/95 (January), 34024/98 (February), 34096 (April), 34097/109 (March), 34104/8 (May).

Route availability remained exceptionally good in view of the increased axle-loading and was almost as wide as that enjoyed by the original design. They were, however, prohibited over the lines in North Devon and Cornwall and until 1960 to Plymouth, but east of Exeter permission was now granted for both varieties to work routes hitherto barred to the original locomotives, e.g., Topsham to Exmouth, Seaton Junction to Seaton, Lymington Junction to Lymington Pier and Totton to Fawley. The Grately to Bulford and Bentley to Bordon branches were barred to the rebuilds while remaining open to those not modified, and the latter gained the facility of using the Botley to Bishop's Waltham line. On the Central Section, the only additional prohibition was over the Steyning road between Itchingfield Junction and Shoreham while both varieties were now barred from the Bluebell line between Horsted Keynes and Culver Junction. Later the Steyning restriction was removed, and on 3 October 1960 No. 34003 *Plymouth* of Bricklayers Arms was the first rebuild to use this route when heading the 5.08 a.m. London Bridge-Brighton.

At £670,000 the cost of rebuilding the sixty West Countries was not excessive when related to overall Southern Region expenditure, but nevertheless it constituted a major item and one expected to contribute to general efficiency by reduced running costs and improved performance. How well then did the sixty rebuilds comply with these requirements? Time proved there was little difference in performance between the two series, both steamed freely, rode smoothly, climbed and accelerated well, and gave a good account of themselves in general service. Some loss of free running, in particular on down grades, was apparent with the rebuilds, but this was offset by reduced slipping at starting and none at speed.

Repair costs of the class as built, despite a boiler requiring little maintenance, were exceptionally high and compared unfavourably with other modern express classes, details being as follows:

Repair costs per mile (pence)

Class	*Period*	*Locomotive*	*Boiler*	*Total locomotive and tender*
West Country	**1954/55**	**4.45 pence**	**0.19 pence**	**5.14 pence**
Merchant Navy	1955	5.06 pence	0.24 pence	5.98 pence
A1	1954/55	2.87 pence	0.39 pence	3.55 pence
Britannia	1955	2.97 pence	0.39 pence	3.66 pence
Royal Scot	1955	3.48 pence	0.54 pence	4.75 pence
Rebuilt West Country	***1960/61**	**2.94 pence**	**0.20 pence**	**3.54 pence**

* costs reduced to 1955 standard.

Rebuilding reduced the repair costs by 60 per cent and offered figures for the locomotive and tender very similar to those of the Peppercorn A1's, these being the best for the 1954/55 period. There was a similar improvement in coal consumption, 8.4 per cent less according to figures issued by Eastleigh, although the rebuilds at Nine Elms in April to June 1960 were averaging 40.49 lb. per mile as against 50.41 lb. for those not rebuilt. Oil consumption also showed a marked decrease, the average saving per hundred miles being quoted as 6¼ gallons.

In 1947-9 the mileages run between intermediate and general repairs were similar to those of the Lord Nelsons, Schools and King Arthurs, but over the next decade they were improved to such a degree that mileages of 250,000 were common between general overhauls. Details are as follows:

Mileages between General Repairs

	1949-1951		*1953-1956*	
Locomotive No.	*Miles*	*Months*	*Miles*	*Months*
34001	97,555	24	249,146	59
34002	109,759	29	256,166	60
34003	121,888	32	222,258	63
34005	94,530	29	224,299	64
34010	93,464	26	222,357	59
34011	103,246	29	208,577	58
34035	79,529	20	288,894	68
34046	96,927	25	220,138	60
34050	100,208	24	218,524	57
34054	82,488	25	230,986	63

The average intermediate and general repair mileages of Nos. 34001 to 34055 for 1947-9 and 1953-6 were as follows:

Type of repair	*1947-1949*	*1953-1956*
average mileage to Intermediate Repair	61,747	108,033
average time in months to Intermediate Repair	17	27
average mileage to General Repair	96,486	228,425
average time in months to General Repair	28	61

Undoubtedly much of this improvement was caused by the introduction of TIA, although a proportion was the result of better workshop techniques, harder-wearing materials and numerous minor modifications. No such dramatic mileage increases occurred over the next few years, but the average between successive general repairs for engines not rebuilt rose progressively to 243,000. Representative mileages for 1959 to 1961 are as follows:

	To Intermediate Repairs		*To General Repairs*	
Locomotive No.	*Miles*	*Months*	*Miles*	*Months*
34002	139,186	32	287,239	67
34035	158,632	39	247,047	60
34054	146,387	38	228,370	63
34094	143,235	32	281,701	70
34099	114,282	26	245,861	67
34106	171,230	37	243,025	59
34107	157,168	37	253,923	60

Similar details for the rebuilds are not so easily obtainable for many, including No. 34005 *Barnstaple*, were condemned without undergoing a general overhaul, while others were returned to traffic by Eastleigh Works after mileages ceased being entered on locomotive record cards. Details of those available are as follows:

	To Intermediate Repairs		*To General Repairs*	
Locomotive No.	*Miles*	*Months*	*Miles*	*Months*
34001	122,007	31	222,421	65
34004	111,643	33	215,546	60
34013	102,948	30	210,550	71
34017	101,644	25	298,060	74
34021	120,068	32	230,063	68
34025	113,119	33	220,335	66
34052	171,409	41	257,112	64

The mileages of the two series were generally similar with any advantage being in favour of those running as Bulleid intended. In cost, however, the rebuilds proved considerably cheaper to overhaul in works and maintain at the depots.

Important as they might appear to Waterloo, mileages and costs held scant appeal to enginemen whose interests seldom extended beyond cab comfort, ease of preparation and disposal, reliability, and above all, capability. All manner of evil might be excused locomotives capable of performing their daily tasks with a modicum of ease. Fortunately, whether rebuilt or as Bulleid intended, the Southern Region light pacifics could always be relied upon to give of their best, and few main-line duties required reservation for the larger and more-powerful Merchant Navies. As regards comfort the enclosed Bulleid cab left much to be desired, for in summer it frequently became unbearably hot while at all times it was dirty and dusty. With better ventilation and other modifications the cab of the rebuilds was relatively cool and much cleaner, while the visibility was better. Some riding deterioration could be detected with the rebuilds, but since the class as designed by Bulleid rode exceptionally smoothly the standard remained high and considerably better than other contemporary pacifics.

Opinions concerning the preparation and disposal of locomotives tend to be personal, for they invariably reflect the length of time, inconvenience and type of labour involved. For instance, most drivers preferred preparing a non-rebuild, as the inside motion made no call on their time, the oil-bath and its contents falling to the responsibility of the depot fitters. On the rebuilds, like other multi-cylinder locomotives, the driver had to tend the inside motion, an awkward task and one unlikely to gain much favour. As a result, drivers were inclined to take a jaundiced view of the rebuilds, whereas firemen with thoughts of easier firing and disposal approved of them.

By 1957, crews and running shed staff had accumulated much experience in retaining the class active and high mileages were being worked. The performance was similarly excellent, with few Southern Region express duties calling for greater power. If maintenance, repair, fuel and oil costs had improved likewise, then major design changes were unwarranted, but, unfortunately, such was not the case. Rebuilding was instigated to assure this and since the overall running costs were reduced by 17.4 per cent with other favourable factors remaining constant, then the rebuilds must be considered successful. Whether in view of electrification the full cost of £670,000 was ever entirely recouped is doubtful, but that was no fault of the rebuilds.

The final stages of the Ramsgate electrification engineering and signalling works were completed during weekends 23/24 and 30/31 May 1959, while the first electric train to operate throughout was the 8.00 a.m. Victoria-Ramsgate on 2 June 1959. It was formed of nine steam stock coaches headed by electric locomotive E5004. Steam services continued to operate to Ramsgate, Dover and Sheerness until the night of 14/15 June, when a change over to electric was effected. Of the rolling stock displaced, much was despatched to Maze Hill, Blackheath and Eardley, with four sets going to Horsted Keynes pending breaking-up at Newhaven. Other redundant vehicles were berthed at Headcorn, Tonbridge, Martin Mill, Canterbury West and Grove Park.

The last regular steam train from Victoria over the Chatham line, the 8.52 p.m. Dover, was in charge of L1 class No. 31753 which carried a small wreath on the smokebox door and departed to prolonged whistles from other locomotives in the vicinity. The last up train left Ramsgate at 8.35 p.m. behind No. 34001 *Exeter* which was similarly decorated and sent on its way.

Inevitably, many steam locomotives became redundant and on paper, if not in reality, 106 were transferred to Nine Elms, including three Merchant Navies, nine Class 5's, seventeen King Arthurs and nine Schools. To meet the summer Continental and inter-Regional services only fourteen unrebuilt light pacifics and a handful of Schools remained at Battersea. Rebuilds Nos. 34016/7/21/2/5/6/7/37 were moved from Ramsgate to Bricklayers Arms where they joined Nos. 34001/3/4/5/12/3/4 working the business services via Tonbridge.

Use of the rebuilds on the Western Section became more general as the numbers increased, although only No. 34053 *Sir Keith Park* could regularly be seen at Exeter before April 1959 when No. 34031 *Torrington* made several appearances with the 9.00 a.m. ex-Waterloo. A little later No. 34062 *17 Squadron* returned to Exmouth Junction rebuilt and immediately took its turn with the London expresses, while summer Saturdays brought down Nos. 34010/8/29/47 from Nine Elms, often in place of Merchant Navies. By this date all light pacifics, whether rebuilt or not, were free to run between Okehampton and Plymouth, as well as Yeovil and Dorchester. No. 34062 *17 Squadron* as might be expected was the first rebuild to cross Meldon Viaduct on 28 July 1959, but once again there was no hurry to make use of their services and by April 1960 only No. 34026 *Yes Tor* had joined the select band. However, by the following year most of the Exeter-Plymouth passenger services were in their hands, although the North Cornwall line remained out of bounds.

From time to time Portsmouth was used by royal specials, but for a variety of reasons, including security, the Harbour Station had not proved entirely satisfactory. Before the Second World War the South Dockyard line had been regularly employed for this purpose, but its closure and lifting of the track made any further use of its facilities impossible. Therefore, in November 1960 thought was turned to the using of the North Dockyard branch from Portsmouth & Southsea (High Level) station and on the 20th, following some re-laying and the fitting of improved means of communication Nos. 34039 *Boscastle* (rebuild) and 34075 *264 Squadron* worked a series of trial runs with Pullmans *Niobe* and *Cassandra*, royal saloon 396 and two modern corridor coaches. No serious obstacles were found to forbid either class, though for convenience two minor track modifications and the removal of several bollards were recommended. These, however, were never fully implemented, as changing travel patterns made it more convenient to employ aircraft for royal and other important visitors, and Gatwick or Heathrow became the usual venues for arrival or departure.

Over the years the up slow road at St. Denys proved a veritable death trap for locomotives of all classes, including the Bulleid rebuilds. No. 34022 *Exmoor* on 12 December 1960 with the 1.00 p.m Cardiff-Brighton overran the up slow signal at about 20 m.p.h. and ploughed through the sand-drag provided for such eventualities, until brought to a halt by the platform ramp. The leading coach became derailed and by fouling the adjacent up through line threw all services in the area into absolute chaos for two hours. Several up expresses including the "Bournemouth Belle" had to reverse direction at Southampton Central and proceed via Redbridge to Romsey, where a second reversal was necessary to reach Eastleigh. There a third reversal set the much-delayed trains off up the main line to Waterloo, the "Bournemouth Belle" arriving 78 minutes late. The offending rebuild was re-railed after considerable trouble during the early hours of 13 December by the combined efforts of the Eastleigh and Salisbury breakdown cranes and towed away to Eastleigh Works for repair. Considering the speed of impact, locomotive damage was surprisingly light, but the bottom of the tender tank was ripped open by a broken rail and the leading axle buckled. At the subsequent inquiry the driver admitted misreading the signals where the two up lines converged, an error so many other crews had made that one wonders why action was not taken to remove such a persistent source of danger. On 29 October 1959, No. 34020 *Seaton* similarly had come to grief with the 6.30 p.m. Weymouth-Waterloo. Once again the platform ramp halted further progress, but fortunately no fouling occurred of the up road, and subject to severe speed restriction it could be used until late evening. The stock was then drawn back to Bevois Park while the Eastleigh crane unsuccessfully struggled to re-rail *Seaton*. Further assistance was called from Salisbury, but it was 4.00 a.m. on 1 November 1959 before this was finally achieved, and only then after piles had been driven for jacks, and a bulldozer employed widening and strengthening the ballast.

Waterloo, with its complicated layout and signalling, also proved an accident black spot, although, fortunately, of a minor nature. An instance on 11 April 1961 involved No. 34040 *Crewkerne*, which had worked up on the 1.25 p.m. Weymouth and was running back light engine to Nine Elms when it was struck on the west crossing by the incoming 4.38 p.m. electric from Effingham Junction. Speeds were not high, but the impact was practically head on and the leading coach of the electric was badly crushed, killing the driver and injuring several passengers. For a time the evening rush-hour traffic was brought to a standstill until a signal cable could be repaired, but from 6.00 p.m. a trickle of heavily overloaded trains recommenced running over the up relief main and the Windsor lines. The chaos was such that, contrary to all rules and regulations, passengers forced their way into the intermediate and rear motormen's compartments as well as filling the guards' vans. At the scene of the accident Schools No. 30939 *Leatherhead* was standing by to remove No. 34040 *Crewkerne*, which was not badly damaged. Suburban services were back to normal the following morning, but main-line steam trains out of Waterloo remained erratic following the derailment of No. 34095 *Brentor* at the exit of Nine Elms shed.

For steam traction in Kent, 1961 was the year of destiny, with No. 34077 *603 Squadron* heading the last regular 9.30 a.m. steam boat train via Chatham on 25 March, and electric working commencing on 12 June between London and Folkestone, Dover and Ramsgate via Tonbridge and Minster. As often happens towards the end of an era, some interesting workings occurred. In May No. 34059 *Sir Archibald Sinclair* appeared on Battersea Continental services via Tonbridge, while over the Whitsun holiday No. 30926 *Repton* performed similar duties prior to working the

Royal Derby special. Another stranger in early June was Brighton's No. 34008 *Padstow* which headed a twelve-coach Cook's Tour special from Victoria to Dover Marine and returned with vans. The last steam "Golden Arrow" on 11 June 1961 was in charge of the gleaming No. 34100 *Appledore*, its progress for posterity being recorded by numerous photographers and watched from vantage points by sizeable crowds.

Transfers were extensive, and included Nos. 34001/17/71/7/82/7/8 to Nine Elms, Nos. 34021/37/85 to Bournemouth, Nos. 34003/5 to Salisbury and Nos. 34004/16/22/5 to Eastleigh. Some movements anticipated electrification by several months while others were delayed until the new services were fully operational. At Eastleigh Nos. 34004/16/22/5 relieved Lord Nelsons on the London and Southampton Docks services. Another transfer took No. 34027 *Taw Valley* from Bricklayers Arms to Brighton where it joined No. 34008 *Padstow* on the 7.17 a.m. Brighton-London Bridge and the 4.40 p.m. return. The former's load was not heavy, only six or seven coaches, but Brighton's Schools had gained the undesirable habit of stalling on the curving 1 in 60 climb out of Lewes and following numerous complaints the pacifics were substituted with instant success.

By 1960 Nos. 34050 *Royal Observer Corps* had been in traffic for twelve years and therefore was entitled to the long-service medal. To mark the event, on 2 July 1961 it was presented with the appropriately-coloured plaques which were mounted on the cabsides below the numerals. The unveiling took place at Waterloo prior to the working of a special ROC train to Bournemouth.

On the Eastern Section electric locomotives with varied success had worked the "Night Ferry" regularly since the beginning of 1961, but on 1 January 1962, on a day of heavy snow, freezing temperatures and abject confusion, Nos. 34100 *Appledore* and N-class 31412 were commandeered for the unenviable task, and passed up through Canterbury in grand style. On the following day Nos. 34089 *602 Squadron* and 31404 were in charge, but thereafter its working reverted to electricity.

Bricklayers Arms since mid-1961 had solely been concerned with Central Section duties which called for the maintenance of four light pacific rebuilds, six N's, three 2-6-4 tanks, three C's and one H. This obviously was far from satisfactory, and at the beginning of 1962 summer services the shed closed to steam and the duties were shared between Battersea, Norwood and Brighton depots. The four pacifics, Nos. 34012/3/4/101, went to join Nos. 34008/27 at Brighton and this, together with the unrebuilt Nos. 34019/38/55/7, gave an unprecedented strength of ten pacifics. However, it was not long before the new arrivals became afflicted with the malaise which seemed to characterise Brighton-based locomotives in the post-war years and by December 1962 only two of ten were at work. Throughout the 1950's and early 1960's the entire allocation was always well cleaned, but mechanically the standard was poor, probably lower than any other Southern Region depot, except perhaps, Bournemouth in the last years of steam. To ease the position two more rebuilds, Nos. 34089/100 were transferred from Battersea towards the end of the year, both being in exemplary order and for several months fought off Brighton's derangements.

For some years the 5.25 p.m. London Bridge to Reading and Tunbridge Wells West with its ten-coach load had proved a difficult train to work because it had to be hustled down to Redhill at the peak of the business exodus without delaying the electric services. At Redhill the Tunbridge Wells portion was detached, making the journey onwards to Reading less taxing. Since their arrival at Redhill the Schools had solved the problem, but with their withdrawal substitutes had to be found. Therefore, the beginning of 1963 saw the 5.25 p.m. entrusted to Maunsell's 2-6-0's with most indifferent results, for time could only be kept with a clear run and a crew able and willing to thrash their locomotive from the outset. Such men in 1963 were hard to find. Trials were thereupon made with Nos. 34012/9 before the end of the month, followed by No. 34055 in February 1963. Surprisingly, Nos. 34019/55 did marginally better than rebuild No. 34012. The pacifics worked down to Reading with the 5.25 p.m., stabled there for the night and worked the 7.27 a.m. Reading-London Bridge in the morning. Although time was kept, they were not popular at Reading owing to difficulties with the primitive coaling stage, so the Maunsells reappeared for a week or so before advantage could be taken of the national fuel crisis to cancel both through trains. Due care was taken to ensure they were not resumed when fuel supplies returned to normal.

This, of course, was the beginning of the Beeching era when service cuts and economies were the order of the day, especially if they were non-standard. The various inter-Regional and inter-Divisional trains became early victims, and by 1962 the long-standing daily Hastings-Birkenhead service had been trimmed back at either end to run between Eastbourne and Wolverhampton only, and in September 1962 was withdrawn completely. The Brighton-Bournemouth train disappeared at the same time while a year later the Brighton-Cardiff went the same way. This, and the introduction in early 1963 of D65XX diesel locomotives (Class 33) and more diesel multiple-units made it quite obvious that steam operation on the Central Section was drawing rapidly to a close. On 29 June 1963 came the last regular rostered pacific run over the Oxted line, No. 34013 *Okehampton* with the 7.17 a.m. Brighton-London Bridge. There were a few special workings after that date, including No. 34012 *Launceston* on a ramblers' excursion to Uckfield on 21 July 1963, No. 34057 *Biggin Hill* on a similar train to Heathfield on 4 August 1963, No. 34079 *141 Squadron* on yet another to Groombridge on 29 September 1963, and No. 34089 *602 Squadron* on the 4.40 a.m. London Bridge-Eastbourne diverted via Heathfield on 28 July 1963.

September 1963 saw Battersea closing as a steam depot, while the run-down at Brighton took a dramatic step forward with the transfer of the entire pacific allocation, Nos. 34012/3/4/9/27/57/63/89/100, to Salisbury. As a result, Exmouth Junction became responsible for the last remaining through service, the Plymouth, the pacific coming up one day and returning the next, having spent the night hours on Central Section freight and van duties. On Saturdays it worked the 3.27 a.m. London Bridge-Eastbourne before going light engine to Brighton for the 11.30 a.m. Plymouth. The locomotive that came up from Exmouth Junction on a Saturday was employed on Sundays working the 10.00 a.m. Brighton-Bournemouth West. During the first few weeks Nos. 34030/61/5/9/70/9/86/107/8 all made appearances, those not rebuilt apparently being preferred. These workings were short-lived, for commencing on 6 January 1964 the service was diverted to Portsmouth to avoid having to join and separate the Brighton and Portsmouth portions at Fareham. Henceforth the pacific stabled overnight at Fratton, and the Brighton coaches were transferred to electric locomotive haulage. Officially this was considered the end of steam traction on the Central Section main line, although for several months there were plenty of steam-headed specials, with Nine Elms often, at short notice, providing the pacifics to meet a variety of requirements. These included Nos. 34010/30/50 on Newhaven reliefs over the Easter weekend, No. 34066 on the "Sussex Downsman" rail tour of 22 March 1964, Nos. 34052/77 on Derby specials and No. 34088 with the "Regency Belle" excursions. The latter ran from Victoria to Brighton to give patrons a sight of the night life and should have been formed of a 5-BEL unit, but it was found that the return from the coast at 2.15 a.m. usually clashed with engineering works on the main line and resort had to be made to the Steyning line with steam power and seven Pullmans. Unfortunately for the promoter, Brighton's late-night entertainment had little appeal and fare-paying customers were usually outnumbered by the train crew.

By the late summer of 1964 pacifics really had practically vanished from the Central Section main line, where the remaining steam duties were largely inter-Regionals from the LMR and worked by its locomotives. The Bulleids did make a comeback on the coast line in October 1964, when re-scheduling of the Plymouth brought Salisbury locomotives through to Brighton in place of electric or diesel locomotives. By this date the shed at Brighton was completely closed so servicing had to be obtained at Fratton. In the morning the down train was taken-over from the electric or diesel locomotive at Chichester and worked to the West Country. This remained the traffic pattern until May 1965, when diesels took charge in both directions, only to give way again to steam in the autumn when carriage heating became necessary. Finally, in April 1966, steam was ousted for the last time. During 1964-7 pacifics were still to be seen from time to time on the Mid-Sussex line, for whenever engineering works forbade transit of the 3.35 a.m. Waterloo-Portsmouth via Guildford it was transferred to the alternative route.

In the West Country at the end of 1962 regional boundary adjustments gave control of the depots at Yeovil Town, Exmouth Junction, Barnstaple and Wadebridge to the Western Region. At the same time over a hundred Southern Region locomotives, including light pacific rebuilds Nos. 34024/32/6/56/8/9/60/2/96/108/9, were transferred to the Western Region. The complete allocation of the West Countries and Battle of Britains at this time was as follows:

Depot	*Rebuilds*	*Non-Rebuilds*
Nine Elms	34001/9/10/7/8/31/50/71/7/82/7/8/90/3/5	34006/7/64/73/94
Bournemouth	34040/2/4/5/6/53/85	34041/3/102/3/5
Exmouth Junction	34024/32/6/56/8/9/60/2/96/108/9	34002/11/5/20/3/30/3/5/63/5/6/9/70/2/4/5/6/8/9/80/1/3/4/6/106/7/10

Depot	Rebuilds	Non-Rebuilds
Salisbury	34003/5/26/9/47/8/52	34049/51/4/67/8/91/2/9
Brighton	34012/3/4/27/89/100/1	34019/55/7
Eastleigh	34004/8/16/21/2/5/8/34/7/9/97/8/104	34038/61

At first few changes were apparent in the West of England, but in June 1963 the Western Region commenced withdrawing non-rebuilds, while in the late autumn Nos. 34024/32/6/56/8/60/108 were returned to the Southern Region in exchange for non-rebuilds Nos. 34049/54/61/7/8/84. More significant was the crew-training with Western (Class 52) and Hymek (Class 35) diesels between Exeter and Okehampton and Plymouth in the spring of 1964, and the replacement of steam on many of these services in the summer. This was followed on 7 September 1964 by the dieselisation of all the Exmouth Junction duties and the virtual ending of steam in the West of England, except when failures or shortage of diesels necessitated the recall of steam locomotives to main-line duty. Withdrawal and transfers had materially reduced the stock of pacifics at Exmouth Junction, and only a handful of non-rebuilds remained available for further service on the Southern Region where, following mass withdrawals in December 1962, practically all steam express work was in the hands of the surviving Merchant Navies, light pacifics and Class 5 4-6-0's. Indeed, the time was fast approaching when non-rebuilt pacifics were seldom seen at Waterloo.

To save expense all general repairs ceased in February 1964, the last received by the rebuilds were as follows:

Locomotive No.	*Mileage worked since rebuilding*	*Date returned to traffic*
34001	222,421	6/7/1963
34004	215,546	14/12/1963
34013	210,550	12/1/1964
34017	298,069	26/1/1964
34021	230,063	9/11/1963
34025	220,335	25/5/1963
34052	257,112	29/2/1964

Thereafter, repairs were either casual or intermediate, apart from Nos. 34005/12/8/37/42/58/82/101 which received heavy intermediate repairs and a repaint of dark green, the last being No. 34012 *Launceston* in September 1964. Inevitably this policy led to extensive exchanges of driving wheels, bogies, motion parts, tenders, etc., during 1964/66 in order to keep those locomotives in best mechanical order at work.

Withdrawal of the rebuilds commenced in May 1964 with No. 34028 *Eddystone*, which had run a mere 286,962 miles and 69 months since reconstruction in August 1958, and by the end of the year the services of Nos. 34003/16/27/9/45/58/62/96/109 had similarly been dispensed with. Details of the final mileage are as follows:

Locomotive No.	*Mileage to rebuilding*	*Mileage after rebuilding*	*Total mileage*	*Withdrawn*
34003	543,328	300,759	844,087	9/1964
34016	554,230	257,444	811,674	6/1964
34027	503,085	261,231	764,316	8/1964
34028	564,587	286,962	851,549	5/1964
34029	580,259	248,230	828,489	9/1964
34045	521,841	239,509	761,465	6/1964
34058	639,472	173,114	812,586	10/1964
34062	543,488	293,088	836,576	6/1964
34096	511,280	173,218	684,498	9/1964
34109	557,217	162,601	719,818	9/1964

No. 34016 had a cracked inside cylinder, No. 34109 a condemned firebox and the others severe frame fracturing. The last-mentioned was a common failing of both rebuilds and non-rebuilds, especially between the rear bogie wheels and the leading coupled wheels. The front end stiffening and the improved vertical and horizontal stretchering introduced after the September-October 1950 trials with No. 34041 *Wilton* apparently had very little effect on the main frames, for of forty-three pacifics inspected at Eastleigh Works in 1960-4, all but four had evidence of deep fractures ahead of the leading coupled

No. 21C164 at Brighton, 9 July 1947, after being fitted with convex smoke-deflector plates and the original cab given a V-front (*Real Photographs Co. Ltd.*)

No. 34064 *Fighter Command* at Newington, 31 July 1948. Painted apple green and heading the chocolate-and-cream liveried coaches of the 1.15 p.m. Cannon Street-Ramsgate (*D. L. Bradley*)

The Giesl ejector light pacific, No. 34064 *Fighter Command* at Southampton Central, 27 July 1963 (*E. W. Fry*)

No. 34081 at Brighton, 6 September 1948. Full-width V-cab, 5,500-gallon tender, and painted malachite green with transfer front numerals and spaces left in the centre lining bands for the squadron plaques (*D. L. Bradley*)

No. 34082 *615 Squadron* with the 9.35 a.m. Margate-Charing Cross, 5 May 1949. Both front numerals and smokebox door numberplate carried (*D. L. Bradley*)

The "Golden Arrow" passing down through Tonbridge behind No. 34083 on 15 April 1949. Smokebox door numberplate and no front numerals (*D. L. Bradley*)

No. 34089 *602 Squadron* stands at Exmouth Junction shed, 27 August 1965.
(*S. C. Nash*)

The nameplate of rebuild No. 34095 in March 1962 (*D. L. Bradley*)

The end approaches. No. 34095 without nameplates heads the 10.20 a.m. Weymouth-Crewe (perishables) away from Yeovil (PM) on 9 September 1967 (*S. C. Nash*)

No. 34096 *Trevone* at Eastleigh, 5 April 1952. Sanding to centre and trailing coupled wheels with hinged circular covers (*E. W. Fry*)

No. 34101 *Hartland* pauses at Southampton Central with the through Brighton-Plymouth on 6 April 1963 (*D. L. Bradley*)

No. 34101 *Hartland* at the front of Eastleigh shed, 7 March 1964. Modified 5,500-gallon tender, speedometer, electric warning flashes, AWS and red nameplate backgrounds (*E. W. Fry*)

No. 34103 *Calstock* at Eastleigh, 8 September 1956, with the casing removed ahead of the cylinders and 5,500-gallon tender (*E. W. Fry*)

No. 34103 *Calstock* at Southampton Central, 31 March 1961, with AWS, speedometer, electric warning flashes, red background to nameplates and modified 4,500-gallon tender (*E. W. Fry*)

No. 34104 *Bere Alston* passing Folkestone Junction with the "Golden Arrow", 5 August 1950. Sliding covers to the sandboxes (*D. L. Bradley*)

At work on the Somerset & Dorset, No. 34105 *Swanage* on 16 August 1958, piloting Class 4 No. 75071. No fairing to chimney, safety-valves reduced to two and re-positioned on rear of boiler barrel (*D. L. Bradley*)

wheels. Some required welds of over 2½ft. to remedy the defects, although most were of the order of six to ten inches. Other vulnerable areas were at the rear of the third coupled axle, and above and to the front of the centre coupled axle; these fractures, however, were only of some three to five inches in depth and not as serious or prevalent as those found at the leading end. Generally, the frames of locomotives not rebuilt were in better condition than those rebuilt, this being especially so of the 34091 to 34110 series. Much trouble was also met from the new inside cylinders, with 23 per cent of the 1964-6 withdrawals being from this cause.

By this date so many locomotives were being withdrawn that the Southern Region was unable to break them up at Eastleigh and most were sold for scrap after various useful items had been salvaged or exchanged, details being as follows:

Locomotive No.	*Purchaser*	*Broken-up*
34003	P. Ward, Queenborough	12/1964
34029	P. Ward, Queenborough	1/1965
34016	Woodham Bros., Barry	preserved
34027	Woodham Bros., Barry	still intact 4/1974
34028	Woodham Bros., Barry	still intact 4/1974
34045	Woodham Bros., Barry	4/1965
34058	Woodham Bros., Barry	still intact 4/1974
34062	Birds Commercial Motors, Bridgend	7/1962 (by R. S. Hayes, Bridgend)
34096	Birds Commercial Motors, Bynea	3/1965
34109	Birds Commercial Motors, Morriston	8/1964

No. 34016 *Bodmin* rusticated at Barry for eight years and then was purchased by the Quainton Railway Society. On 29 July 1972 it was delivered with 5,500-gallon tender T3339 to the Society and restoration commenced at Quainton Road Station.

The start of the 1964 summer timetables brought few changes to the Bournemouth line, where on Saturdays pacifics had charge of most services with Class 33 diesels limiting themselves to the 11.30 a.m. to Bournemouth and the Lymington and Swanage trains. As previously mentioned, steam also retained its grip on the West of England services until 17 August, when Warship (Class 42) diesels took over some of the Waterloo services, including the up "Atlantic Coast". This in effect was the prelude to full dieselisation on 7 September 1964, when all the London expresses and many of the semi-fasts were rostered for Warship haulage. Most of the slow services fell to diesel multiple-units while steam was restricted to goods duties and the Bude, Okehampton and Padstow trains. However, the inevitable teething troubles led to pacifics appearing daily at Exeter for the remainder of the year, and equally inevitably the running of the commandeered Merchant Navies and West Countries was of the highest order.

Withdrawals, dieselisation and shed closures led to numerous transfers and by January 1965 the distribution of the rebuilds was as follows: Eastleigh Nos. 34001/4/8/9/10/7/8/21/2/5/31/4/6/7/9/42/50/60/71/7/82/7/8/90/3/5/7/8/101/4; Salisbury Nos. 34005/12/3/4/26/32/48/52/6/9/89/100/8; Bournemouth Nos. 34024/40/4/6/7/53/85.

Throughout 1965/66 the Bournemouth line was beset by engineering and re-laying works of varying magnitude and duration as preparations for electrification gathered momentum. Lengthy slacks, single-line workings and diversions were commonplace, while complete occupation at weekends over lengthy sections of track made Sunday travel a veritable nightmare. Footplate crews found their daily tasks frustrating and tedious, for seldom could time lost be recouped by smart running or keen station work, while poor fuel and indifferent maintenance added to their difficulties. Nevertheless, most crews gave of their best and obtained surprisingly high speeds and good performances from their grimy and often decrepit locomotives. Some easement of restrictions came with the summer services, while the availability of Type 3 (Class 33) diesels at Eastleigh made it possible on Sundays to dispense with steam on most of the Bournemouth services and at the same time offer depots the opportunity of grappling with the arrears of maintenance. In the autumn the onset of colder weather and the need to provide carriage heating found a greater demand for steam power.

Nos. 34005/12/8/37/42/58/82/101 all received heavy intermediate repairs and repaints between March and September 1964; thereafter only lighter repairs were given, which led to further withdrawals with Nos. 34010/4/22/31/9/42/6/50/3/85 going in 1965, and Nos. 34005/9/12/7/26/32/48/59/82/101 in the following year. To maintain the survivors serviceable it was frequently necessary to resort to extraordinary measures with condemned locomotives being ruthlessly stripped of items capable of further use and tenders from those stopped for maintenance being transferred to ones still in steam.

By 1966, last steam runs and rail tours had become regular events, with the Central Section gaining its share. On 20 February, No. 34013 *Okehampton* headed a last steam journey down the Uckfield line from Victoria to Brighton and thence along the coast to Fareham before coming off for servicing and returning to Portsmouth to take the tour back to London Bridge via Guildford and Epsom. The same locomotive also worked an Isle of Wight farewell trip on 31 December 1966, while on 5 June 1966 another tour took No. 34089 *602 Squadron* to Epsom Downs over the Sutton-Wimbledon line.

Incidentally, it is noteworthy how often No. 34013 *Okehampton* contrived to be present at historic events of one kind or another. For in addition to those just mentioned, it headed the last steam 5.14 p.m. Cannon Street-Ramsgate "City Express" on 12 June 1959, the last steam 6.10 p.m. Victoria-Uckfield-Brighton on 10 August 1962, partnered No. 34057 *Biggin Hill* on the Somerset & Dorset farewell tour of 6 March 1966, and the last steam 5.30 p.m. Weymouth-Waterloo on 7 July 1967. Drivers found *Okehampton* a "goer", while firemen found their task unexpectedly easy, which probably accounted for its being chosen for so many important occasions. A general repair and repaint at Eastleigh in January 1964 ensured that its enviable reputation was maintained until electrification.

Withdrawal by 1 January 1967 had reduced the sixty rebuilds by half and the allocation had become: Nine Elms Nos. 34001/8/18/21/34/6/7; Eastleigh Nos. 34060/71/7/87/8/90/3/5/7/8/104; Salisbury Nos. 34013/52/6/89/100/8; Bournemouth Nos. 34004/24/5/40/4/7. Many of these would also be made redundant before mid-year, for on 2 January the Waterloo-Basingstoke services were electrified, while from 3 April it was possible to operate electric stock right through to Bournemouth, and only a handful of expresses were officially rostered for steam haulage. Full use was made of the Bulleid pacifics on the Ocean Liner services, the Nine Elms-Southampton Docks fitted freights and the Poole-Newcastle through trains, as well as substitutes for diesels or electric multiple units. Indeed, such important duties as the "Bournemouth Belle" and "Royal Wessex" were more often than not steam-powered with Nos. 34024/34/60/89/90/100/8 on various occasions making their presence felt, for with most speed restrictions removed, crews took advantage of the circumstances to prove conclusively that steam had been overtaken by science, not morbidity.

On the West of England services Warship failures were less frequent, but on 10 June 1967 D866 came to grief at Salisbury with the 10.15 a.m. Exeter (St. Davids)-Waterloo and No. 34108 *Wincanton* had hurriedly to be summoned from the shed to take the ten-coach train on to London. Departure was 15½ minutes late, but by Porton speed had risen to 59 m.p.h., to be followed by 87 m.p.h. after Grately, and the stop at Andover made in 19 minutes. The next stage to Basingstoke occupied 19½ minutes and that to Woking, including a p.w. slack, 21¾ minutes with an 88 m.p.h. maximum at Fleet, while the final leg to Waterloo took 26 minutes, and all the lost time would have been made up but for some poor station work at Basingstoke. The return working, 5.00 p.m. out of Waterloo, was taken through to Exeter and No. 34108 *Wincanton* had no difficulty in maintaining the diesel schedule.

During the last week of operation the "Bournemouth Belle" was steam-powered on several occasions, No. 34025 *Whimple* being in charge on 3 July, while on 5 July No. 34024 *Tamar Valley* worked the down train and No. 34036 *Westward Ho* the up. For the final workings on 9 July a Merchant Navy was diagrammed down and a West Country rebuild up, but at the last moment this was vetoed by Waterloo and the "Belle" ended its career behind a grimy diesel.

The Southern Region official "Farewell to Steam" specials ran on Sunday 2 July 1967, and were headed by Merchant Navies Nos. 35008 *Orient Line* and 35028 *Clan Line*. On the same day No. 34025 *Whimple* worked the 9.33 a.m. Waterloo-Bournemouth excursion and No. 34021 *Dartmoor* a fruit special from Weymouth to Westbury. Similar trains on 4 and 5 July gave work to Nos. 34001 *Exeter* and 35003 *Royal Mail*, while on the last-mentioned date No. 34095 *Brentor* headed the 9.40 a.m. Poole-Newcastle. On the evening of 7 July, No. 34093 *Saunton* had charge of the last 5.23 p.m. Waterloo-Bournemouth and No. 34025 *Whimple* the 6.54 to Basingstoke, while the 5.30 p.m. from Weymouth came up 9½ minutes early behind No. 34013 *Okehampton*.

Steam workings on Saturday 8 July included No. 34037 *Clovelly* on the 2.30 a.m. Waterloo-Portsmouth and No. 34095 *Brentor* on the 2.45 a.m. Waterloo-Bournemouth. The former later worked a return holiday special for Colne as far as Willesden and came home with vans. The last steam workings of all occurred on Sunday 9 July 1967, when No. 34021 *Dartmoor* brought up the 11.00 a.m. boat train from Southampton, and Nos. 34052 *Lord Dowding* and 34095 *Brentor* headed special perishables to Westbury and later returned light to Weymouth.

During the last week, locomotives were worked in batches to Salisbury and Weymouth for storage pending disposal, and by the evening of 9 July 1967, both depots presented a crowded appearance, reminiscent of earlier and less sophisticated times. By the end of the month rebuilds Nos. 34018/21/4/5/37/40/4/56/60/71/7/87/9/90/8/104/8 were at Salisbury, Nos. 34004/36/52/93/5 at Weymouth and Nos. 34001/8/13/34/47/100 at Nine Elms. Over the next few months they were sold in batches for scrap and towed away by diesel locomotives, this at Nine Elms during July, August and September becoming a regular Sunday morning duty with D6555 taking away Nos. 34008/34 and 35007 on 25 August and D6517 Nos. 34001/13 and 35030 the following weekend. Sales details are as follows: Cashmore, Newport Nos. 34001/4/12/3/8/21/4/5/31/4/6/7/40/4/8/52/6/60/71/7/82/7/8/9/90/3/5/7/100 (all broken-up by September 1968); J. Buttigieg, Newport Nos. 34005/8/9/17/26/32/42/7/85/98/104/8 (all broken-up by December 1968); P. Ward, Queenborough Nos. 34003/29 (broken-up by January 1965); Hayes, Bridgend No. 34014 (broken-up by January 1966); Birds Commercial Motors, Bridgend No. 34062 (broken-up mid-1966); Birds Commercial Motors, Bynea No. 34096 (broken-up March 1965); Birds Commercial Motors, Morriston Nos. 34050/109 (broken-up by March 1965); Woodfield, Newport No. 34022 (broken-up by August 1965); Woodham Bros., Barry Nos. 34010/6/27/8/39/45/6/53/8/9/101. Of the last-mentioned only Nos. 34045 had been broken-up by 1975. No. 34016 was purchased by the Quainton Road Society and delivered in July 1972 to Quainton Road station for preservation, while No. 34039 was rescued by the Main Line Preservation Group in January 1973 and conveyed to Loughborough Central station to be similarly prepared for service.

LOCOMOTIVE SUMMARY

No.	*Name*	*Built*	*Rebuilt*	*Renumbered*	*Withdrawn*
21C101	*Exeter*	5/1945	11/1957	3/1949	7/1967
21C102	*Salisbury*	6/1945	—	11/1948	4/1967
21C103	*Plymouth*	6/1945	9/1957	5/1948	9/1964
21C104	*Yeovil*	7/1945	2/1958	5/1948	7/1967
21C105	*Barnstaple*	7/1945	6/1957	5/1948	10/1966
21C106	*Bude*	7/1945	—	5/1948	3/1967
21C107	*Wadebridge*	8/1945	—	3/1949	10/1965
21C108	*Padstow*	9/1945	7/1960	4/1949	6/1967
21C109	*Lyme Regis*	9/1945	1/1961	3/1949	10/1966
21C110	*Sidmouth*	9/1945	2/1959	1/1950	3/1965
21C111	*Tavistock*	10/1945	—	5/1948	11/1963
21C112	*Launceston*	10/1945	1/1958	6/1948	12/1966
21C113	*Okehampton*	10/1945	10/1957	6/1948	7/1967
21C114	*Budleigh Salterton*	11/1945	3/1958	11/1949	3/1965
21C115	*Exmouth*	11/1945	—	4/1948	4/1967
21C116	*Bodmin*	11/1945	4/1958	7/1948	6/1964
21C117	*Ilfracombe*	12/1945	11/1957	5/1948	10/1966
21C118	*Axminster*	12/1945	10/1958	6/1948	7/1967
21C119	*Bideford*	12/1945	—	5/1948	3/1967
21C120	*Seaton*	12/1945	—	5/1948	9/1964
21C121	*Dartmoor*	1/1946	1/1958	7/1948	7/1967
21C122	*Exmoor*	1/1946	12/1957	6/1948	4/1965
21C123	*Blackmoor Vale*	2/1946	—	4/1948	7/1967
21C124	*Tamar Valley*	2/1946	2/1961	6/1948	7/1967
21C125	*Whimple*	3/1946	11/1957	10/1948	7/1967
21C126	*Yes Tor*	3/1946	2/1958	5/1949	9/1966
21C127	*Taw Valley*	4/1946	9/1957	7/1948	8/1964
21C128	*Eddystone*	4/1946	8/1958	12/1948	5/1964
21C129	*Lundy*	5/1946	12/1958	2/1949	9/1964
21C130	*Watersmeet*	5/1946	—	11/1948	9/1964
21C131	*Torrington*	6/1946	12/1958	1/1949	2/1965
21C132	*Camelford*	6/1946	10/1960	4/1948	10/1966
21C133	*Chard*	7/1946	—	12/1948	12/1965

No.	Name	Built	Rebuilt	Renumbered	Withdrawn
21C134	*Honiton*	7/1946	8/1960	7/1948	7/1967
21C135	*Shaftesbury*	7/1946	—	1/1949	6/1963
21C136	*Westward Ho*	7/1946	9/1960	5/1948	7/1967
21C137	*Clovelly*	8/1946	3/1958	3/1949	7/1967
21C138	*Lynton*	9/1946	—	2/1949	6/1966
21C139	*Boscastle*	9/1946	1/1959	6/1948	5/1965
21C140	*Crewkerne*	9/1946	10/1960	10/1948	7/1967
21C141	*Wilton*	10/1946	—	1/1949	1/1966
21C142	*Dorchester*	10/1946	1/1959	6/1948	10/1965
21C143	*Coombe Martin*	10/1946	—	9/1948	6/1963
21C144	*Woolacombe*	10/1946	5/1960	1/1949	5/1967
21C145	*Ottery St. Mary*	10/1946	10/1958	12/1948	6/1964
21C146	*Braunton*	11/1946	2/1959	1/1949	10/1965
21C147	*Callington*	11/1946	10/1958	1/1949	6/1967
21C148	*Crediton*	11/1946	3/1959	8/1948	3/1966
21C149	*Anti-Aircraft Command*	12/1946	—	4/1949	12/1963
21C150	*Royal Observer Corps*	12/1946	8/1958	1/1949	8/1965
21C151	*Winston Churchill*	12/1946	—	10/1948	9/1965
21C152	*Lord Dowding*	12/1946	9/1958	2/1949	7/1967
21C153	*Sir Keith Park*	1/1947	11/1958	6/1949	10/1965
21C154	*Lord Beaverbrook*	1/1947	—	3/1949	9/1964
21C155	*Fighter Pilot*	2/1947	—	7/1949	6/1963
21C156	*Croydon*	2/1947	12/1960	5/1948	5/1967
21C157	*Biggin Hill*	3/1947	—	6/1949	5/1967
21C158	*Sir Frederick Pile*	3/1947	11/1960	12/1948	10/1964
21C159	*Sir Archibald Sinclair*	4/1947	3/1960	3/1949	5/1966
21C160	*25 Squadron*	4/1947	11/1960	10/1948	7/1967
21C161	*73 Squadron*	4/1947	—	2/1949	8/1964
21C162	*17 Squadron*	5/1947	4/1959	1/1949	6/1964
21C163	*229 Squadron*	5/1947	—	1/1949	8/1965
21C164	*Fighter Command*	7/1947	—	6/1948	5/1966
21C165	*Hurricane*	7/1947	—	6/1948	4/1964
21C166	*Spitfire*	9/1947	—	2/1949	9/1966
21C167	*Tangmere*	9/1947	—	7/1949	11/1963
21C168	*Kenley*	10/1947	—	9/1948	12/1963
21C169	*Hawkinge*	10/1947	—	6/1948	11/1963
21C170	*Manston*	11/1947	—	3/1949	8/1964
34071	*601 Squadron*	4/1948	5/1960	—	4/1967
34072	*257 Squadron*	4/1948	—	—	10/1964
34073	*249 Squadron*	5/1948	—	—	6/1964
34074	*46 Squadron*	5/1948	—	—	6/1963
34075	*264 Squadron*	6/1948	—	—	4/1964
34076	*41 Squadron*	6/1948	—	—	1/1966
34077	*603 Squadron*	7/1948	7/1960	—	3/1967
34078	*222 Squadron*	7/1948	—	—	9/1964
34079	*141 Squadron*	7/1948	—	—	2/1966
34080	*74 Squadron*	8/1948	—	—	9/1964
34081	*92 Squadron*	9/1948	—	—	8/1964
34082	*615 Squadron*	9/1948	4/1960	—	4/1966
34083	*605 Squadron*	10/1948	—	—	6/1964
34084	*253 Squadron*	11/1948	—	—	10/1965
34085	*501 Squadron*	11/1948	6/1960	—	9/1965
34086	*219 Squadron*	12/1948	—	—	6/1966
34087	*145 Squadron*	12/1948	12/1960	—	7/1967
34088	*213 Squadron*	12/1948	4/1960	—	3/1967

No.	Name	Built	Rebuilt	Renumbered	Withdrawn
34089	*602 Squadron*	12/1948	11/1960	—	7/1967
34090	*Sir Eustace Missenden Southern Railway*	2/1949	8/1960	—	7/1967
34091	*Weymouth*	9/1949	—	—	9/1964
34092	*City of Wells*	9/1949	—	—	11/1964
34093	*Saunton*	10/1949	5/1960	—	7/1967
34094	*Mortehoe*	10/1949	—	—	8/1964
34095	*Brentor*	10/1949	1/1961	—	7/1967
34096	*Trevone*	11/1949	4/1961	—	9/1964
34097	*Holsworthy*	11/1949	3/1961	—	4/1967
34098	*Templecombe*	12/1949	2/1961	—	6/1967
34099	*Lynmouth*	12/1949	—	—	11/1964
34100	*Appledore*	12/1949	9/1960	—	7/1967
34101	*Hartland*	2/1950	9/1960	—	7/1966
34102	*Lapford*	3/1950	—	—	7/1967
34103	*Calstock*	2/1950	—	—	9/1965
34104	*Bere Alston*	4/1950	5/1961	—	6/1967
34105	*Swanage*	3/1950	—	—	10/1964
34106	*Lydford*	3/1950	—	—	9/1964
34107	*Blandford Forum*	4/1950	—	—	9/1964
34108	*Wincanton*	4/1950	5/1961	—	6/1967
34109	*Sir Trafford Leigh-Mallory*	5/1950	3/1961	—	9/1964
34110	*66 Squadron*	1/1951	—	—	11/1963

All were constructed at Brighton Works, except Nos. 34095/7/9, 34101/2/4 which came from Eastleigh Works. After Nationalisation Nos. 21C101 to 21C170 were renumbered 34001 to 34070, although prior to this Nos. 21C105/6/7/8/9/10/2/6/21/9/31/6/42/6/8/9/50/7/8/9/67/70 carried the temporary "S" prefix. Nos. 34071 to 34110 built by British Railways never ran with the Bulleid numbering. The West Country class consisted of Nos. 34001 to 34048, 34091 to 34108, and the Battle of Britain class Nos. 34049 to 34090, 34109/10.

Renamings:

34023	*Blackmoor Vale* to *Blackmore Vale*, 4/1950
21C125	*Rough Tor* 11/4/1948 to 23/4/1948, to *Whimple*, 3/5/1948
34071	*615 Squadron* to *601 Squadron*, 8/1948
34092	*Wells* to *City of Wells*, 3/1950
34107	*Blandford* to *Blandford Forum*, 10/1952
	Changes also occurred with the plaques and included:
21C106	Coat of arms of Cornwall changed to a full achievement (Bude)
21C110	Coat of arms of Devon changed to town coat of arms (Sidmouth)
21C115	Coat of arms of Devon changed to a full achievement (Exmouth)

Other oddities included the two-line nameplates of No. 21C114 *Budleigh Salterton* in which 3in. lettering was employed instead of the standard 6in., the fitting of the Devon coat of arms to No. 21C121 *Dartmoor*, and the alteration of No. 34023's nameplates to read *Blackmore Vale* instead of *Blackmoor Vale*. New nameplates were cast but by a misunderstanding were identical with those to be discarded and had to be adjusted to give the correct reading. Royal Air Force badges were carried by Nos. 34055/6/7/64/5/6/7/8/9/70, 34109, but not No. 34110 *66 Squadron*.

When rebuilt in the autumn of 1957 Nos. 34013 *Okehampton* and 34017 *Ilfracombe* were refitted with their correct nameplates, but exchanged plaques and coats of arms. The error was rectified on Eastleigh shed in March 1958. Similarly, in November 1960 Nos. 34058 *Sir Frederick Pile* and 34068 *Kenley* left Eastleigh Works with each other's plaques, the former carrying the RAF badge and the latter Sir Frederick's coat of arms. No exchange was made before withdrawal.

Last official naming ceremonies:
West Country class No. 34091 *Weymouth*, 29/12/1949
Battle of Britain class No. 34082 *615 Squadron*, 8/10/1948

Last to receive names:
West Country class No. 34026 *Yes Tor*, 14/10/1955
Battle of Britain class No. 34085 *501 Squadron*, 30/7/1955
British Railways Power Classification: 1/1/1949 6MT
British Railways Loading Classification: 1/12/1953 7P5F
Non-rebuilds altered to 7P6F: 11/1957
Rebuilds altered to 7P6F: 11/1961

Final Mileages for Non-Rebuilds

34002	1,003,613
34006	1,099,338
34007	823,193
34011	800,455
34015	903,245
34019	701,316
34020	789,688
34023	921,268
34030	744,279
34033	884,916
34035	764,306
34038	819,984
34041	626,417
34043	749,112
34049	723,947
34051	807,496
34054	737,443
34055	706,607
34057	939,597
34061	701,443
34063	736,984
34064	759,666
34065	730,489
34066	652,908
34067	688,269
34068	700,417
34069	673,643
34070	702,614
34072	698,843
34073	684,325
34074	639,592
34075	643,241
34076	803,425
34078	779,643
34079	765,302
34080	749,863
34081	741,511
34083	737,467
34084	663,249
34086	700,982
34091	469,073
34092	502,864
34094	672,346
34099	628,771
34102	593,438
34103	629,172
34105	623,405
34106	691,443
34107	665,130
34110	609,147

Mileages of Rebuilds

Locomotive No.	*To Rebuilding*	*Final Total*
34001	584,794	1,079,957
34003	543,328	811,674
34004	573,593	920,972
34005	489,808	837,332
34008	597,083	961,734
34009	662,481	959,762
34010	578,944	922,906
34012	500,788	847,523
34013	559,411	944,928
34014	573,677	837,477
34016	554,230	811,674
34017	459,309	856,641
34018	547,303	974,317
34021	541,097	950,142
34022	527,822	793,647
34024	689,964	839,964
34025	512,484	872,938
34026	563,491	916,244
34027	503,085	764,316
34028	564,587	851,549
34029	580,259	828,489
34031	552,594	841,182
34032	649,155	853,398
34034	636,999	942,133
34036	582,544	894,546
34037	480,115	810,658
34039	466,238	745,508
34040	500,397	769,624
34042	477,413	726,761
34044	571,638	894,998
34045	521,956	761,465
34046	515,391	779,210
34047	513,822	845,991
34048	539,988	847,615
34050	509,320	796,814
34052	507,986	936,502
34053	529,129	825,317
34056	634,179	957,081
34058	639,472	812,586

Locomotive No.	*To Rebuilding*	*Final Total*
34059	569,583	877,107
34060	645,723	934,417
34062	543,488	836,576
34071	437,599	782,028
34077	478,162	745,642
34082	424,406	697,386
34085	441,609	661,415
34087	415,738	704,638
34088	377,016	656,583
34089	402,834	661,252
34090	444,011	743,948
34093	528,389	888,004
34095	566,629	796,614
34096	511,280	722,326
34097	500,111	743,659
34098	535,630	819,105
34100	409,318	712,916
34101	330,106	568,479
34104	425,977	678,853
34108	583,780	808,361
34109	557,217	719,818

These mileages have been taken from the Engine Cards from entry to traffic until recording ceased in late 1964. Thereafter reference was made to the Repair Sheets until mid-1966 when the mileages of those engines remaining in service were collected from the Motive Power Depots. Consequently the figures quoted for the late withdrawals are probably less than their actual final mileages.

West Country/Battle of Britain Boilers

Number constructed:—

Eastleigh Works 12, North British Locomotive Company 12, Brighton Works 96. Total 120.

Boiler numbers 1261 to 1380.

Locomotives Nos. 34071/82/3 entered traffic new with second-hand boilers (1280, 1278 and 1285 ex-Nos. 21C124, 21C121 and 21C127), which left thirteen replacement boilers available. These were used on the following:

Boiler No.	*Locomotive No.*	*Date*
1319	21C102	12/1947
1320	21C124	9/1947
1336	21C104	12/1947
1337	S21C110	1/1948
1355	34029	2/1949
1356	34040	3/1949
1357	34054	3/1949
1370	34064	6/1950
1372	34055	5/1951
1375	34007	5/1951
1377	34005	5/1950
1378	34048	8/1953
1380	34044	3/1954

Boiler No. 1380 undoubtedly had the lowest mileage of any carried by the Bulleid pacifics, for it only amassed 491,994 (253,621 with No. 34044 and 238,373 with No. 34101) before being condemned.

Printed by Ratnett & Co. Ltd.
Knighton Junction Lane,
Welford Road, Leicester